POSTCARD HISTORY SERIES

Babylon Village

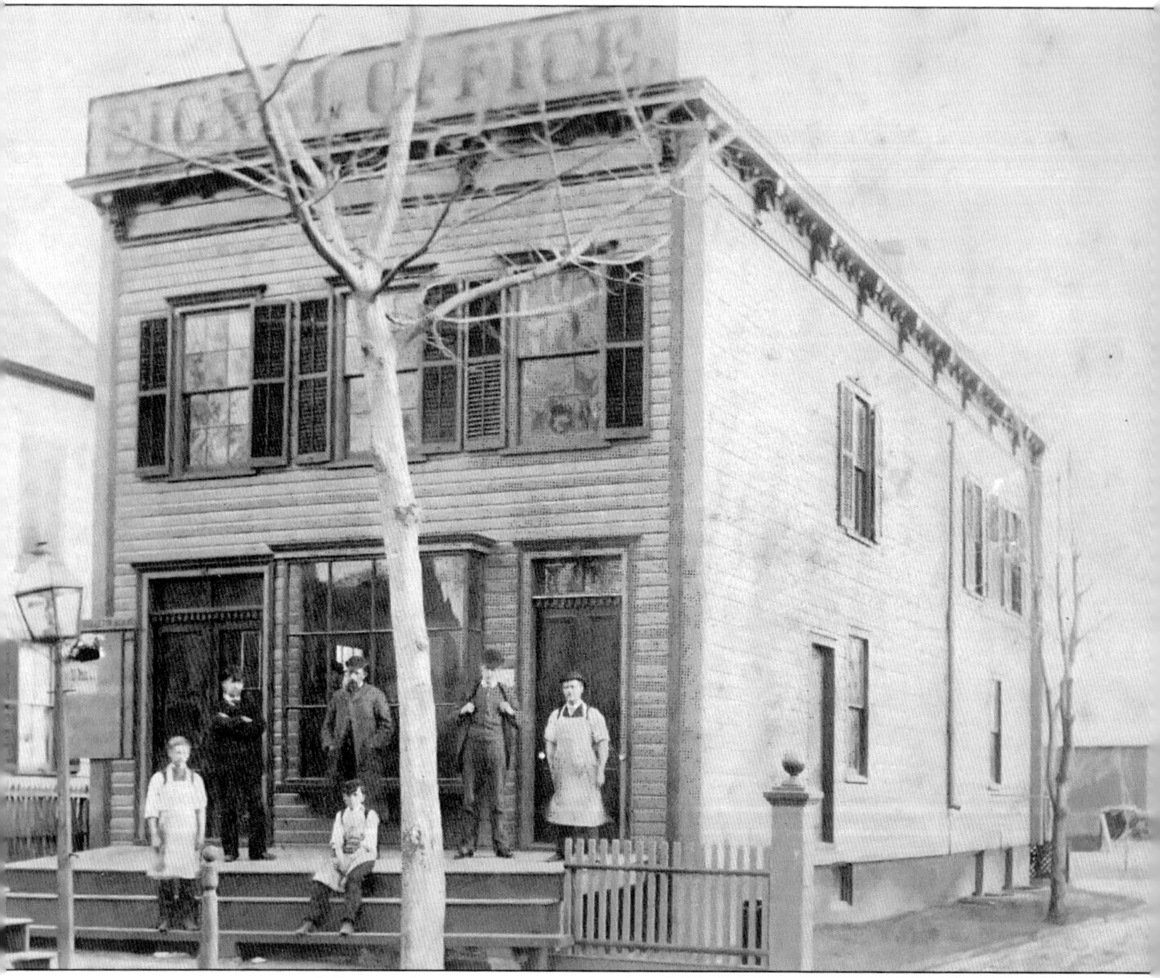

Henry Livingston debuted the *South Side Signal* on July 7, 1869, declaring, "Our Signal lamp is lighted, and it is our intention to . . . prove a faithful beacon . . . [to] make plain the ways of honor, happiness and virtue." The *Signal* building was erected in December 1869 adjacent to Livingston's West Main Street residence. It operated as the Red Lion English Pub from the 1960s to the 1980s and was relocated to Mansfield Place by attorney Patrick Kevin Brosnahan in 1990. (Town of Babylon, Office of Historic Services.)

ON THE FRONT COVER: The intersection of Main Street at Fire Island and Deer Park Avenues is pictured around 1905. The original public fountain erected by the Women's Exchange in 1897 is prominent in the foreground. The steeple of the Presbyterian church and the Provost Building with a Heffley Drug advertisement are visible in the background, two prominent landmarks that still adorn the village. (Village of Babylon Historical and Preservation Society.)

ON THE BACK COVER: Deer Park Avenue is pictured looking north from Main Street in the 1920s with an officer from the Babylon Village Police Department standing guard near the rudimentary traffic signal. By this time, the old Heffley Drug advertisement had given way to Liggett's Drug Store, on the right. Winegar's Pharmacy (left) was situated at the northwest corner of Deer Park Avenue and Main Street. The pharmacy and adjacent stores suffered a devastating fire in December 1931. (Village of Babylon Historical and Preservation Society.)

POSTCARD HISTORY SERIES

Babylon Village

Village of Babylon Historical and Preservation Society
with Mary Cascone

ARCADIA
PUBLISHING

Copyright © 2017 by Village of Babylon Historical and Preservation Society with Mary Cascone
ISBN 978-1-4671-2475-1

Published by Arcadia Publishing
Charleston, South Carolina

Printed in the United States of America

Library of Congress Control Number: 2016956676

For all general information contact Arcadia Publishing at:
Telephone 843-853-2070
Fax 843-853-0044
E-mail sales@arcadiapublishing.com
For customer service and orders:
Toll-Free 1-888-313-2665

Visit us on the Internet at www.arcadiapublishing.com

In memory of the generations of Babylonians who helped shape and develop this village, and for the generations of Babylonians to come.

Contents

Acknowledgments

This book is the result of a collaborative project between the Village of Babylon Historical and Preservation Society (VBHPS) and the Town of Babylon History Museum (TOBHM) to organize and preserve the historical society's photograph and postcard collections. Many thanks to the VBHPS board for having the foresight to protect and share these visual treasures and to the TOBHM staff for their diligent, and often monotonous, labors: Georgia Cava, Kelly Filippone, Renee Leone, museum volunteers Samantha Parmely and Jason Cascone, volunteer researcher Steven Clampit, 2016 Ujima summer intern Jahron Causey, deputy historian Thomas B. Smith, and town historian Mary Cascone. Current VBHPS board members are Jackie Marsden, Judy Skillen, Donna Consola, Marie Bohrer, Janine Logan, Richard Vultaggio, Carolyn Gutmann, Wayne Horsley, Karen Petz, Jack Conroy, George Pozderec, and Carolyn Romaine. Many Babylonians have inspired and made contributions toward this project, including former museum curator Ruth Albin; Westminster Kennel Club researcher Joanne Anderson; the Babylon Public Library for supporting the maintenance of an excellent microfilm machine and printer, and reference librarian Inez Foster and library director Vicki Lever for just being excellent; Gus Fishel; St. Joseph's Church researcher Dr. Rick Hess; Karen Kennedy; Scott Lockwood; Oak Island and Oak Beach researcher Tom "Tinker" Morris; Bert Pedersen; Stephen Quigley of the Long Island Sunrise Trail Chapter, National Railway Historical Society; Theresa Santmann, whose generous funding for digitization of the *South Side Signal* in 2010 has made local research much more convenient; Sumpwams Creek researcher Tom Stock; village historian Alice Zaruka; Rev. Leonard M. Davis, Bethel A.M.E. Church (Bethel AME); Rev. Wayne Griffiths, First Baptist Church; and William Holmes of the United Methodist Church. All images are from the collections of the Village of Babylon Historical and Preservation Society, except as noted. Additional images were graciously provided by Edward Kauf, Herbert Ketcham, Steve Loudon, Lindenhurst Historical Society (LHS), Babylon Masonic Lodge No. 793 (Masons) and the Town of Babylon, Office of Historic Services (TOB).

Introduction

Welcome to our postcard collection. Presenting a prime selection of nearly a century of collecting and developing, the Village of Babylon Historical and Preservation Society proudly offers this historic homage to our village. In doing so, we gratefully acknowledge the Muncy and Howell families, to name but two, who generously donated their personal collections to the historical society, expanding the collection so that we may now share them with you, the public.

Postcard collecting and the sending of postcards was a popular way to connect with friends and assemble souvenirs of places visited. Many postcards in our collection were never mailed, just treasured by locals and kept in the community. Others were, however, mailed from Babylon with pleasant notes to friends and family around the country. It is remarkable when postcards sent away from Babylon long ago make their way back to us. Today, websites such as eBay can facilitate the return of some old-time postcards. Sadly, the act of sending a postcard via the postal system has fallen victim to the contemporary trend of taking a selfie in Argyle Park and posting it on a social media website.

But a word, first, about the history of our lovely village. Babylon Village has been an incorporated village since 1893, but its history began with the Native Americans who occupied Long Island and thrived off the bounty of the Great South Bay. Their historic presence is reflected in the names of community streets and creeks, which were derived from their culture and language—*sumpwams* (a just man), *annuskemunaka* (planted land), *ketewamoke* (crab meadow), and *araca* (furthermost).

The abundance of fish and salt hay that sustained the original indigenous peoples brought new settlers to Huntington's South Shore, known as Huntington South, originally part of the town of Huntington, established by English settlers in 1653. As the southern portion of Huntington grew and fashioned its own identity, citizens voted to secede from the northern territory in 1872. The name given to the new town, bordered at four corners by Amityville, East Farmingdale, Deer Park, and our village, was Babylon. The new town took its name from the community where some of the secession movement's most ardent supporters lived. The communities of North Babylon and West Babylon assumed their names from proximity to the village. Reminders of prominent citizens from that time live on in local street names: Elbert Carll, Henry Livingston, David S.S. Sammis, James B. Cooper, E.B. Litchfield, Judge John R. Reid, and William R. Foster. They took great pride in their newly formed town and in their village community, from the bucolic neighborhood streets to the verdant shores of the barrier beaches, many of which appear as postcard images within this book.

Postcards were an important advertising tool, highlighting sights to be seen and places at which to be seen. In the 19th century, during Babylon Village's resort era, the village and surrounding area was what the Hamptons and the east end of Long Island are today, an idyllic vacation haven for the well-heeled and a fun home for the residents involved in the waterfront trades, hospitality industries, and general business. Promoted by real estate investors as within commuting distance to Manhattan, Babylon boasted a growing year-round commuting population that helped sustain the village's vitality when the resort era concluded around the 1920s. The village continued to thrive and grow with the changing times but always managed to maintain its historic character.

Unlike photographs, postcard images can sometimes be deceiving. Long before photo editing software and digital photographs were commonplace, early-20th-century postcards were often hand colored or edited. Postcard artists frequently smoothed out street ruts, repainted worn buildings, or added pleasant people ambulating through town. Postcards were meant to represent the best and most beautiful aspects of a community and make a good representation, acting like an invitation to come and visit the place.

The postcard images contained within these pages depict an idyllic world of a quaint, charming village and seaside cottage communities; of uncomplicated lazy days filled with laughter, sunshine, and entertainment; and sailboats and motorboats cruising across the Great South Bay. Many things have evolved, but many others have remained much the same. The marinas and houses along the creeks and bayfront teem with watercraft. There are more people, the storefronts have been updated, and technological advances have taken place, but stroll down Deer Park Avenue or Main Street today and you will see many original buildings are still here, proudly displaying their dates of construction inlaid in stone or brass plaques. What was once a bank is now a high-end restaurant, the town municipal building is a museum, and the village library has become home to our historical society. In spring and summer, baskets brimming with ivy geraniums hang from the decorative street lamps, replaced by pine boughs and lights in December. J. Stanley Foster's grand gift to the village of Babylon, Argyle Park, still enchants lovers, children, and dog walkers alike. Family picnics are laid with care beneath the shade of the old trees while the swans and geese glide across the surface of the lake. The gazebo across the way houses live music on sultry summer evenings and an occasional wedding ceremony. Every weekend, the park hosts brides and other celebrants posing for heirloom photographs while a myriad of church bells ring out.

More than two centuries after its naming, there are people who still question association with ancient Babylon and its biblical description, many without ever having visited our village. Today, we like to think that the name Babylon is no longer about a notorious city but rather about a community that honors its past while keeping pace with the future, one that always strives to make a good impression. That good impression is facilitated through works of our community members and organizations, from the village's public works department and chamber of commerce to our historical and beautification societies and not least our houses of worship, school groups, and civic and fraternal organizations. Together, we are proud of our community and its splendid history.

We hope you will enjoy this compilation of historic postcards and the story it tells of our village. When you are in the village, we hope you stop by for a visit and tour of our museum.

Board of Trustees
Village of Babylon Historical and Preservation Society

One

Early Years
"New Babylon" and Huntington South

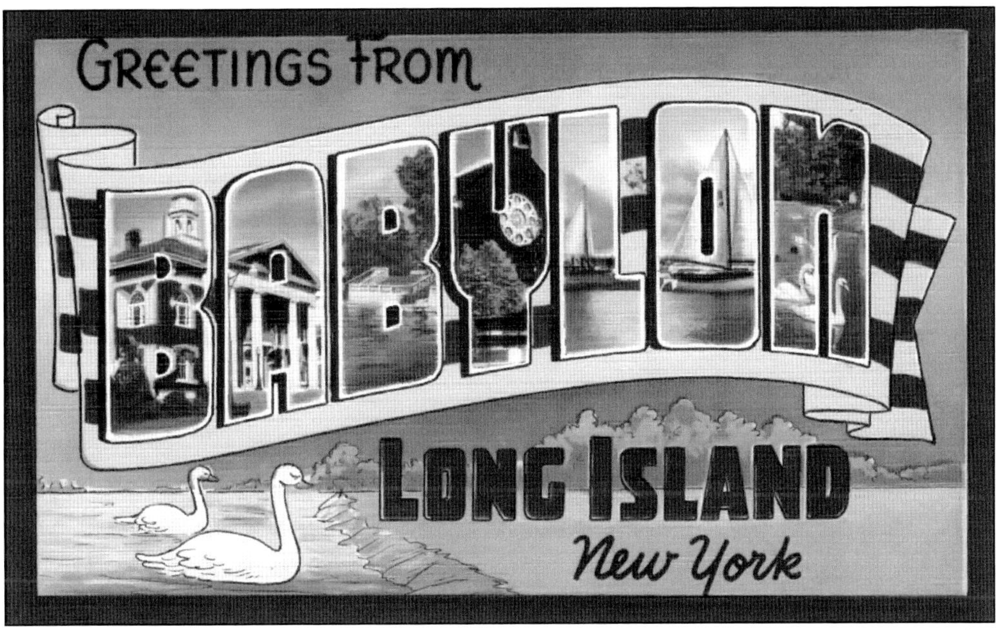

Welcome to Babylon village, a modern suburban community of about 12,000 residents with a rich history. The community has long been heralded for its charming downtown, quaint and historic homes, proximity to the amenities of the Great South Bay, and ease of commuting to New York City and points west. The village of Babylon was incorporated in 1893 and is part of the town of Babylon, which separated from the town of Huntington in 1872.

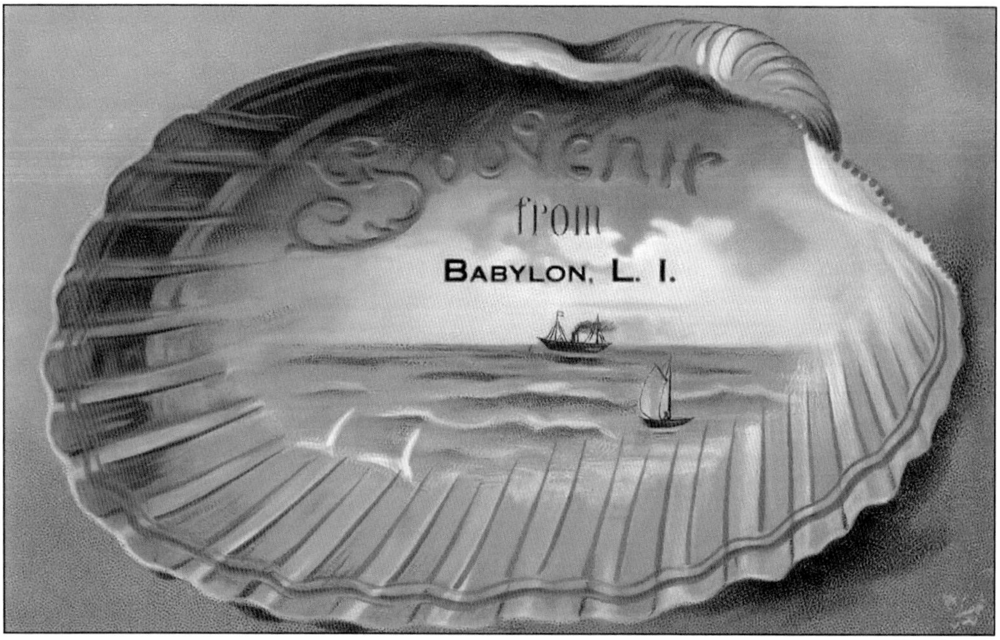

The town of Huntington dates to 1653. Prior to the town division, the communities of the town of Babylon were known as Huntington South. During the late 1800s and early 1900s, Babylon was a summer resort town. Weary city dwellers traveled to Babylon by stagecoach and later by railroad to escape the city heat. First horsecars and then trolleys transported passengers to steam ferries bound for the barrier beaches and oceanfront hotels. (TOB.)

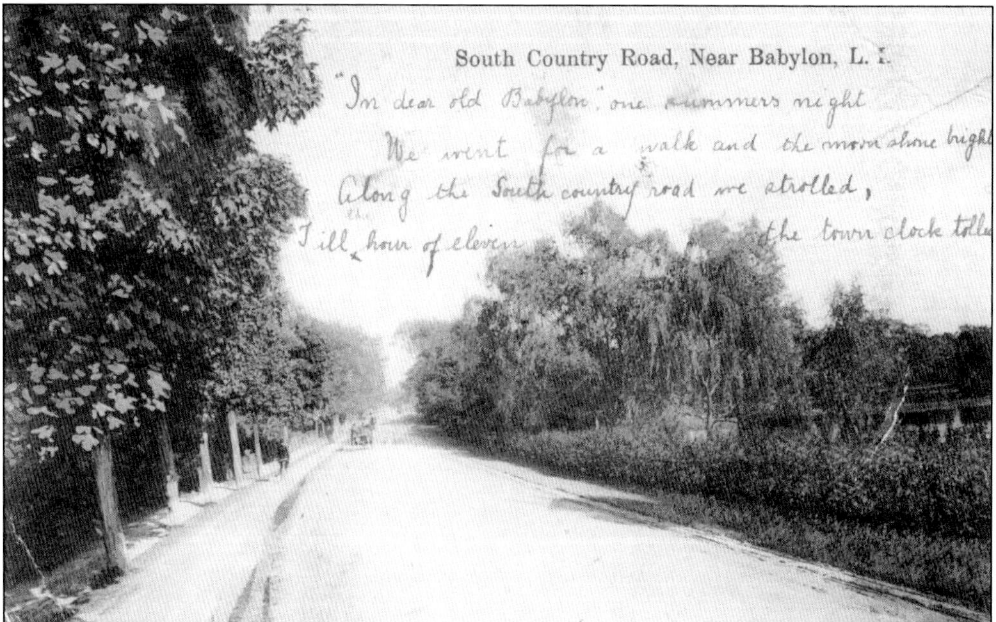

The former South Country Road, now known as Montauk Highway or New York State Route 27A through most of Suffolk County, is named Main Street through Babylon village. Running along the north end of Little East Neck and Sumpwams Neck, Main Street also passes over Carll's Creek and Sumpwams Creek.

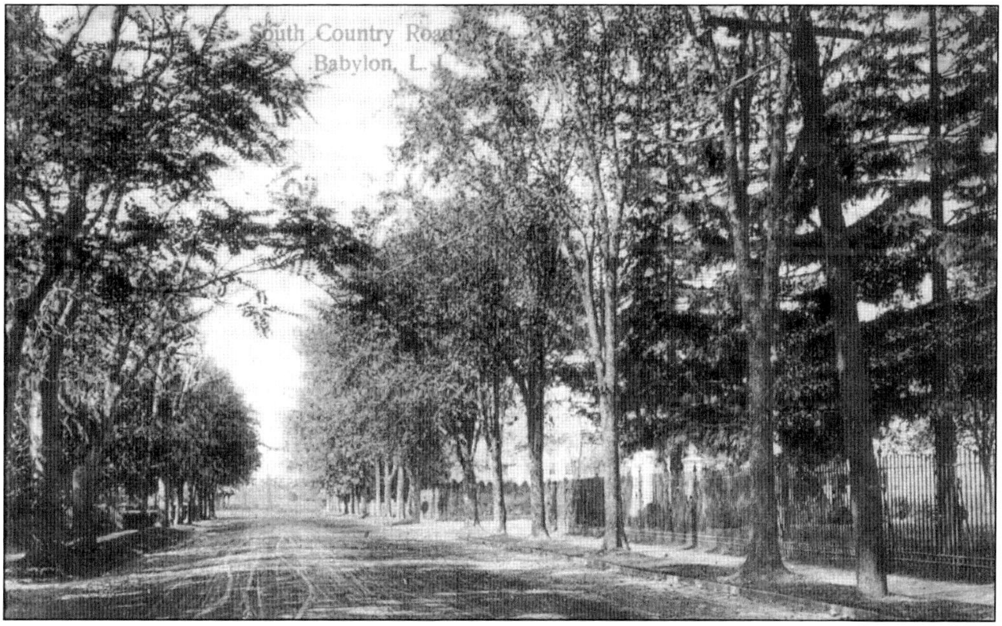

Montauk Highway extends about 26 miles west to Jamaica, New York. In the borough of Queens, the road is known as Merrick Boulevard. In Nassau County and the Suffolk County village of Amityville, it is known as Merrick Road. East of Babylon village, Montauk Highway continues approximately 90 miles to Montauk Point, the easternmost end of Long Island.

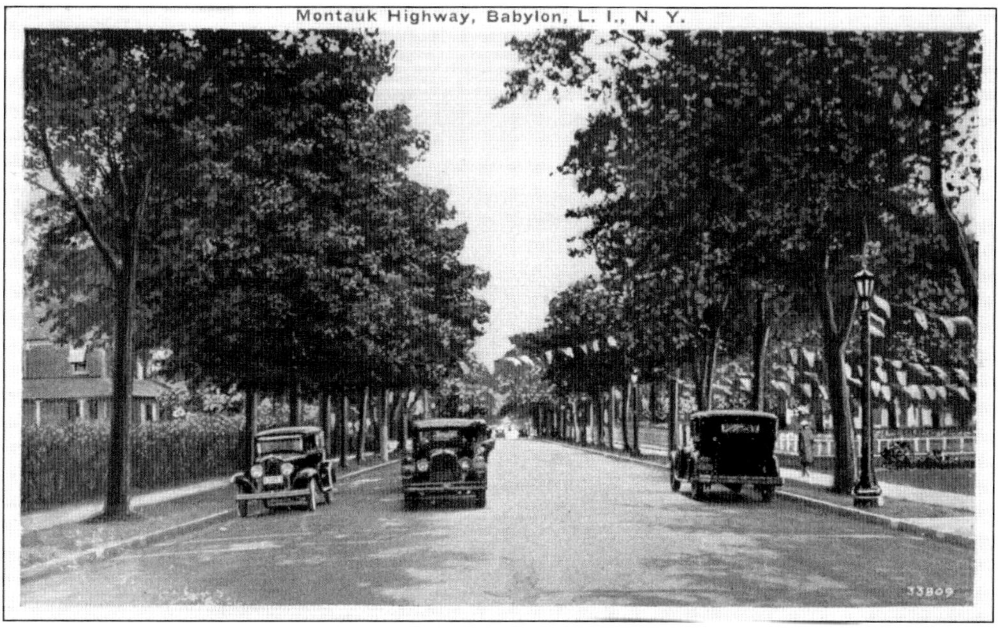

The rise of automobiles brought increased traffic to Montauk Highway; however, the expansion of Sunrise Highway in 1940 alleviated some congestion. Around 1967, community fervor defeated a road widening proposal that included filling part of Argyle Lake and paving over the picturesque overflow. Condemning the road plans, a *Newsday* reporter commented that "the pool under the waterfall is a popular spot with local youngsters who fish there for trout, perch and whatever else they can catch."

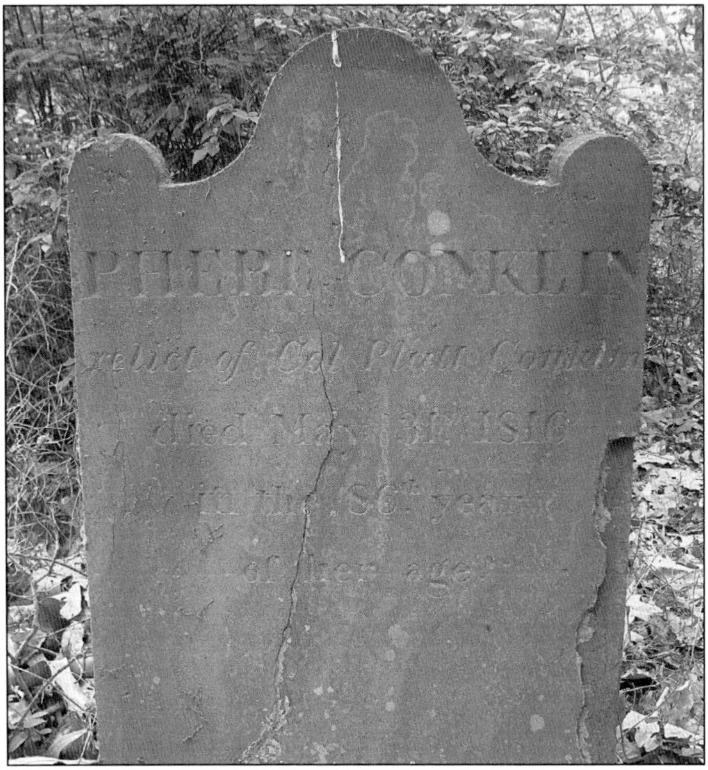

Credited with the naming of Babylon, Phebe Smith Conklin and her only child, Nathaniel Conklin, are buried in the Conklin family cemetery in Wheatley Heights alongside six generations of Conklins, including her Revolutionary War solider husband Col. Platt Conklin; Nathaniel's wife, Mary Wickham; and sons William and Wickham. Legend states that Nathaniel's grandfather, Jacob Conklin, sailed with the pirate captain William Kidd, though stories disagree over whether Jacob was a captive or willing participant. (TOB.)

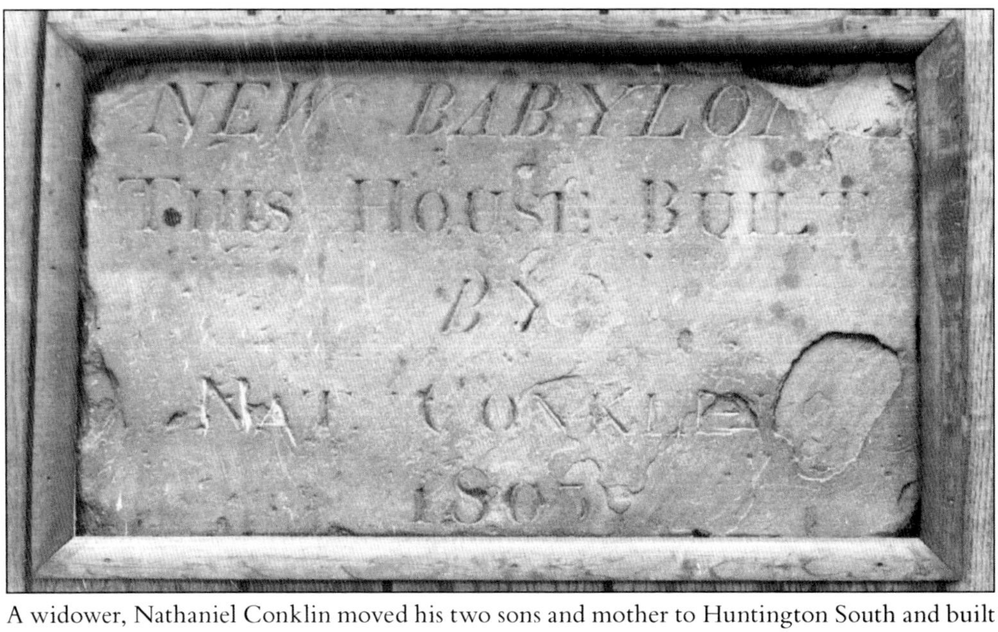

A widower, Nathaniel Conklin moved his two sons and mother to Huntington South and built a home at the northeast corner of Main Street and Deer Park Avenue in 1803. Situated across the street from the boisterous American House, Phoebe Conklin complained that the town was "another Babylon," referring to the sinful and debaucherous biblical city. Nathaniel countered by stating that the town was a "New Babylon" and inscribed the name on the cornerstone of his home. (TOB.)

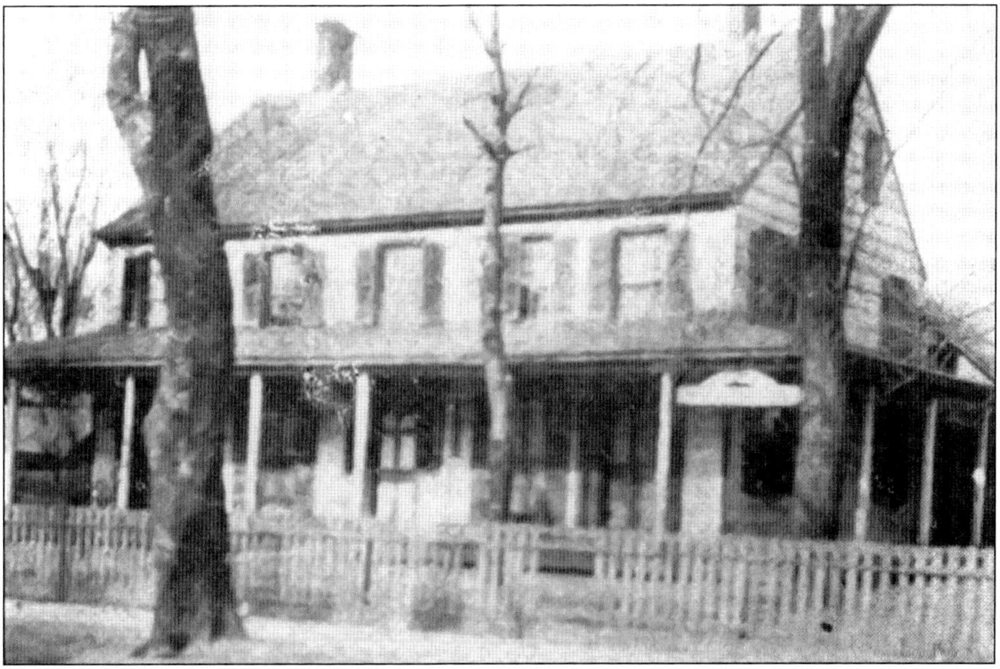

Nathaniel Conklin moved his family to West Islip, and the house passed through many owners until 1871, when David S.S. Sammis sold it to John Lux for $2,000. Lux moved the house to the west side of Deer Park Avenue, just south of the railroad tracks, where it remains. Situated next to his Washington Hotel, Lux occupied the house with his family. By 1915, the hotel had closed, and the house became a boardinghouse.

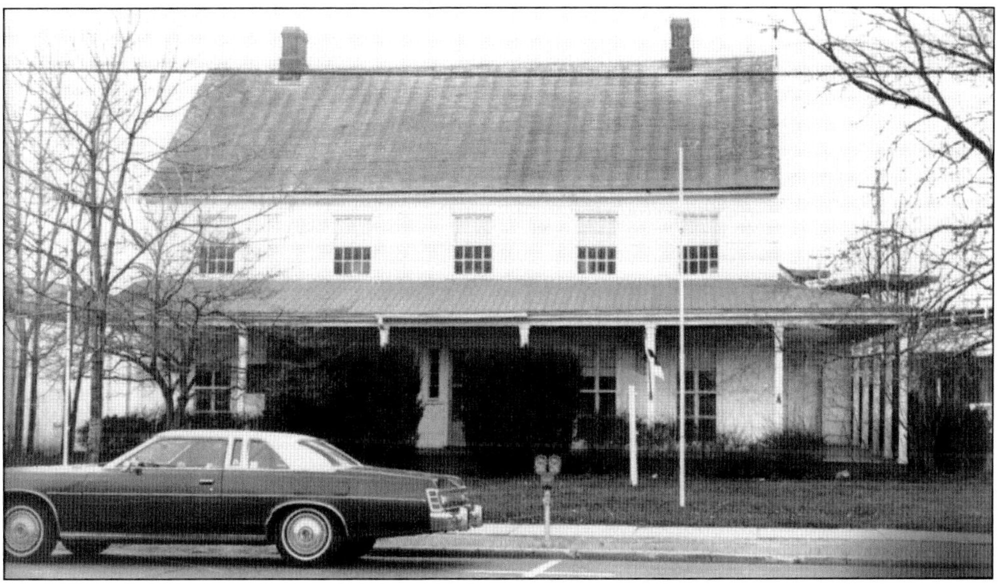

The local Red Cross chapter was headquartered in the old Conklin home through World War II. In 1945, the vacant house was donated to the Red Cross by descendants of the Sammis family in memory of their grandmother, Antoinette Wheeler Sammis, and mother, Emeline Sammis Norton. Recognizing its importance in local history, the house was purchased by Babylon village and listed in the National Register of Historic Places in 1988; it is now a museum. (TOB.)

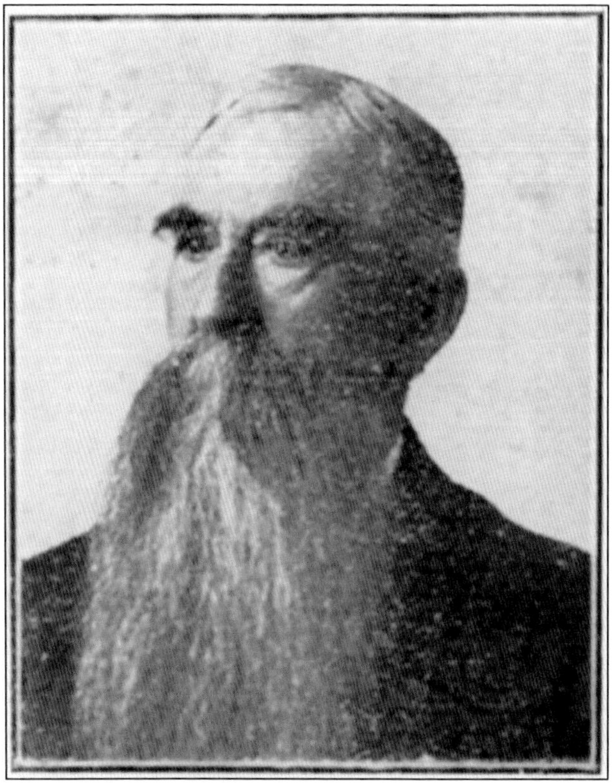

Benjamin Prince Field came to Babylon in 1831. During his 60-some years in Babylon, Field became a well-known resident, working in the tinsmith trade and marrying Mary Ann Purchase, with whom he had eight children. In 1911, at the age of 80, Field left an indelible imprint on Babylon history by chronicling his adopted hometown in *Reminiscences of Babylon*.

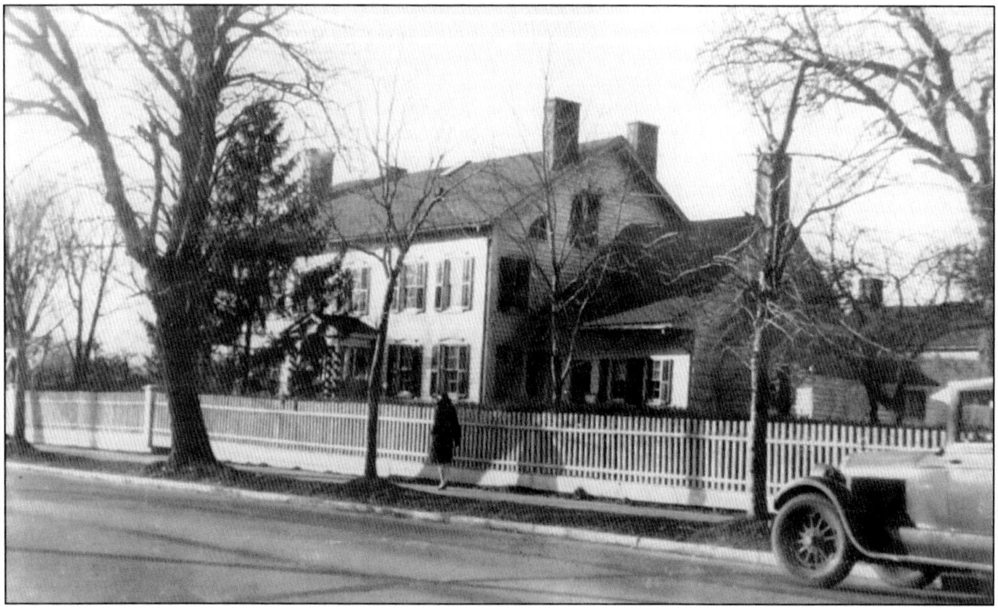

After six years of construction, Maj. Timothy Carll completed his Main Street home in 1801; it is commonly known as the 1801 House. The house remained in the Carll family for over 100 years until the title passed to Ernest Wiltsie. In 1957, owing to what he called its "sentimental and historical value," Francis B. Garvey had the building moved northwest alongside Argyle Lake and renovated it for offices next to the Argyle Square professional development. (TOB.)

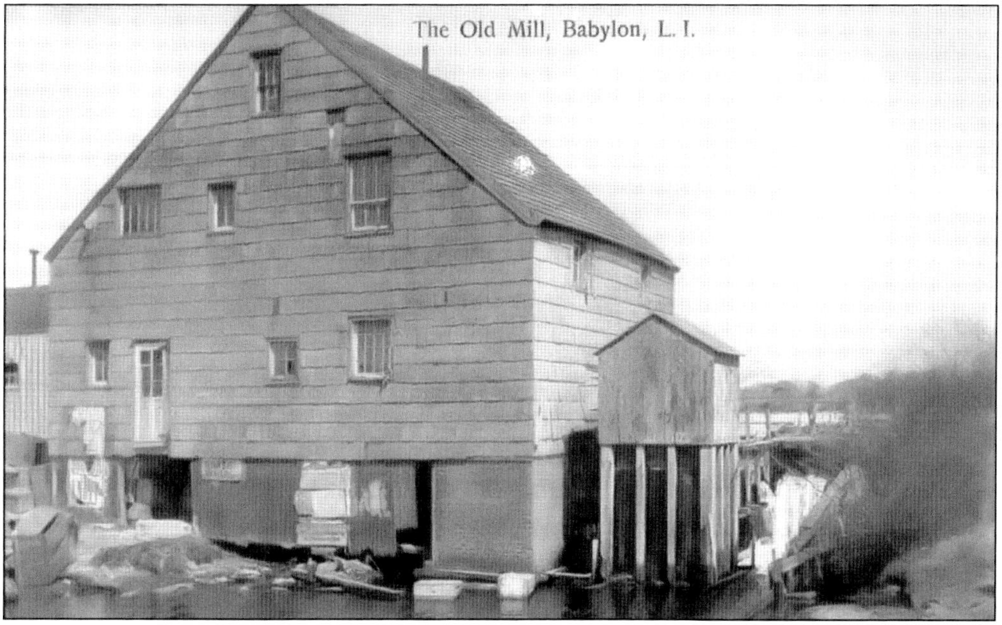

Around 1750, the Oakley family built a wooden gear gristmill on Sumpwams Creek, just north of present Montauk Highway. In his 1911 book, Benjamin P. Field recalled the mill in the 1850s when it was operated by Nathaniel Oakley, who wore a long smock and tall beaver hat, "all well covered with miller's dust, white flour." Eliphalet W. Oakley succeeded his father Nathaniel in the milling business, changing from a gristmill to a sawmill.

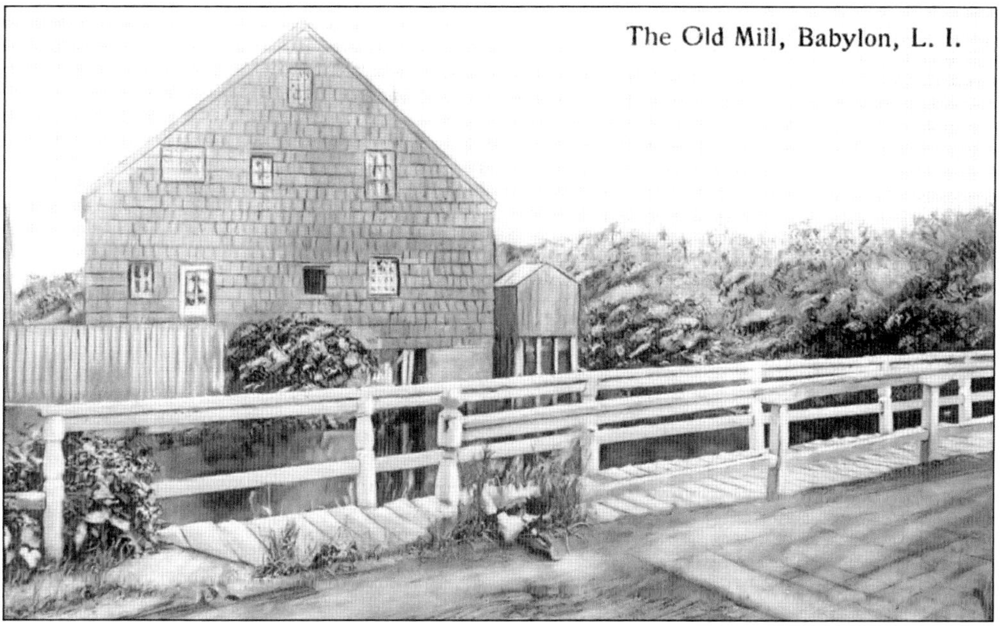

The mill passed out of the Oakley family and later became a manufactory for buggy whips under the direction of David C. Ricketts and his son Walter. Ricketts moved his factory to George Street around 1903, but the rise of automobiles meant the end for many such whip factories. In 1910, Edwin Hawley purchased the property and directed the construction of a decorative spillway on the north side of Montauk Highway.

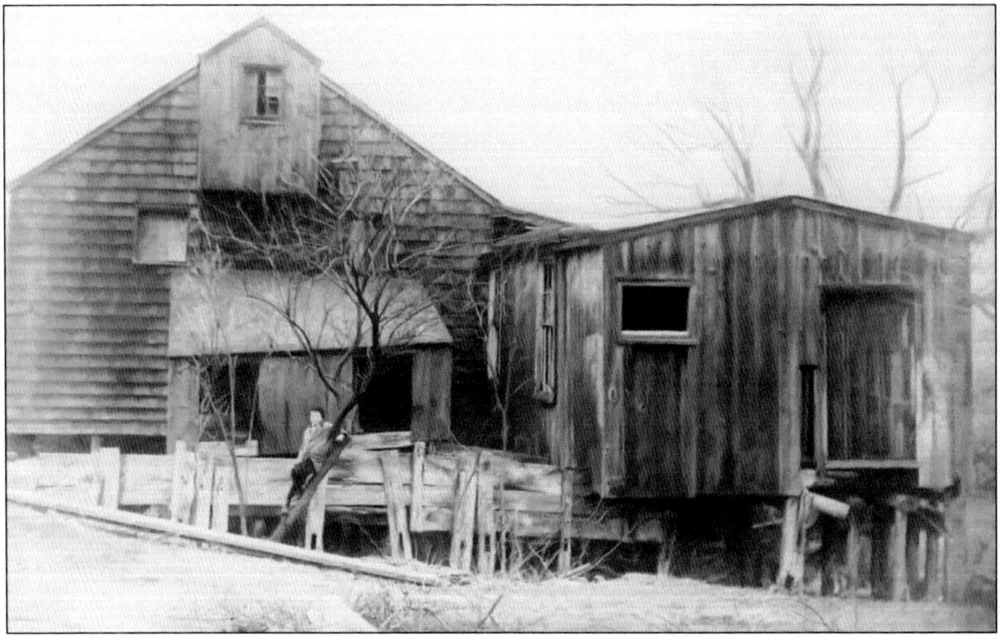

The Southard family owned their namesake lake property for at least three generations and operated a gristmill on the south end of Southard's Pond. In 1905, the *Brooklyn Daily Eagle* reported that the then century-old mill was "no longer used as a grist mill, but the big saws still eat their way through a tree trunk now and then, although not as frequently as in days gone by."

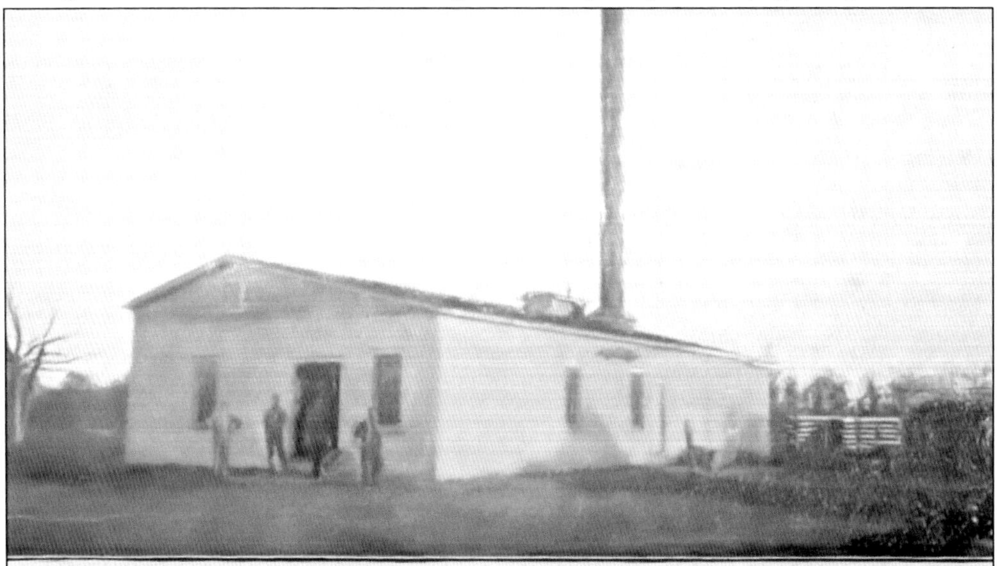

Babylon was first lit by electric light on November 24, 1886, with the illumination of eight businesses and three street lights. The *South Side Signal* proclaimed that "others will no doubt avail themselves of the privilege . . . until the old-fashioned kerosene lamp is entirely superseded by the electric light." Electric illumination came just 15 years after the *Signal* pondered "Shall Babylon be Lighted with Gas?" after the installation of the first gas generator at the Watson House.

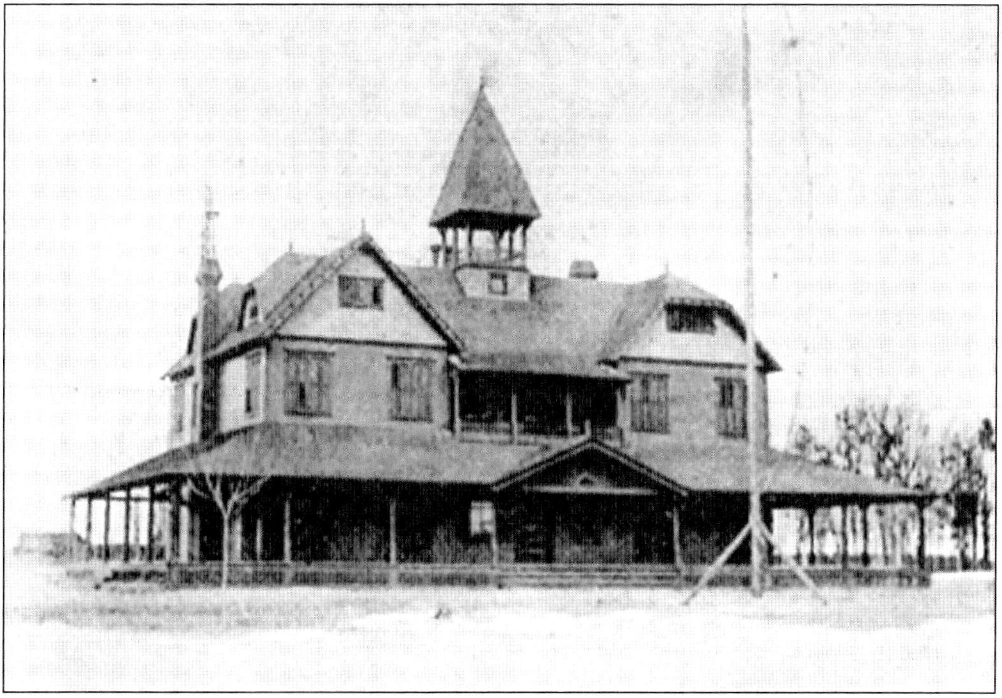

Formed around 1876 and named in honor of their regular meeting place in the bar of Manhattan's Westminster Hotel, the renowned Westminster Kennel Club was headquartered in Babylon from 1880 until 1904. Formed as a sportsman's club, the organization occupied a 64-acre site at the southwest corner of Southard's Pond that included kennels for 200 dogs, a clubhouse with a dozen bedrooms, and a shooting house.

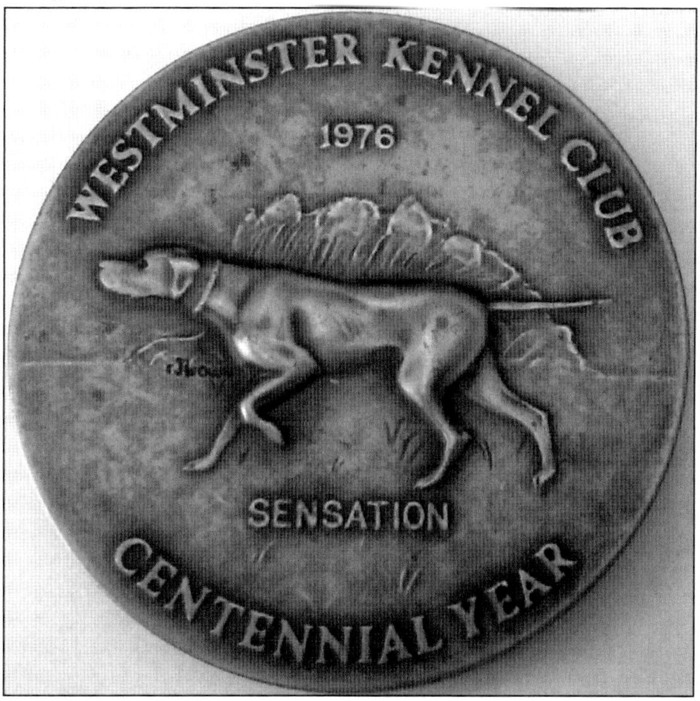

An English-born pointer, originally named Don, was brought to America by George deForest Grant to support the breeding stock of the club's hunting dogs. To promote the new club, Don was renamed Sensation and became a superstar. The lemon-and-white pointer, immortalized as the Westminster Kennel Club logo, was buried at the base of the Babylon club's flagpole in 1887. The club relocated to New Jersey after New York State outlawed pigeon shooting. (TOB.)

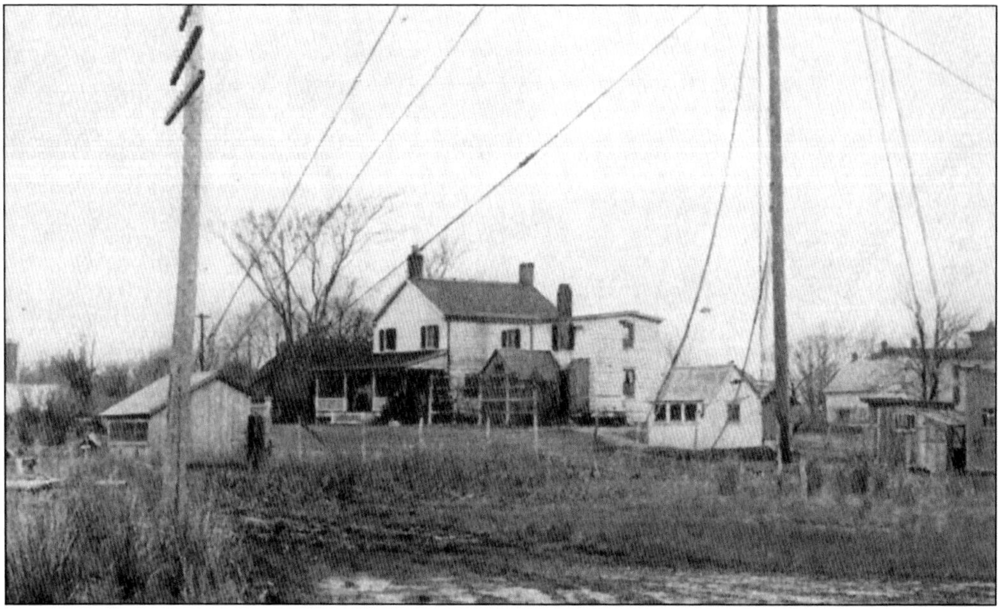

In September 1902, the Marconi Wireless and Telegraph Company established its fourth New York land station under a five-year lease of the Andrew Jacobs property on Fire Island Avenue. The station instructed students in wireless operations using three 160-foot transmission poles that conveyed messages to and from the Marconi station at Sagaponack, New York, or passing steamers outfitted with the system within a 100-mile range.

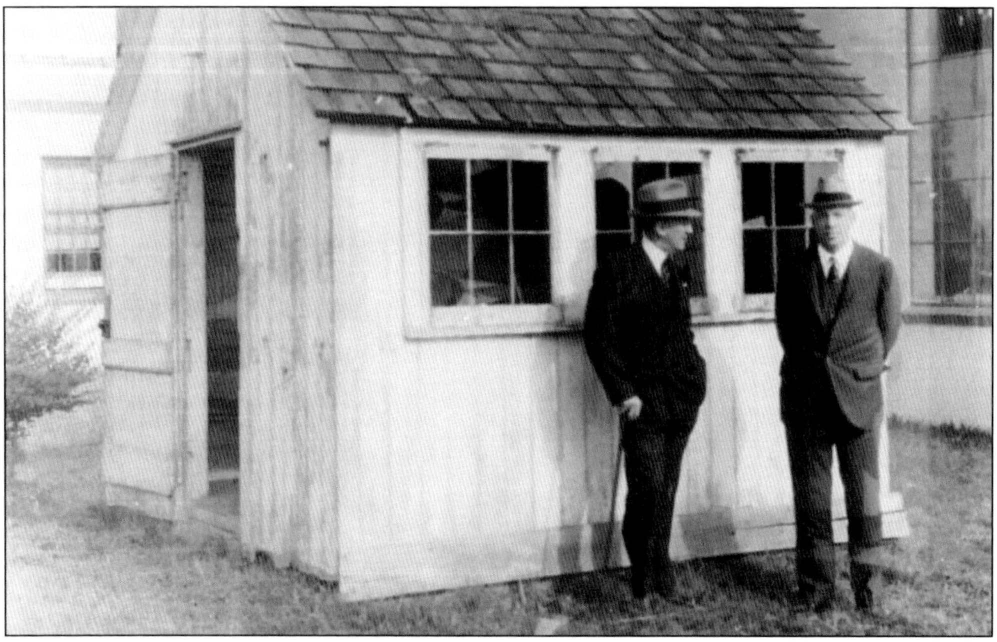

In 1930, FM radio inventor Edwin Howard Armstrong purchased the old wireless building from a local farmer during a visit to Capt. H.J. Round, who had worked at the Marconi school and transmitting station. Armstrong was an admirer of Marconi's work and gave the building to the Radio Corporation of America in tribute to Marconi. Marconi (left) and Armstrong are pictured with the building at RCA in Rocky Point on October 17, 1927. (TOB.)

Two

Waterfront Community
Living along Great South Bay

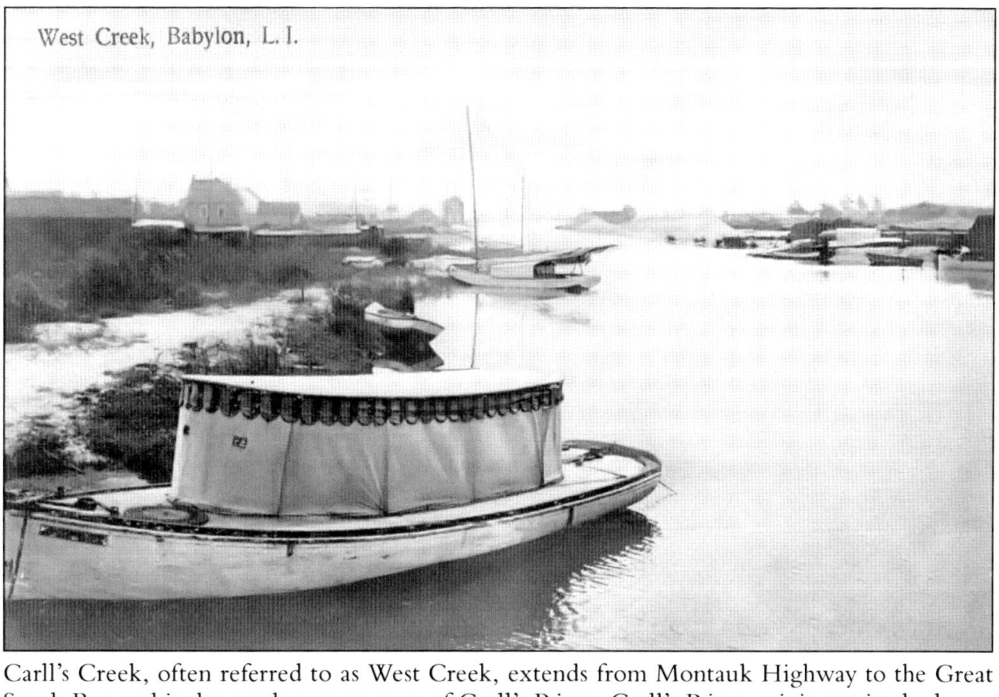

Carll's Creek, often referred to as West Creek, extends from Montauk Highway to the Great South Bay and is the southernmost part of Carll's River. Carll's River originates in the lower Half Hollow Hills, near Deer Park and Wyandanch, flowing about five and a half miles south through Geiger Lake, Belmont Lake, Southard's Pond, and Argyle Lake, continuing through Carll's Creek to the bay.

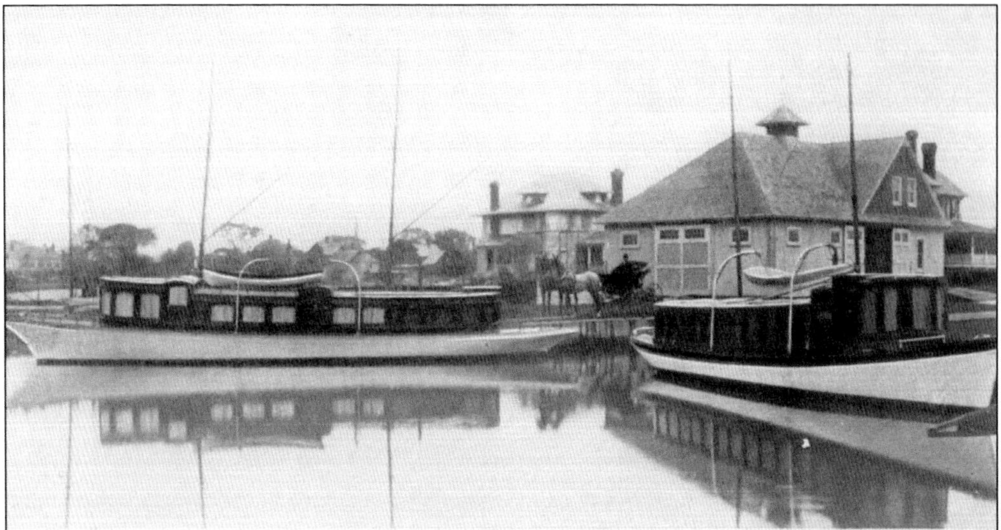

4818 THOMPSON AVE. & CREEK, BABYLON, N Y. PUBL. BY H. P. BISHOP'S MUSIC STORE.

Carll's River was named for the Carll family, who once owned large tracts of land around Babylon. Elbert Carll (1807–1887) was elected the first supervisor of the town of Babylon after its separation from the town of Huntington. He owned most of the land on either side of present Carll Avenue. He also owned much of the property around present Thompson Avenue, and it appears that Elbert Carll named the street in honor of his mother-in-law, Julia Thompson.

A CREEK SCENE AT FREDERICK SHORES, BABYLON, LONG ISLAND, N. Y.

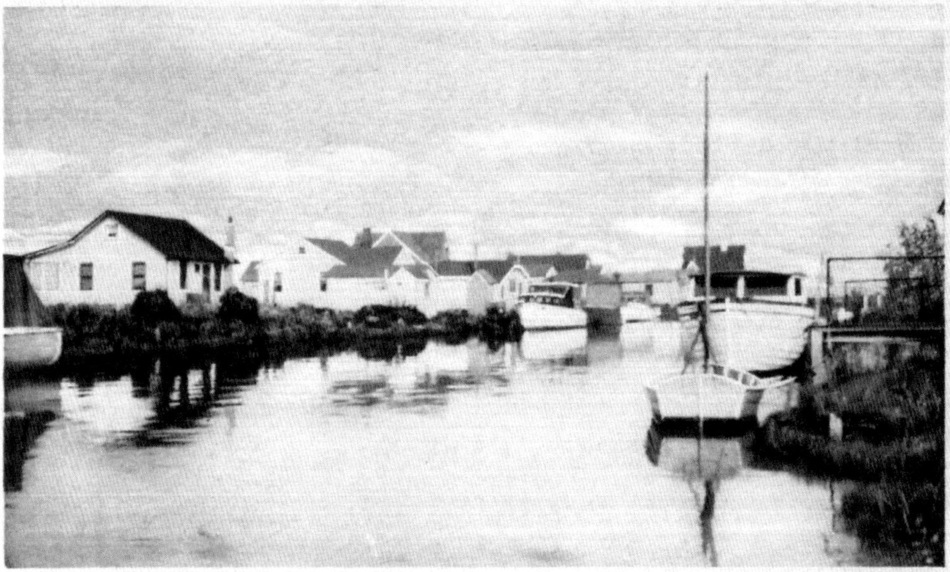

The south shore of Long Island saw a real estate boom in the 1920s, including the development of Frederick Shores, the namesake of its founder Cadman H. Frederick. A 1927 advertisement for Frederick Shores offered lots starting at $285, declaring: "Here is the waterfront chance of a lifetime. Get out of the reeking, heat-drenched city. You owe it to the kiddies and yourself. At last the family of moderate means can enjoy the same privileges as the millionaire."

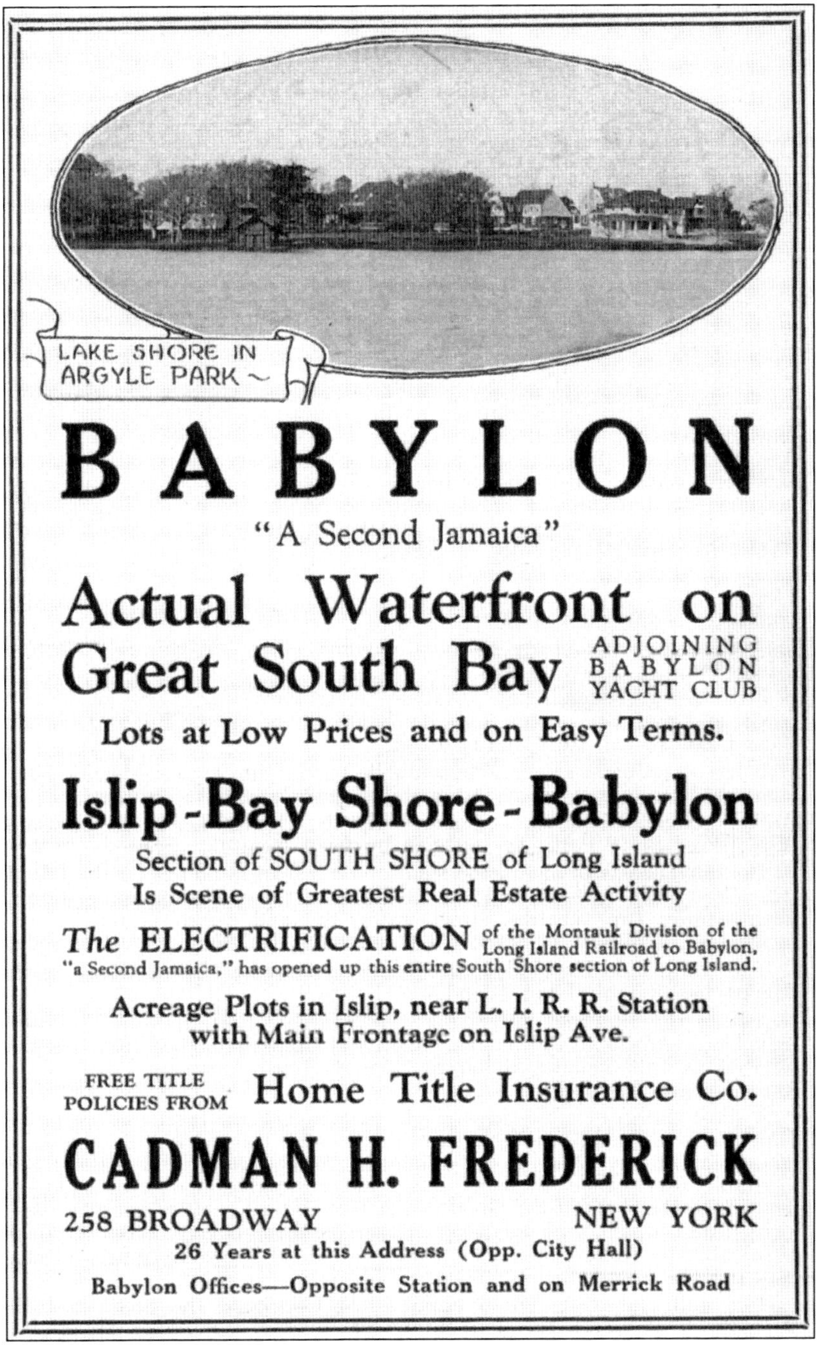

This advertisement for Cadman Frederick's South Shore housing developments appeared in the 1927 real estate booklet *Long Island—"The Sunrise Trail"* published by the Long Island Rail Road. Real estate and the railroad were common advertising partners, touting the proximity of housing developments to railroad stations that would ease commuting to employment and amenities in New York City. The phrase "A Second Jamaica" was meant to highlight the anticipated growth of the Babylon area after the Long Island Rail Road's electrification of the line in 1925. (TOB.)

BAB Y

Is Step pin

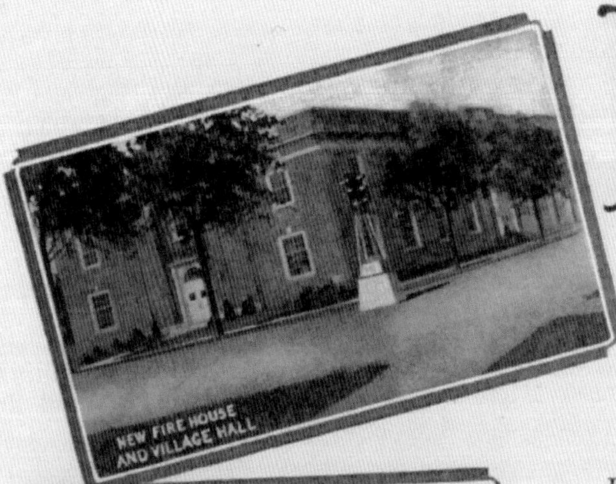

NEW FIRE HOUSE AND VILLAGE HALL

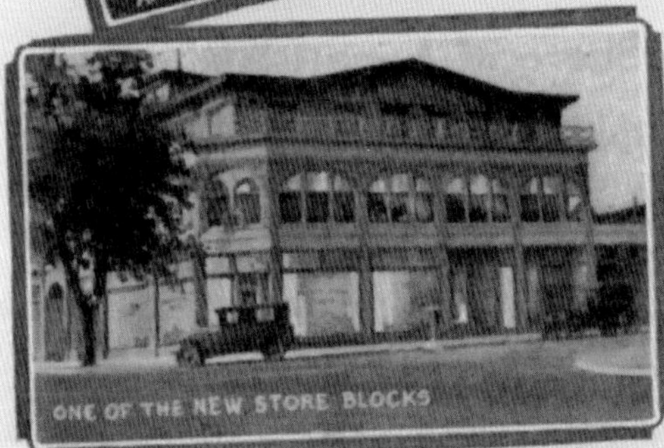

ONE OF THE NEW STORE BLOCKS

BABYLON LIBRARY

—And how!

In one year, a new Fire House and Village Hall, a new Public School, a new Parochial School and new, up-to-date stores everywhere you look.

And then, since play is a big item with us Babylonians, we point with pride to the sightly new home of the Babylon Yacht Club on Great South Bay, the beautiful Southward Ho Club and a new, gigantic bathing beach now nearing completion.

With
new fir
and el
Babylor
conveni
its inco
mosphe
lon has
a charr

If yo
family
of the
out wh
boat an
—out
—step

This space contributed by
Babylon National Bank
John R. Tracey, Nash Agent
E. W. Howell, Builder
W. P. Ketcham, Plumber
E. C. Livingston
Frank Weilbacher
E. Clayton Smith, Auto Replacement Parts
Lyman Estates, Water Fronts
Jeremiah Robbins, Real Estate
William V. Young, Village Plots
George H. Walbridge, Surveyor

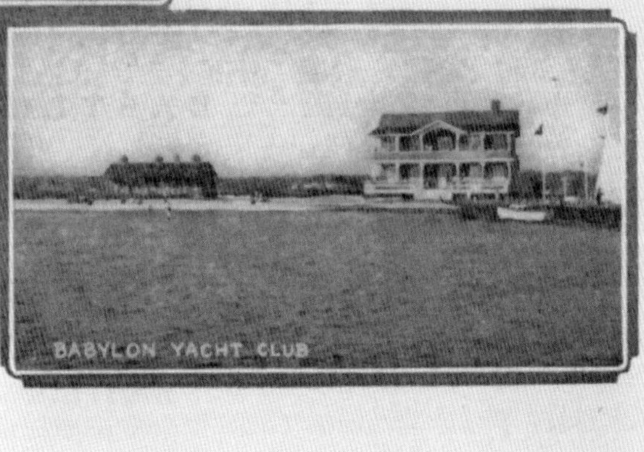

BABYLON YACHT CLUB

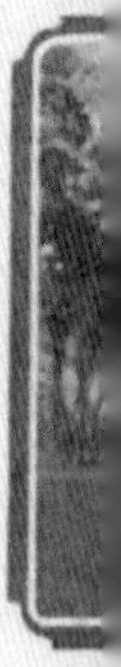

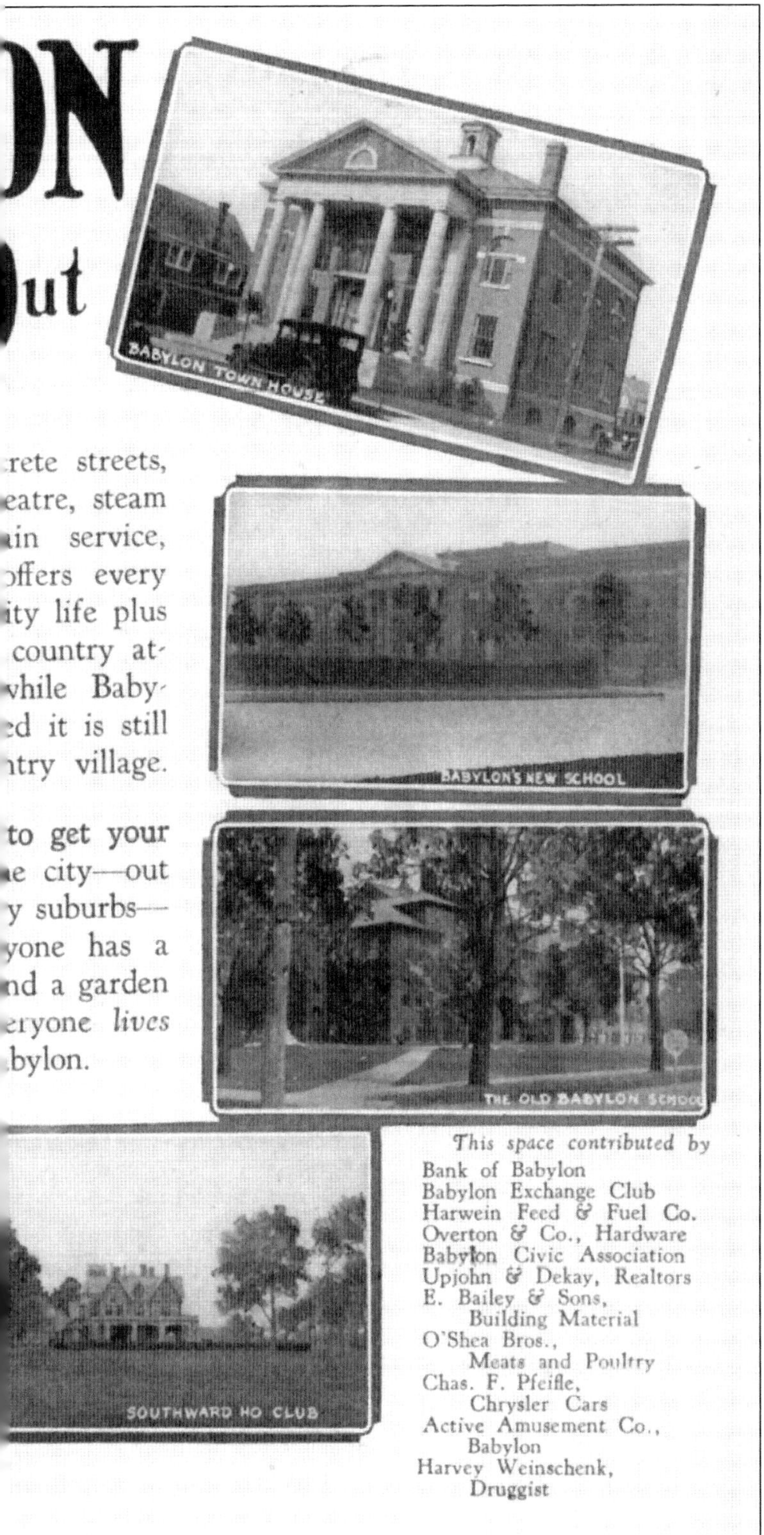

ON

ut

rete streets, eatre, steam ain service, offers every ity life plus country at- while Baby- ed it is still ntry village.

to get your e city—out y suburbs— yone has a nd a garden eryone *lives* bylon.

This space contributed by
Bank of Babylon
Babylon Exchange Club
Harwein Feed & Fuel Co.
Overton & Co., Hardware
Babylon Civic Association
Upjohn & Dekay, Realtors
E. Bailey & Sons, Building Material
O'Shea Bros., Meats and Poultry
Chas. F. Pfeifle, Chrysler Cars
Active Amusement Co., Babylon
Harvey Weinschenk, Druggist

Another Babylon promotion from the 1927 *Long Island—"The Sunrise Trail"* flaunts some of the village's highlights. Clockwise from upper right are Babylon Town Hall, built 1917–1918 on property donated by the Sammis family; the recent high school expansion facing Railroad Avenue; Babylon High School, built in 1893, seen from Grove Place; Southward Ho Country Club, founded in 1923 and situated on the former Bay Shore estate of James Hazen; Babylon Yacht Club on the Great South Bay; Babylon Library, which opened in 1911 on property donated by Elbert Carll Livingston; a commercial block; and the village municipal building, erected in 1926 on property donated by Jay Stanley Foster in 1924. (TOB.)

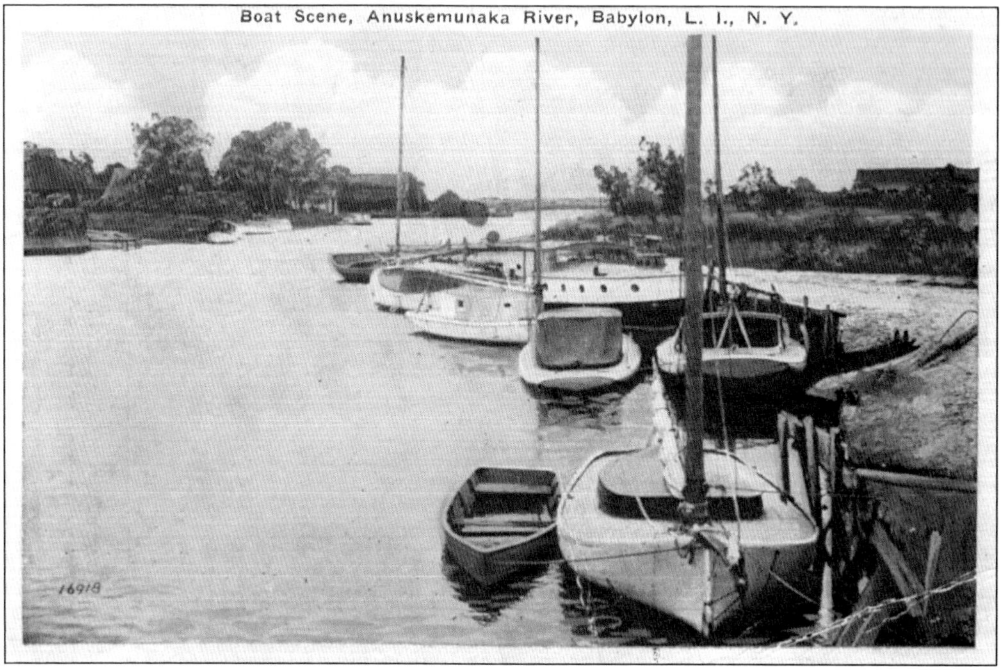

At times, Carll's Creek has also been known as Annuskemunaka River. Annuskemunaka Road is located at the southern end of Sumpwams Neck. Although there have been reports that *annuskemunaka* is a Native American word for "seashell," some scholars have asserted that the word refers to "planting land" or "plowed ground."

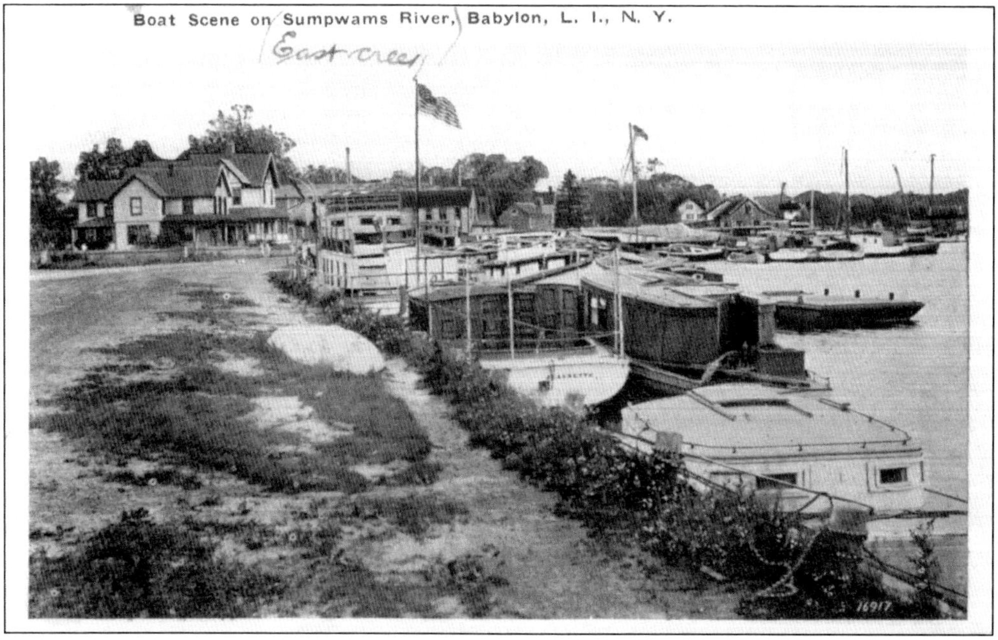

Like Carll's River, Sumpwams Creek originates from headwaters in Deer Park, flowing six miles south through several small ponds and Hawley's Pond to the Great South Bay. The river's path nearly mimics the boundary between the towns of Babylon and Islip. *Sumpwams* is believed to be a Native American word referring to an honest person.

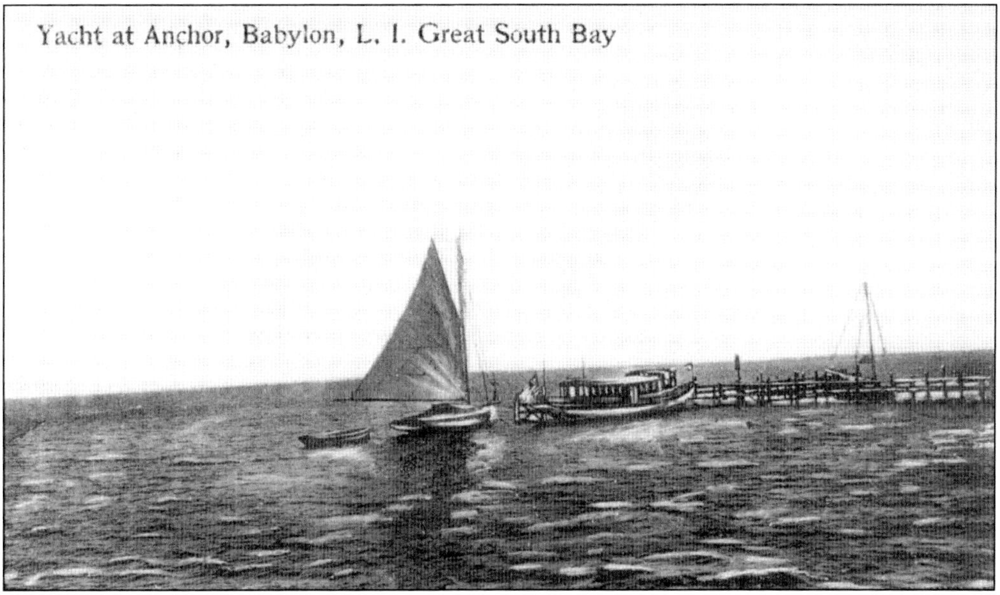

"News from the south shore of Long Island indicates that the season there will soon be fully underway," reported *Brooklyn Life* magazine on June 18, 1898. "A considerable percentage of the cottagers have already arrived and the nautical activity displayed by the yacht owners seems to bid fair for an interesting yachting season. . . . Frank Stephens Eastby, who is settled in his country house on Robbins avenue, Babylon, has the sloop *Auk* already in commission and has entertained a number of guests aboard her."

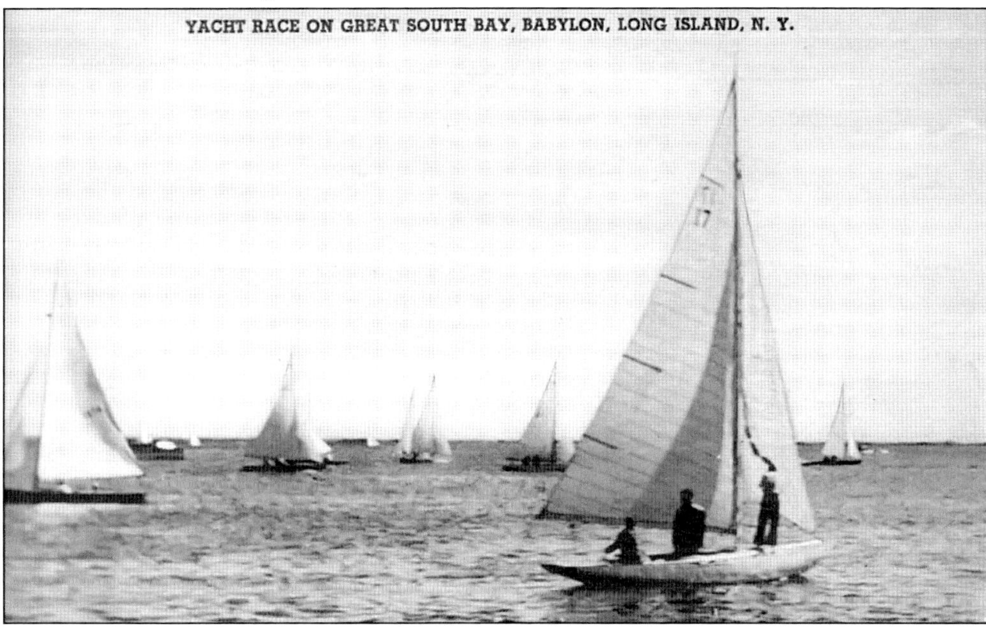

Under the 1910 headline "As a Sportman's Paradise: The Many Ways in Which the Island Lures the Lover of Outdoor Pastimes," the *New York Times* described Babylon as "the station for yachtsmen who rendezvous at Oak Island, near Fire Island Inlet." At Babylon, "stanch sailboats, with competent skippers, can be hired for fishing in the bay or . . . in quest of the fighting bluefish off Fire Island Light."

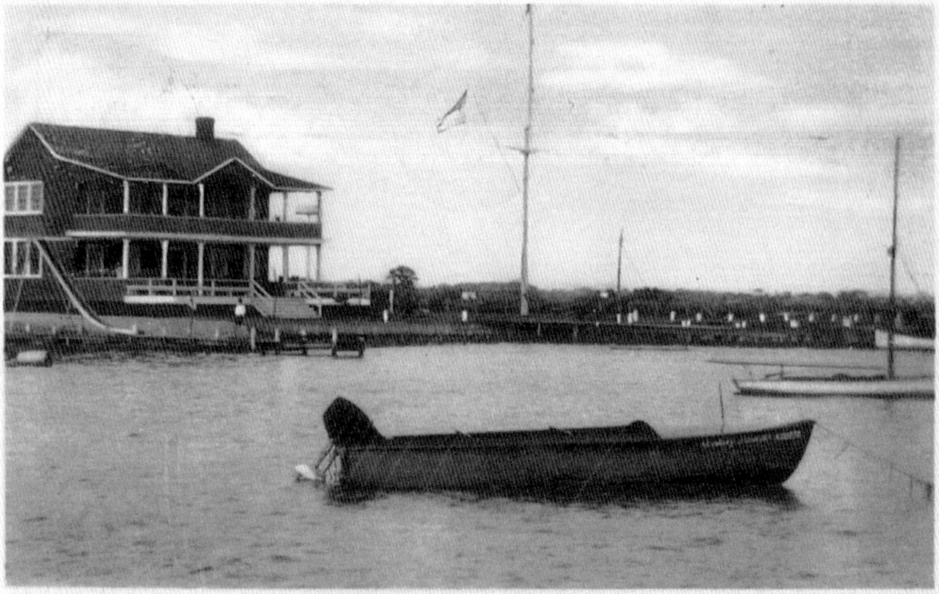

YACHT CLUB, BABYLON, LONG ISLAND, N. Y.

The Babylon Yacht Club incorporated in 1903 "to encourage members to become proficient in the personal management, control and handling of their yachts and to promote sociability and recreation among its members." Schenk Remsen served as the club's first commodore. The following year, the organization built a small clubhouse on Sumpwams Point. (TOB.)

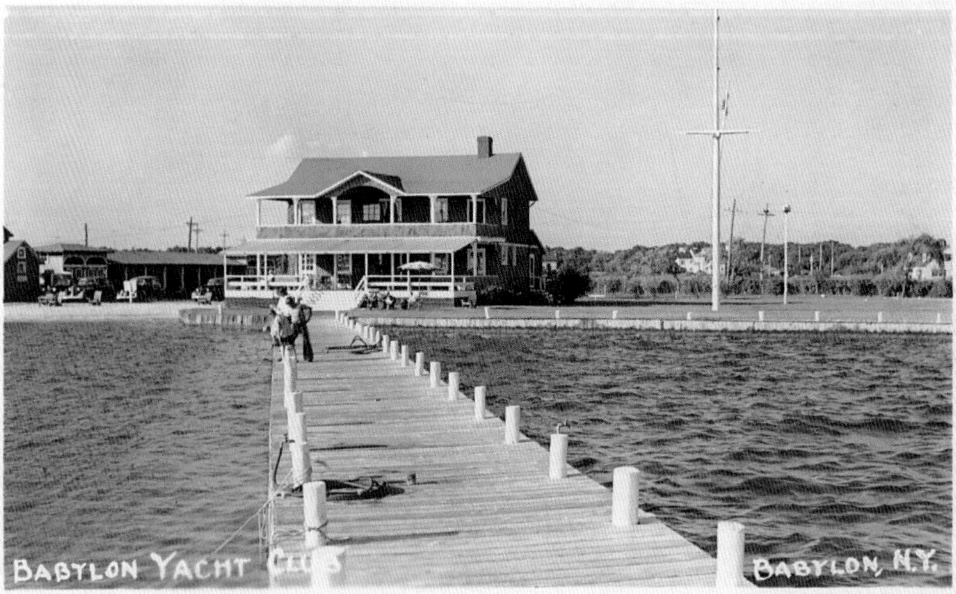

By its third year, the yacht club boasted 55 members and purchased a large lot on the site of the present municipal dock, where it built a larger clubhouse in 1907. The original clubhouse was moved across the Great South Bay and became the Oak Island Yacht Club. In 1929, the clubhouse was moved by scow to the old McCurdy estate, Eaton Lane in West Islip, where it continues to operate.

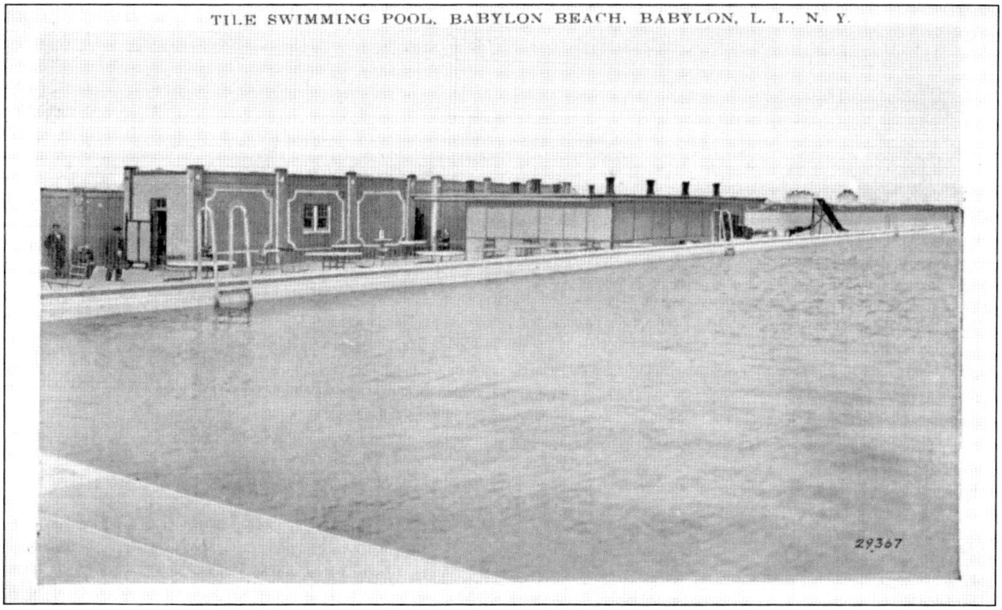

The Babylon Bathing Beach and Swimming Pool, opened in 1927, was the creation of Cadman H. Frederick, a local real estate developer. The pool opened as he began promotion and development of his new Frederick Shores residential community, which lay at the foot of Little East Neck Road, south of the old Foster estate. The 200-foot-by-80-foot pool was one of the largest on the East Coast and widely noted for its tile work.

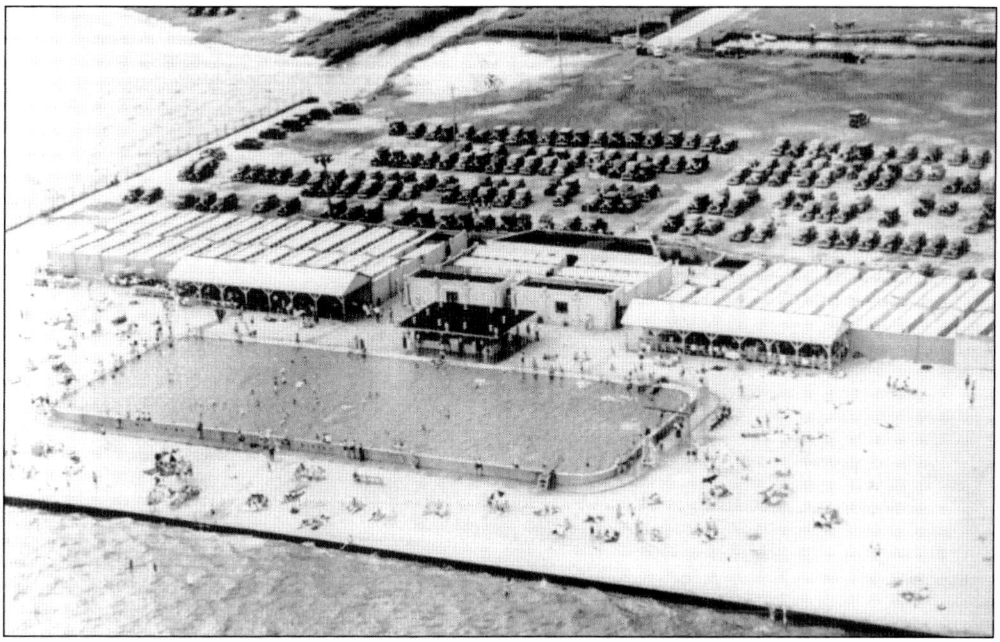

An aerial view shows the pool at the end of Fire Island Avenue around 1927. In 1947, Babylon village residents voted five to one in favor of purchasing the pool, on three-and-a-half acres, from Cadman H. Frederick for $45,000. The pool complex underwent an extensive modernization in 1972. On August 21, 1982, the pool was rededicated as the Gilbert C. Hanse Municipal Pool, "in recognition of his outstanding service to Babylon Village."

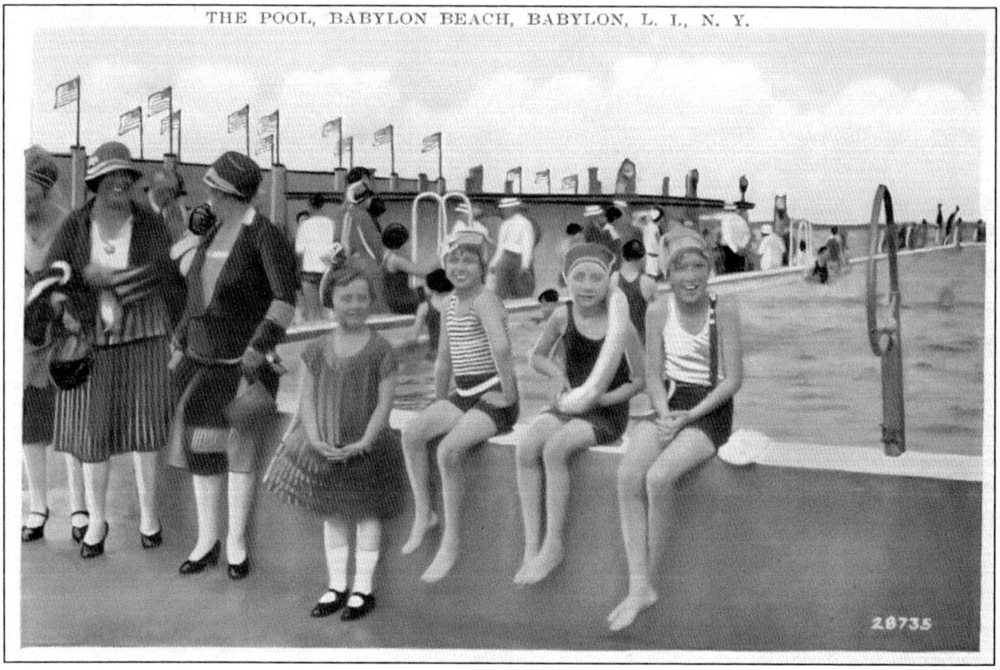

The *Brooklyn Daily Eagle* touted the new recreation facility: "After 18 months of intensive work and the expenditure of approximately $500,000 . . . the work of constructing the new bathing beach, the casino, bathing pool, etc., has been accomplished in record time . . . thousands of dollars have been invested in a playground for children and in beach equipment. Parking space for at least 1,000 automobiles also has been provided."

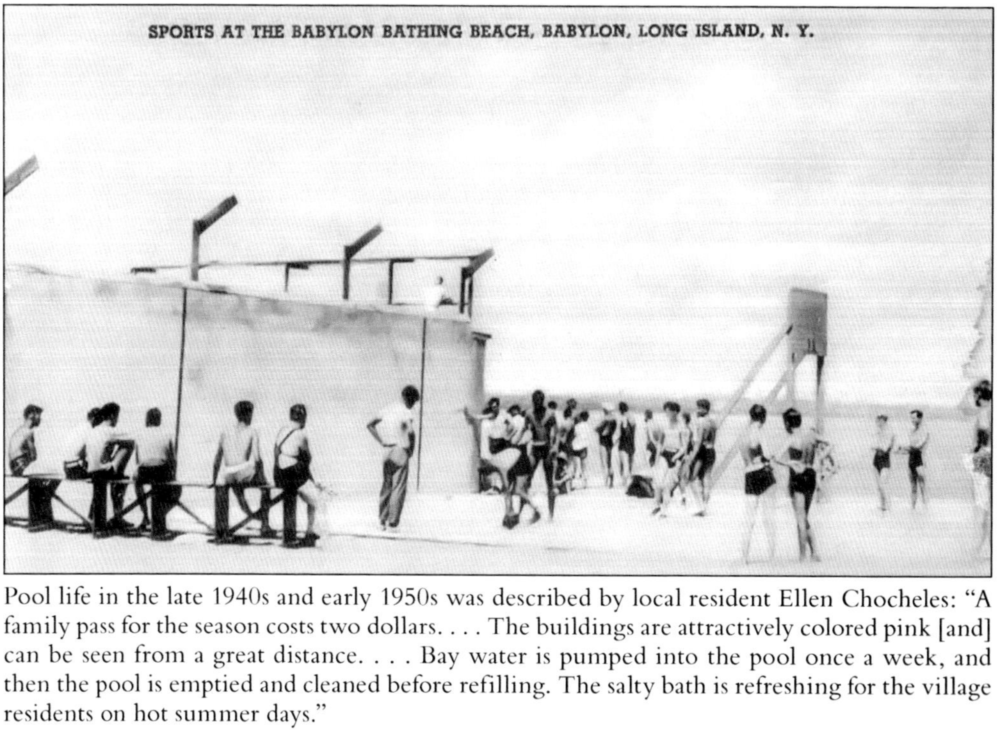

Pool life in the late 1940s and early 1950s was described by local resident Ellen Chocheles: "A family pass for the season costs two dollars. . . . The buildings are attractively colored pink [and] can be seen from a great distance. . . . Bay water is pumped into the pool once a week, and then the pool is emptied and cleaned before refilling. The salty bath is refreshing for the village residents on hot summer days."

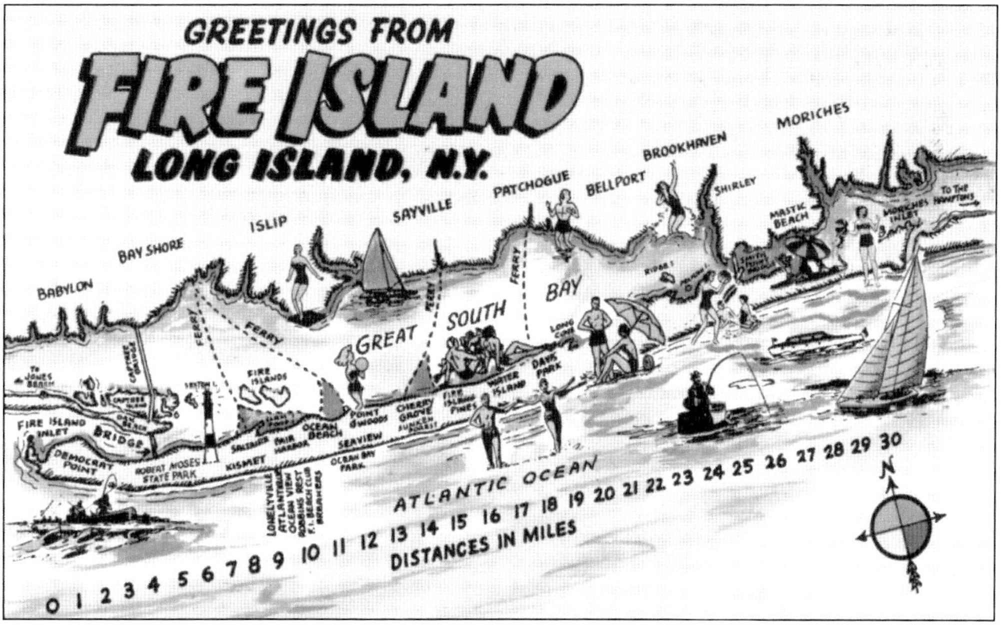

Transport to ocean beaches by private boats and steam ferries was a cottage industry before completion of the Robert Moses Causeway. Summarizing his experiences, Moses recalled "A compelling need . . . for a modern landscaped, restricted and protected parkway system uninterrupted by [railroad] crossings . . . with infrequent entrances and exits, free from hotdog stands and billboards and other disfigureing and distracting structures along its border, and we realistically assumed the burden of determining routes totalling 130 miles." (TOB.)

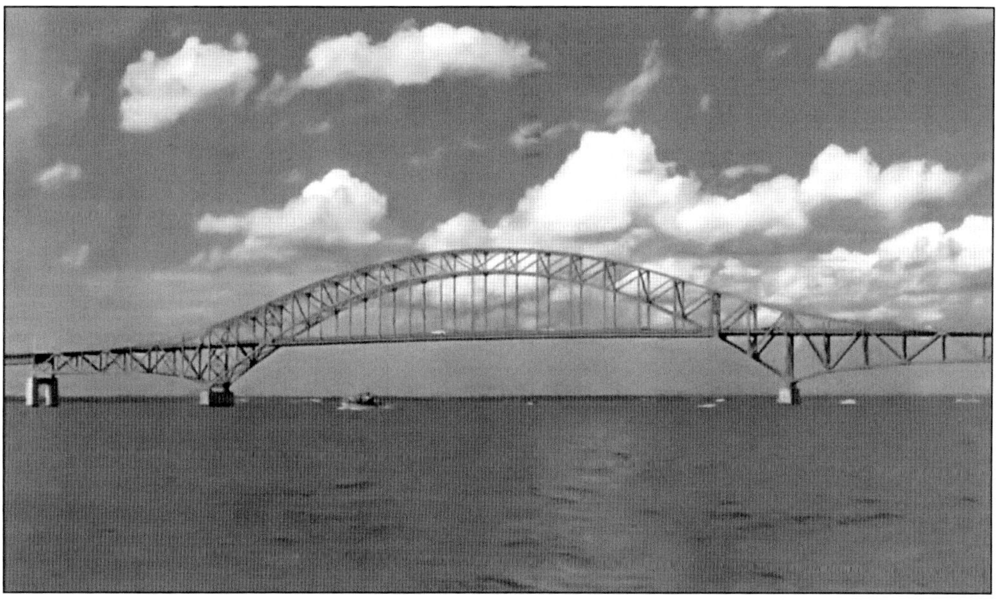

Robert Moses, who oversaw the planning of the New York state parkway system, stated, "Those of us who laid out the state park and parkway program on Long Island twenty-five years ago had no illusions as to the task ahead of us. . . . We anticipated plenty of bitter personal opposition from selfish and misinformed sources and in this respect at least were not disappointed or caught napping. Today we stand at the threshold of completion of the system." (TOB.)

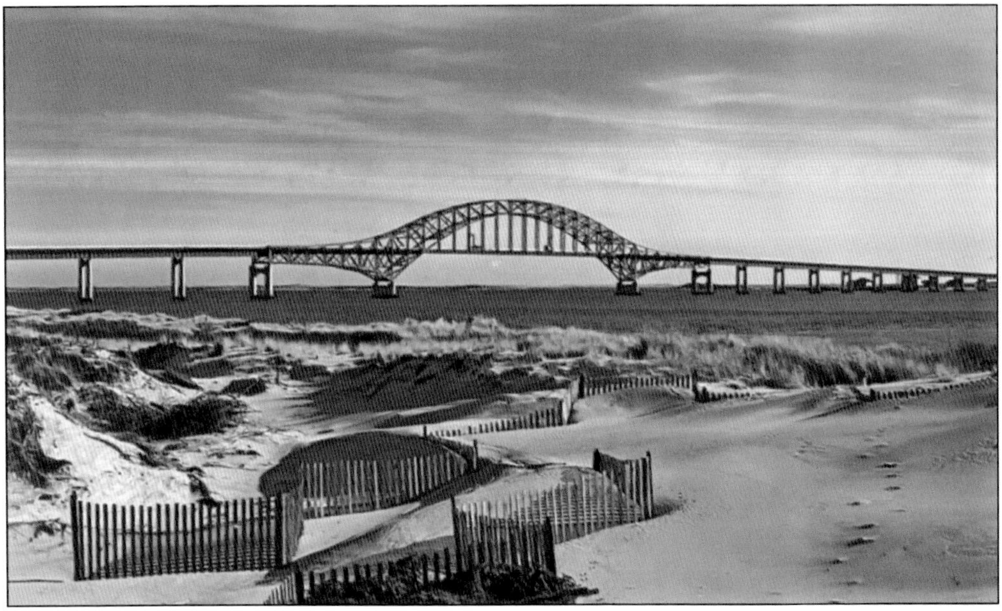

The causeway, joining the Southern State and Ocean Parkways, has three bridges. The northernmost bridge, the Great South Bay Bridge (previous image), formally opened on June 12, 1954. That original bridge is now the southbound bridge. The northbound bascule or drawbridge, State Boat Channel Bridge, opened in 1968. The Fire Island Inlet Bridge (pictured) opened on June 13, 1964. (TOB.)

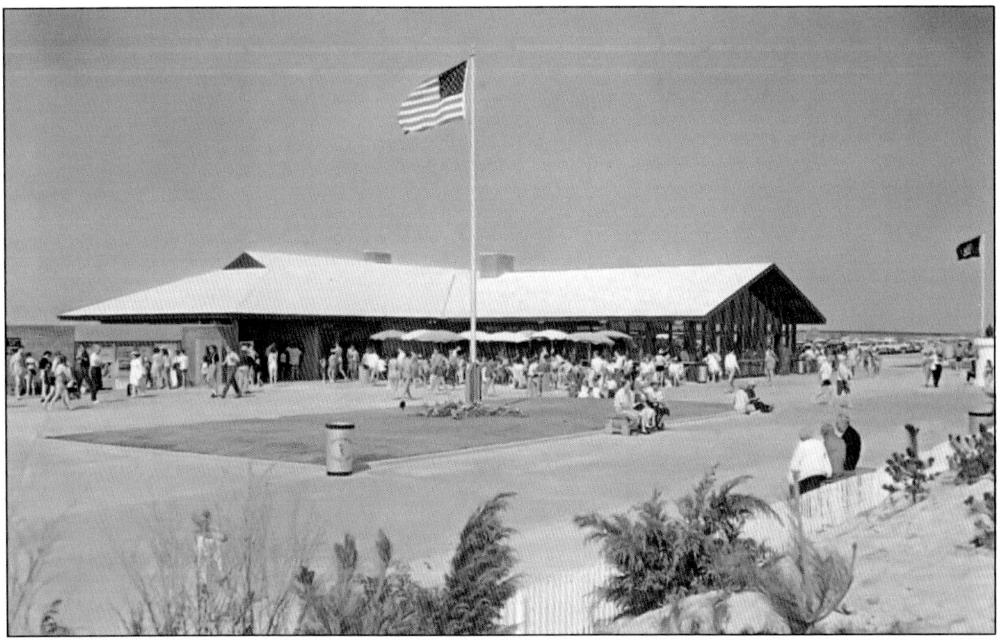

Originally named Fire Island State Park, the park was formally dedicated Robert Moses State Park on the day that the Fire Island Inlet Bridge was opened. The *Islip Bulletin* reported that the park was "expected to increase its average yearly attendance from about 135,000 to an ultimate 6 million. The beach, considered one of the finest on the east coast, has been accessible only by private boat or ferry." (TOB.)

Three

Seaside Resort
The Hotel Era

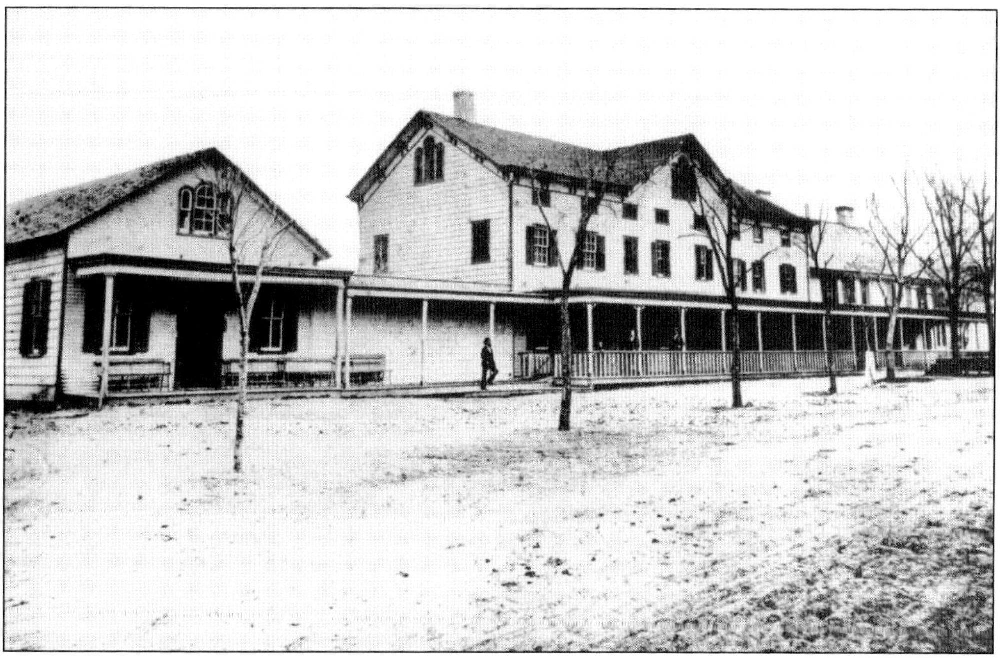

The American House, built around 1780 by Jesse Smith, was a popular stage stop for routes from points west and from the Deer Park railroad station. It stood for over a century before its loss to fire on June 4, 1883. A few days after the fire, the *South Side Signal* reported that the fire started in the ceiling between the first and second floors and offered the opinion that "it originated from mice gnawing matches." (TOB.)

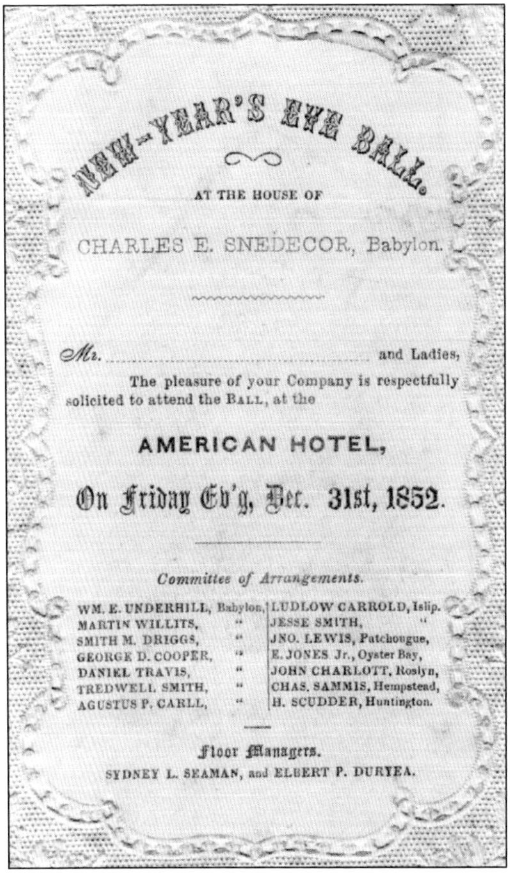

NEW-YEAR'S EVE BALL,

AT THE HOUSE OF

CHARLES E. SNEDECOR, Babylon.

Mr. .... and Ladies,

The pleasure of your Company is respectfully solicited to attend the BALL, at the

AMERICAN HOTEL,

On Friday Ev'g, Dec. 31st, 1852.

Committee of Arrangements.

WM. E. UNDERHILL, Babylon,	LUDLOW CARROLD, Islip.
MARTIN WILLITS, "	JESSE SMITH, "
SMITH M. DRIGGS, "	JNO. LEWIS, Patchougue,
GEORGE D. COOPER, "	E. JONES Jr., Oyster Bay,
DANIEL TRAVIS, "	JOHN CHARLOTT, Roslyn,
TREDWELL SMITH, "	CHAS. SAMMIS, Hempstead,
AGUSTUS P. CARLL, "	H. SCUDDER, Huntington.

Floor Managers.

SYDNEY L. SEAMAN, and ELBERT P. DURYEA.

This invitation is to the 1852 New Year's Eve Ball at the American House, hosted by proprietor Charles E. Snedecor. Joseph Bonaparte, ex-king of Spain and Napoleon's brother, was a weeklong hotel visitor in 1816 during a tour of Long Island, and Daniel Webster spent the night in 1840 when he was a senator from Massachusetts, on his way to Patchogue for a Whig Party event.

In 1855, David S.S. Sammis acquired 120 acres on Fire Island east of the lighthouse, and opened the Surf Hotel the following year. Sammis hired three steam yachts—*Bonita*, *Wave*, and *Surf*—to ferry hotel guests across the Great South Bay from Babylon. The hotel boasted accommodations for 100 guests at a weekly rate of $15. Though it was never full and languished through the end of the Civil War, Sammis carried on with the business. (TOB.)

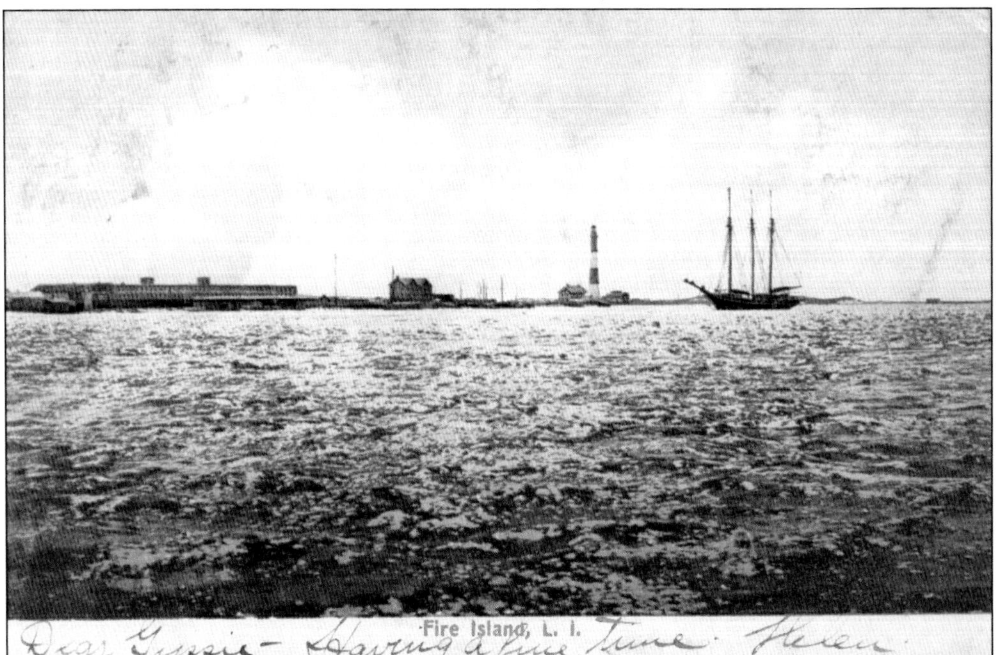

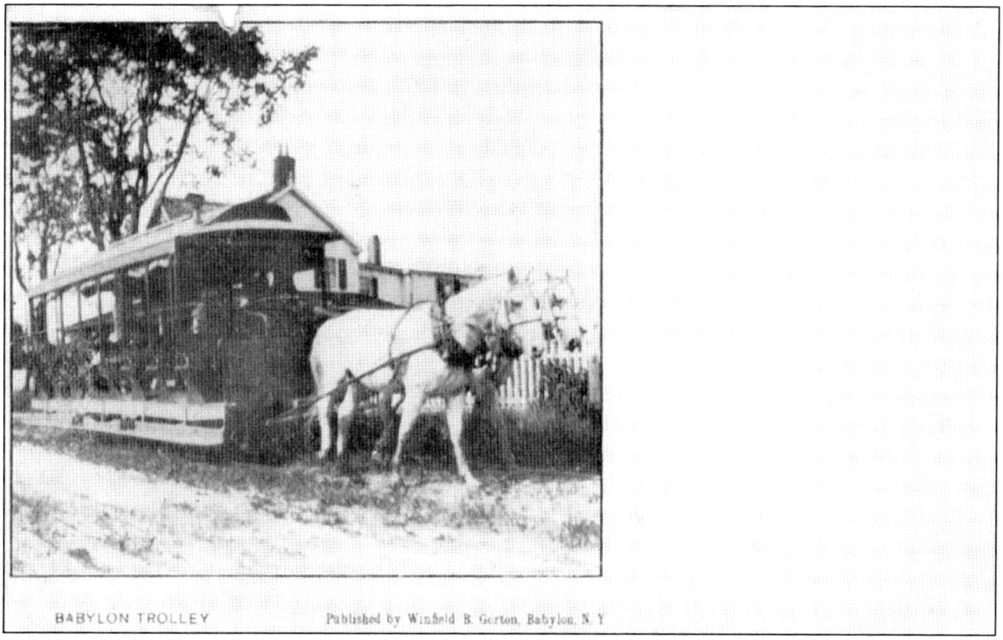

Post-war recovery resumed the anticipated construction of a South Shore rail line, which reached Babylon in October 1867. The 75-minute trip on the South Side Railroad from Jamaica to Babylon offered vacationers convenient transport from the grimy city to the tranquil seaside, and hotel business boomed. In 1871, Sammis installed a horsecar rail line from the Babylon railroad to the ferry docks, ready to whisk guests to the Surf Hotel.

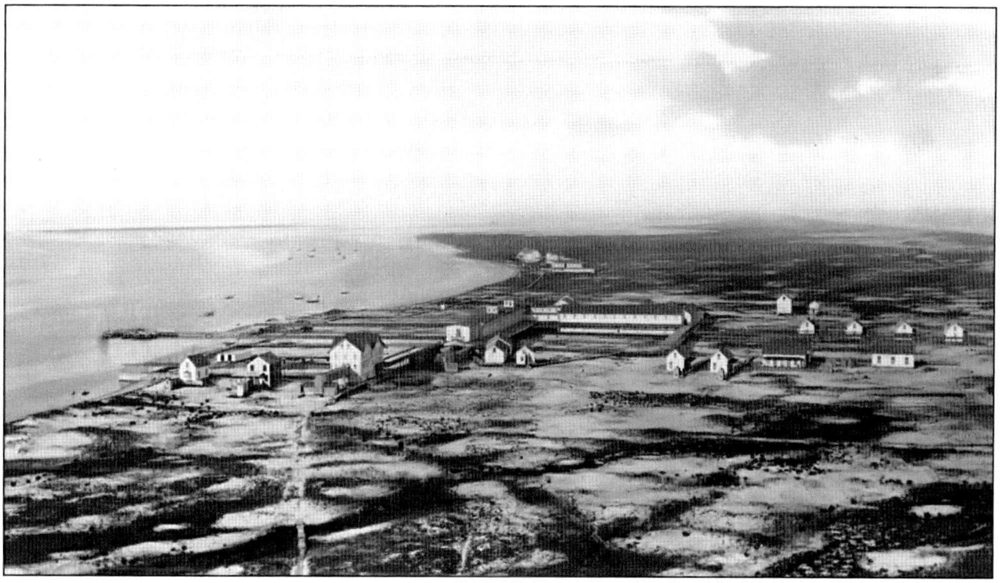

Three US presidents were reportedly visitors to the Surf: James Garfield, Chester Arthur, and Grover Cleveland. It is claimed that Herman Melville wrote portions of *Billy Budd* while staying at the hotel. The hostelry's end came in 1892, when the aging facility was purchased by New York State in anticipation of quarantining cholera patients there. Public outcry prevented this; the property remained in the state's possession, and was later developed as Robert Moses State Park. (LHS.)

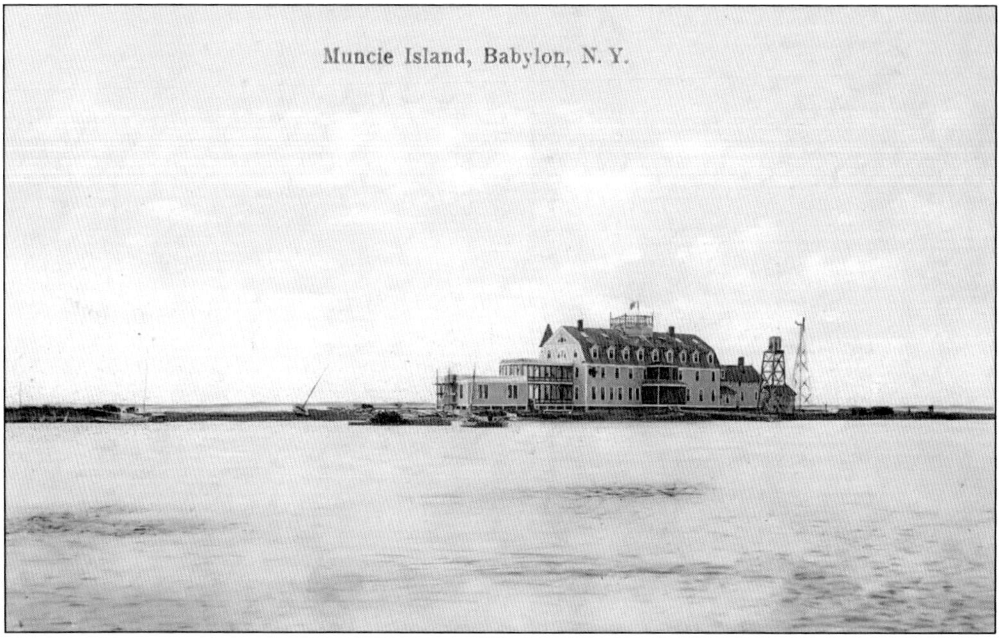

Twins William and Samuel Muncie, both medical doctors who had built a sanitarium, or health spa, in Brooklyn in 1895, also established a seaside sanitarium on their family's namesake island in 1897. Guest rooms at the Towanco Inn, or Muncie's Hotel, rented at a weekly rate of $25. The steamers *Nokomas* and *Senecas* ferried passengers between Babylon and Muncie Island twice a day.

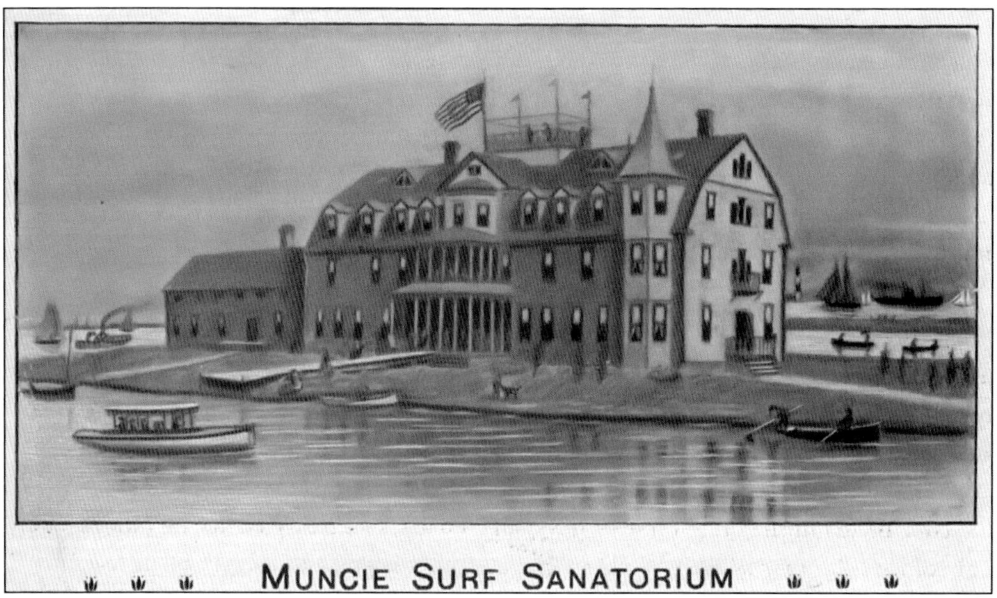

The sanitariums were eventually taken over by Samuel's son Dr. Edward H. Muncie and Edward's wife, Dr. Elizabeth Hamilton Muncie. The resort closed by 1914, and the island was sold for the development of summer bungalows, promoted by Town and Country Estates. The old Towanco Inn was razed by fire in 1925. The popular resort island was decimated by 1933 for construction of Ocean Parkway, leading to and from Jones Beach.

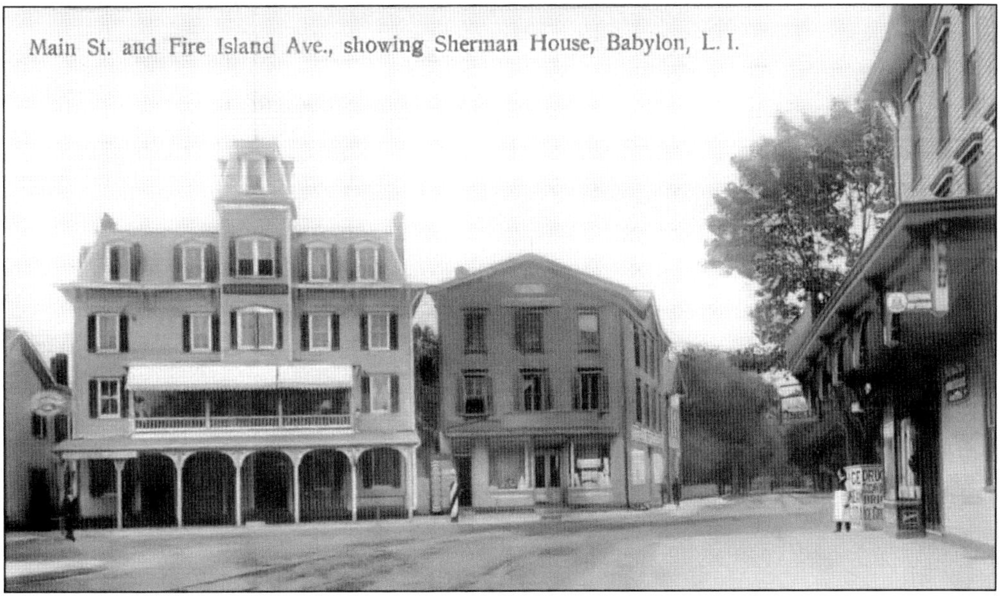

After the 1883 fire at the American House, Sherman Tweedy immediately contracted Samuel Kellum to build a new Main Street hotel on the opposite corner from the old American House, with gas lights, steam heat, and modern plumbing. Tweedy also operated a large horse stable around the corner from the hotel on Fire Island Avenue. The stables were later converted to the South Shore Garage, the present Babylon Carriage House restaurant.

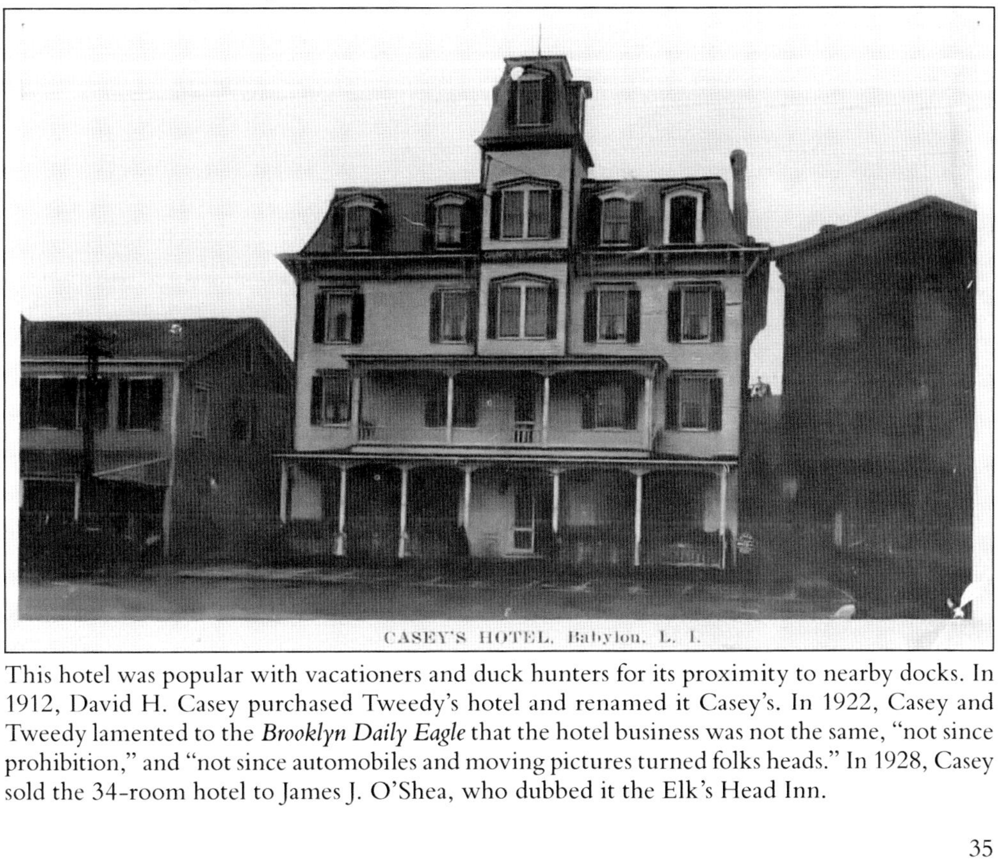

This hotel was popular with vacationers and duck hunters for its proximity to nearby docks. In 1912, David H. Casey purchased Tweedy's hotel and renamed it Casey's. In 1922, Casey and Tweedy lamented to the *Brooklyn Daily Eagle* that the hotel business was not the same, "not since prohibition," and "not since automobiles and moving pictures turned folks heads." In 1928, Casey sold the 34-room hotel to James J. O'Shea, who dubbed it the Elk's Head Inn.

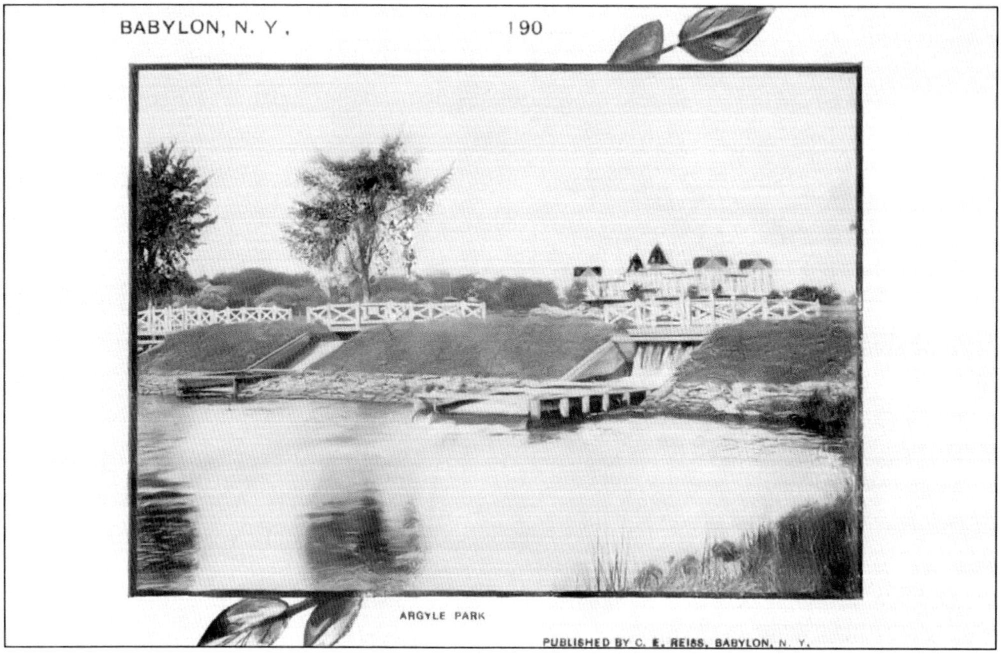

The Argyle Hotel opened near the northeast corner of the lake in the summer of 1882. Described by the *South Side Signal* as "the most eligible site in the town," the complex was built on Blythbourne, the former estate of Brooklyn railroad magnate Electus B. Litchfield. The grand hotel was backed by the Long Island Improvement Company, headed by Long Island Rail Road president Austin Corbin. The name honored the Scottish Duke of Argyll, reportedly an investor in the hotel.

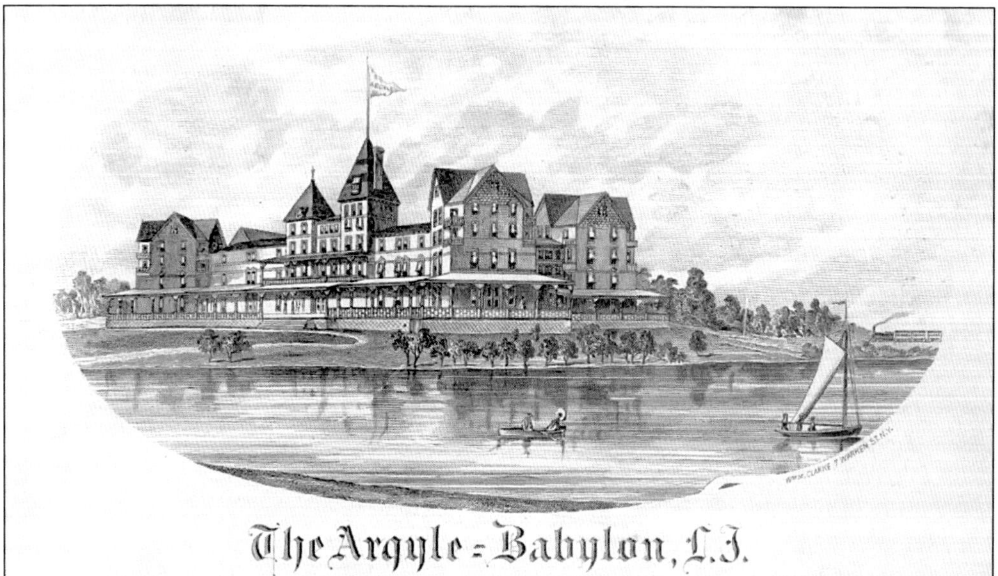

The *Signal*'s description of the Argyle read: "On entering, the visitor is ushered into the grand hall . . . lighted and ventilated by large oval openings through the four floors. . . . The interior is gothic, in natural woods, lighted by large stained glass windows. . . . The view from the top of the towers is grand beyond description—affording a birds-eye view of a vast expanse of sea and shore." The hotel's gas lights offered a brilliant view from Main Street.

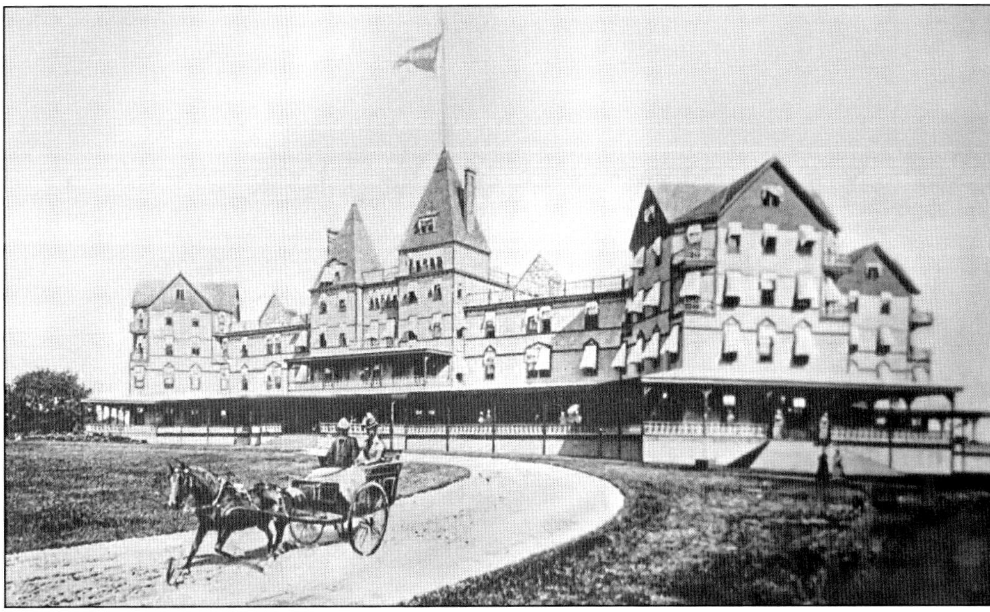

The Argyle Hotel was designed to accommodate nearly 600 guests and 150 employees. However, it has been said that the hotel was never filled to capacity. The hotel may have been the most expensive in Babylon, but it was the least successful. After many attempts, it closed in 1897, and the building was dismantled in 1904. Materials were salvaged and used in many local residences, particularly those in the residential Argyle Park community.

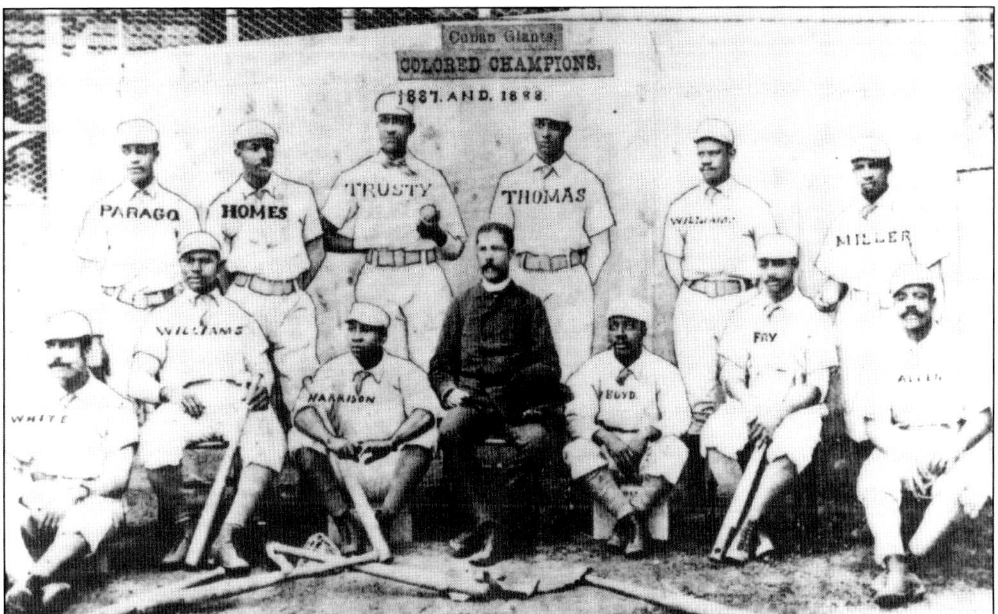

The Argyle Hotel was the 1885 birthplace of the Cuban Giants, the first African American professional baseball team. The team was formed from hotel employees. The name "Cuban Giants" was chosen in an effort to suppress prejudices among audiences that may have preferred to watch a foreign team. Despite the name ruse, the team was one of the best in the Negro Leagues. Members of the Cuban Giants have been inducted into the Baseball Hall of Fame. (TOB.)

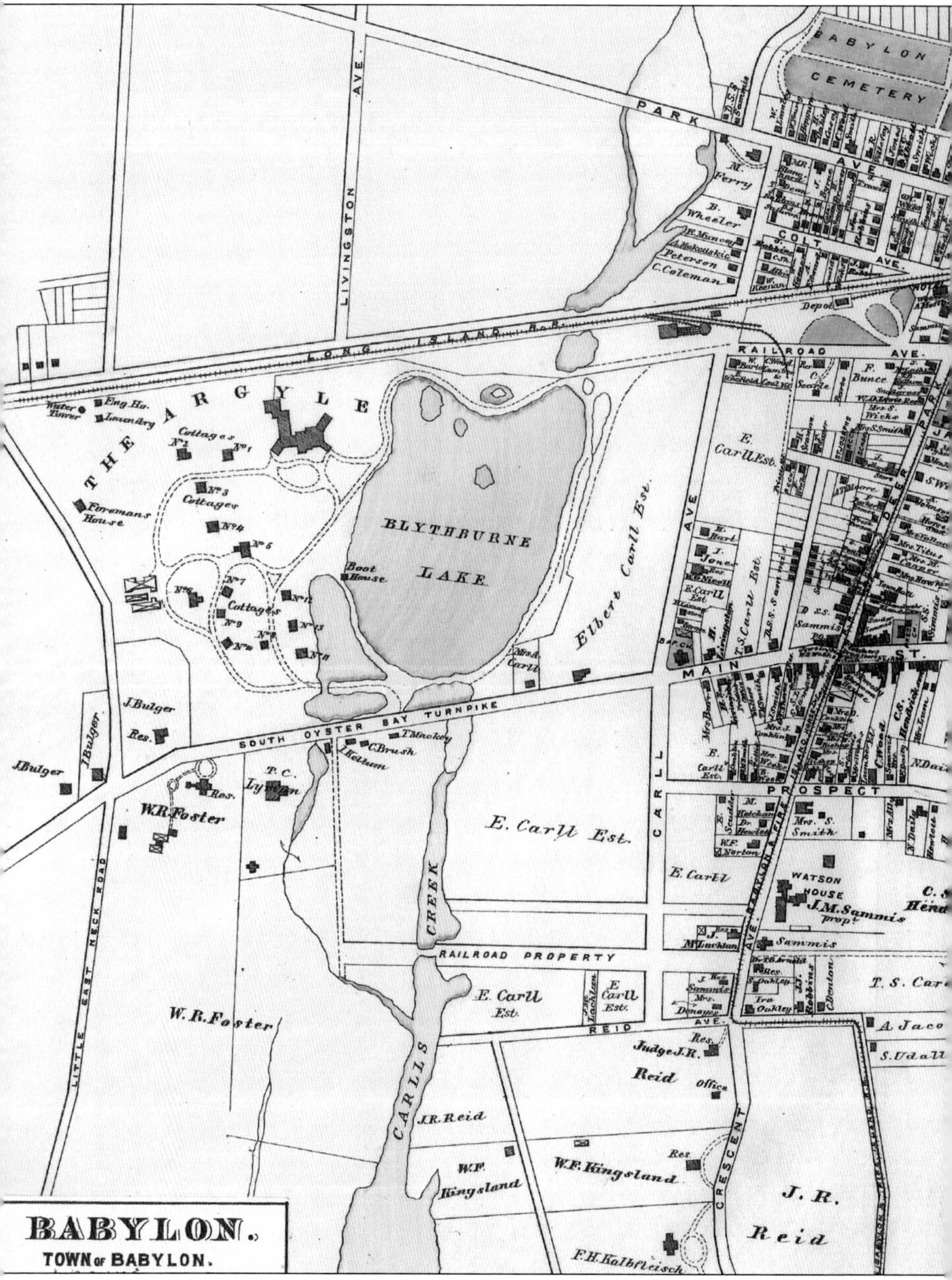
BABYLON.
TOWN OF BABYLON.
BABYLON CEMETERY
PARK AVE.
COLT AVE.
LIVINGSTON AVE.
LONG ISLAND R.R.
RAILROAD AVE.
THE ARGYLE
BLYTHBURNE LAKE
Boat House
Cottages
Foremans House
Water Tower
Eng. Ho.
Laundry
Elbert Carll Est.
E. Carll Est.
CARLL AVE.
MAIN ST.
SOUTH OYSTER BAY TURNPIKE
PROSPECT
WATSON HOUSE
J.M. Sammis propr.
CARLLS CREEK
RAILROAD PROPERTY
REID AVE.
Judge J.R. Reid
J.R. Reid
W.F. Kingsland
F.H. Kalbfleisch
CRESCENT
LITTLE EAST NECK ROAD
W.R. Foster
T.C. Lyman
J. Bulger
Depot
M. Ferry
B. Wheeler
Peterson
C. Coleman
E. Carll
T.S. Carll Est.
A. Jaco
S. Udall

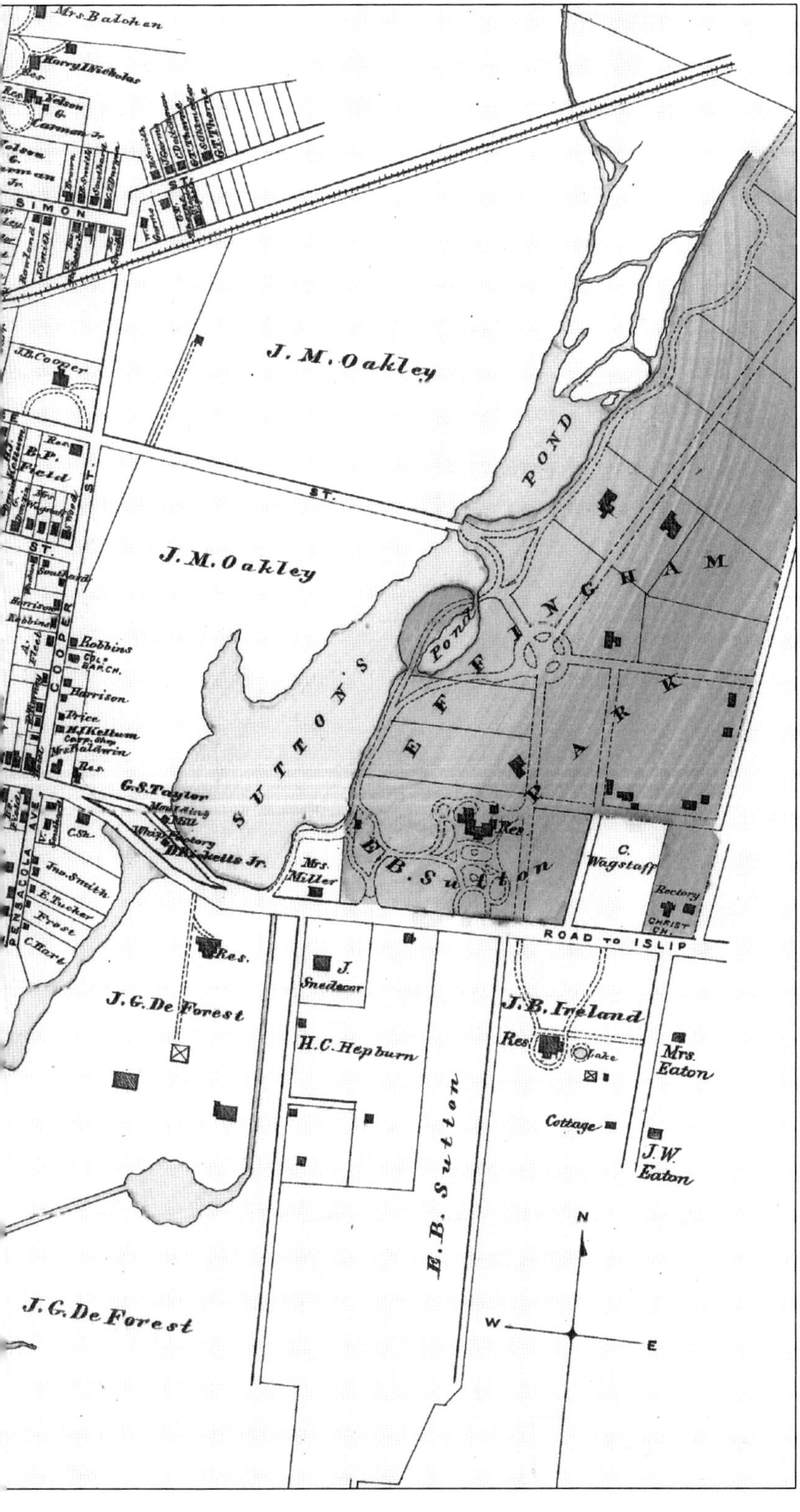

This 1888 map of the village of Babylon from the *Atlas of the Town of Babylon, Islip and the South Part of Brookhaven, in Suffolk County* shows the layout of the sprawling Argyle Hotel on the west side of the lake. The vast estate of banker William R. Foster was on the south side of South Oyster Bay Turnpike (Main Street), opposite the Argyle property. Lands on either side of Carll Avenue are labeled under the ownership of Elbert Carll. The Watson House, on Fire Island Avenue two blocks south of Main Street, is listed under the management of J.M. Sammis. The estates of Judge John R. Reid, attorney Walter F. Kingsland, and chemical manufacturer Franklin H. Kalbfleisch line The Crescent. (TOB.)

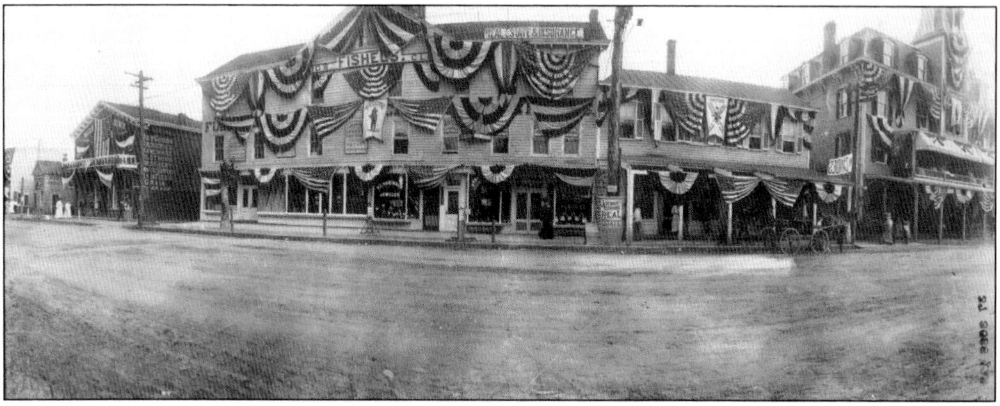

Thomas J. Seaman opened the Sumpwams Hotel around 1850 on the south side of Main Street, east of Fire Island Avenue. After his 1856 death, his wife, Phebe Ann Seaman, managed the hotel until 1875, when she became the hostess of the American House. Leopold H. Fishel purchased the building to relocate his thriving dry goods store. The Fishel Block later housed a myriad of stores before it was destroyed by fire in 1973.

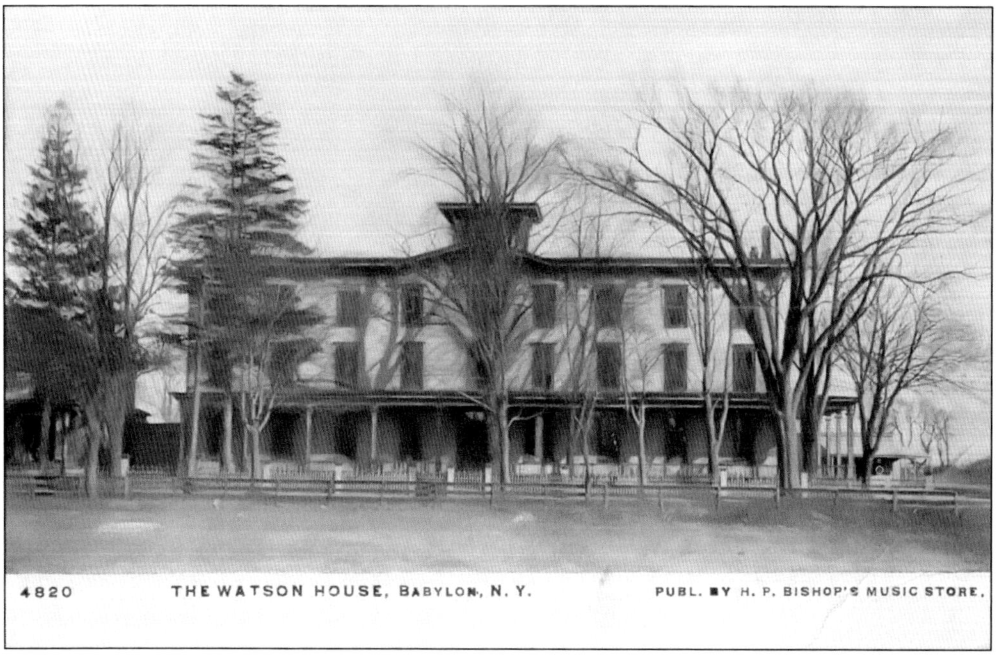

The Watson House opened in 1871, built by Selah C. Smith, grandson of Jesse Smith, who erected the American House. The *South Side Signal* announced that the hotel name honored "George Watson, of Beekman Street, N.Y., who has for many years been a guest of the old American Hotel. Mr. Watson responded, briefly and to the point, thanking the Hotel Proprietor for the honor conferred upon him . . . with the warmest wishes for the success of the enterprise."

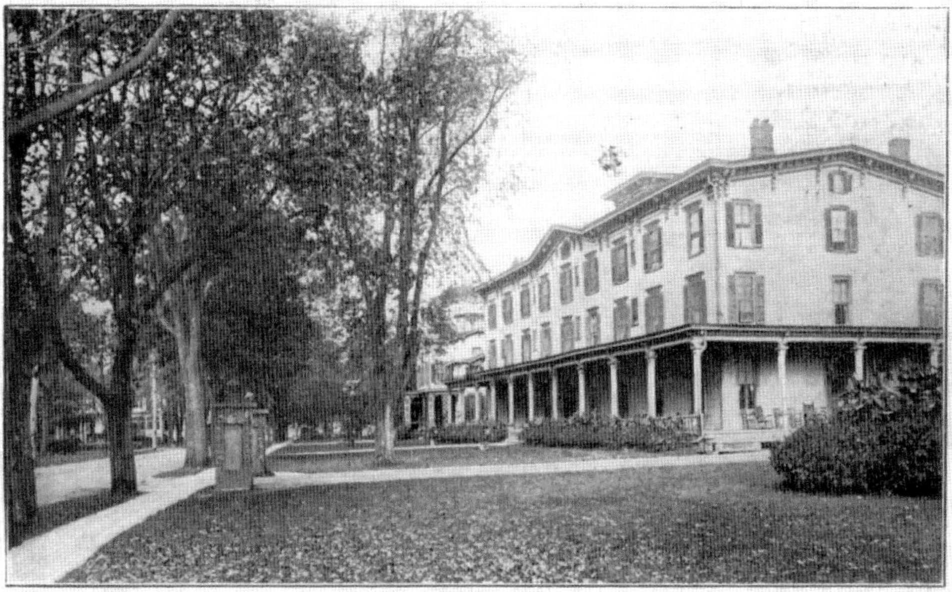

WATSON HOUSE, BABYLON, L. I.

The three-story hotel stood on the east side of Fire Island Avenue, south of Prospect Street, described in a 1906 *Signal* article as "the meeting place for . . . jolly fellows on Sunday afternoons—men who lived along the famous Merrick Road . . . who used to drive to Babylon to exercise their horses." Around 1922, the old hotel became a rooming house. A few years later, the hotel was demolished except for the North Cottage, which became a private residence.

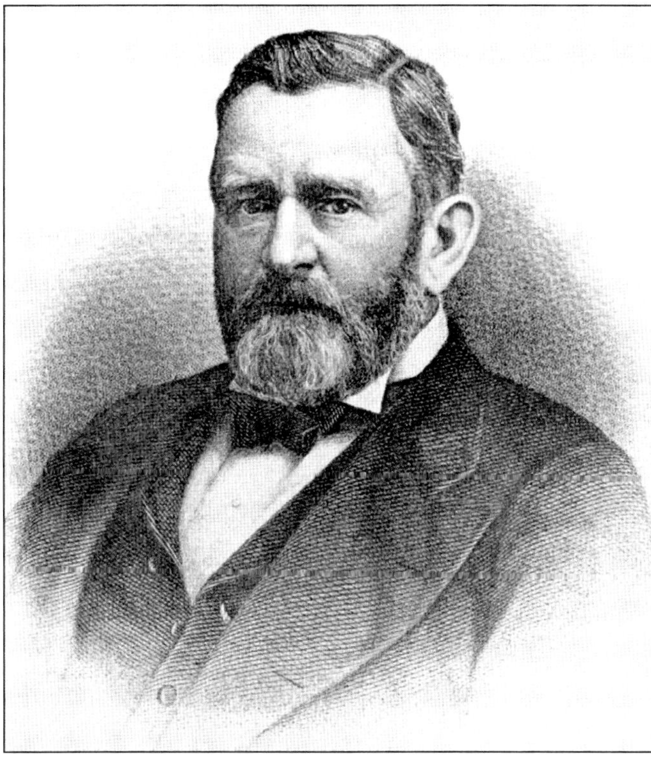

The September 4, 1875, *Signal* reported: "Babylon was honored, on Wednesday, with a visit from President Grant and Gen. Casey, brother-in-law of the President. The party came without previous announcement, taking passage . . . for visiting Gen. Casey's farm at West Deer Park [Wheatley Heights]. After a thorough inspection of the farm and surroundings the party returned to the Watson, where dinner was served in Selah Smith's best style." Future president Chester A. Arthur was a visitor in 1880. (TOB.)

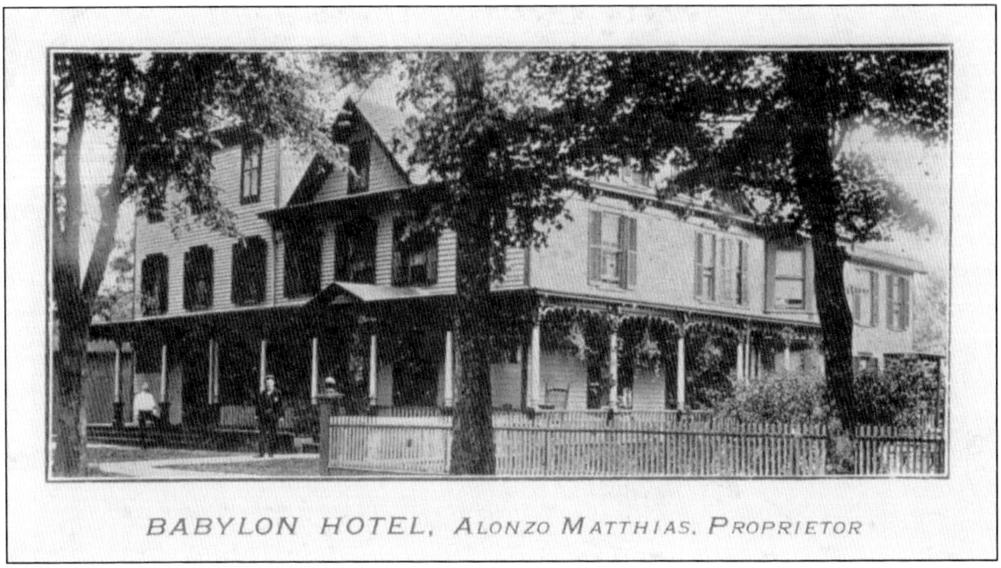

The *Signal* announced the opening of the Babylon Hotel: "Mr. Matthias is sparing no pains to make this affair one that will be long remembered. He has issued the following invitations: 'Alonzo Matthias cordially invites you to attend the opening of the Babylon Hotel at Babylon, Long Island, Wednesday, Aug. 5, 1903.' The Babylon Hotel has been finely furnished and fitted up and is pleasantly situated on Railroad Avenue, convenient to the depot."

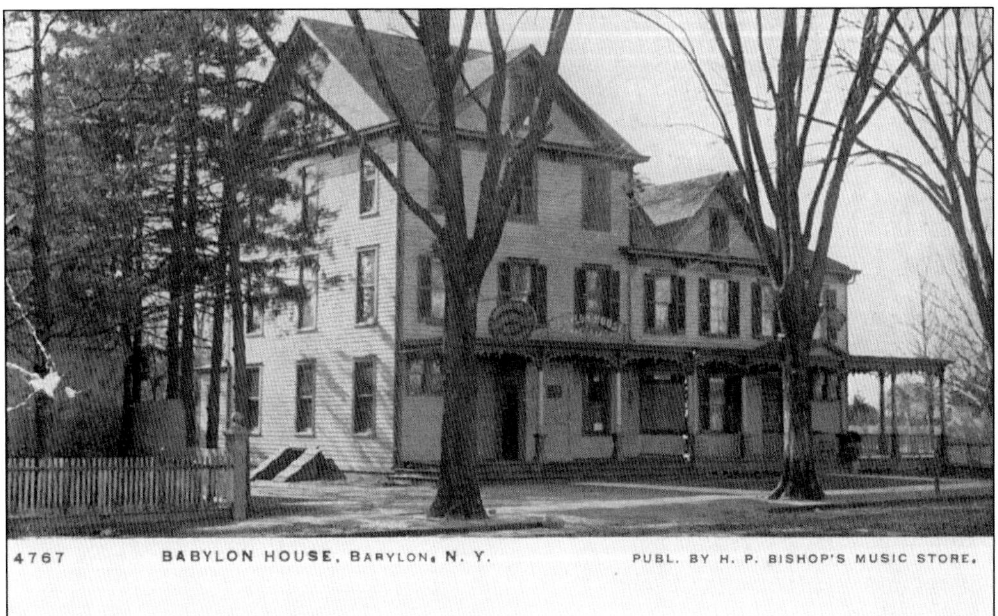

In January 1913, John B. Hoernel purchased the Babylon Hotel from Matthias, but Hoernel died in August of that year. His wife, Bertha, and sons John and William continued management of the hotel and restaurant for many years. The hotel was open for visitors year-round, advertising "Dinner for Auto Parties on Short Notice." The hotel was destroyed by fire in the 1940s.

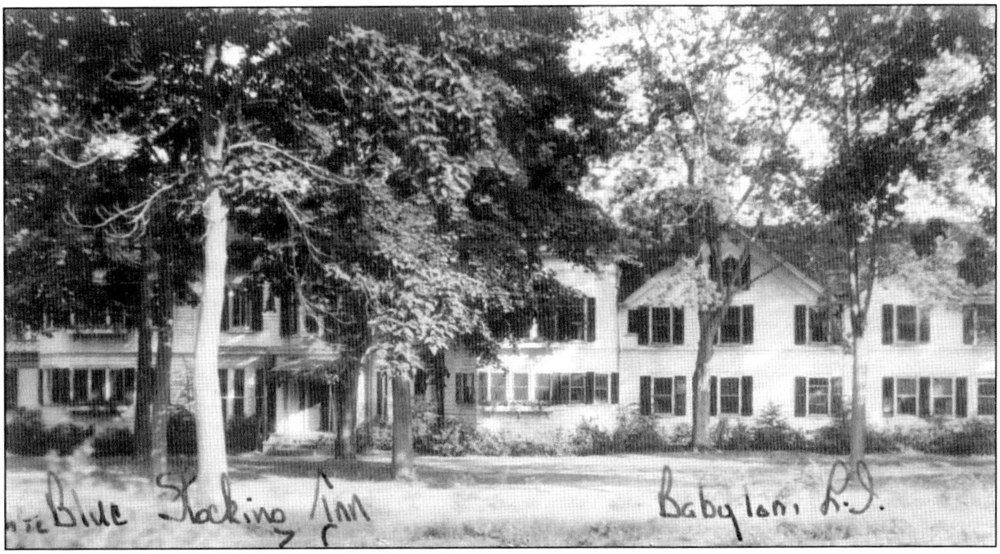

The Blue Stocking Inn, at the corner of Montauk Highway and Little East Neck Road, was supposedly named after the Blue Stocking Inn of London. The 18th-century Blue Stockings Society was an informal organization of educated English women interested in literary discussions, to which they invited equally educated men to take part. The inn closed by the late 1930s, and the building was demolished in 1943, after it had become derelict.

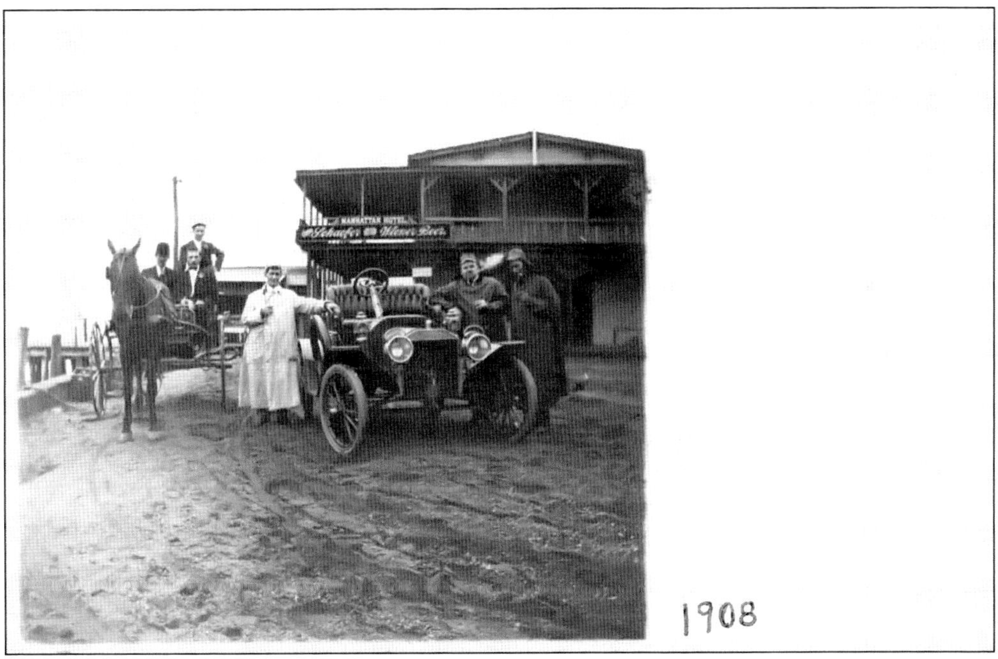

David S.S. Sammis reportedly built the Manhattan House around 1884 near the Babylon steamboat docks. The hotel was soon expanded, and in 1888, proprietor George W. Larned professed the second floor of the hotel was fitted "as sleeping apartments, and is now prepared to entertain guests by the day, week or month . . . in a first class manner."

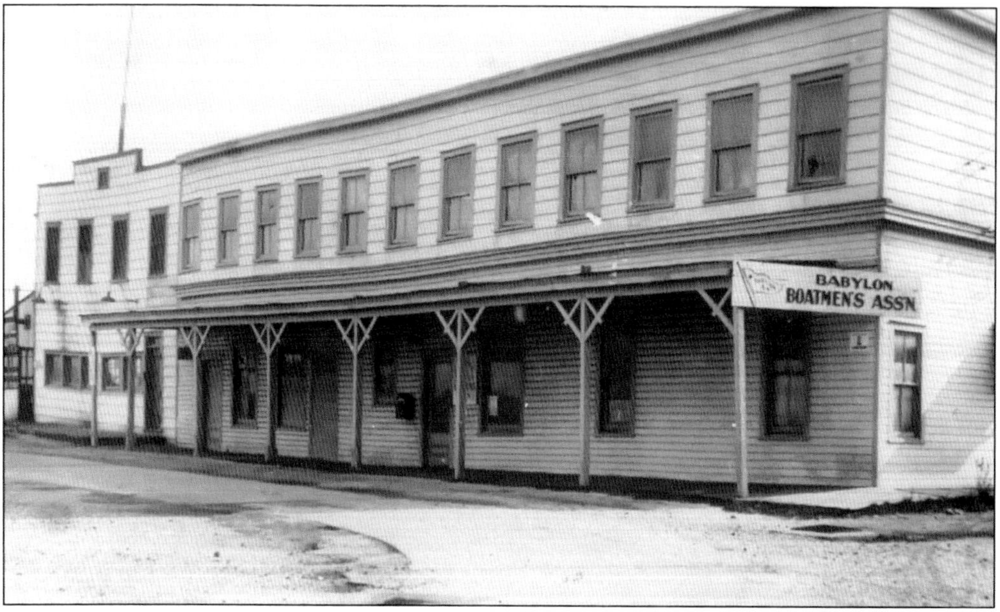

Respectability of the Manhattan House was assured by the *South Side Signal*, which proclaimed that "Ladies accompanied by children will find the hotel a desirable place to visit when at the dock." At that time, it was common for mothers and children to spend several summer weeks near the ocean while fathers came out from the city only on the weekends. Around 1904, the Manhattan House was sold to W. Edward Boyne and renamed Boyne's Hotel.

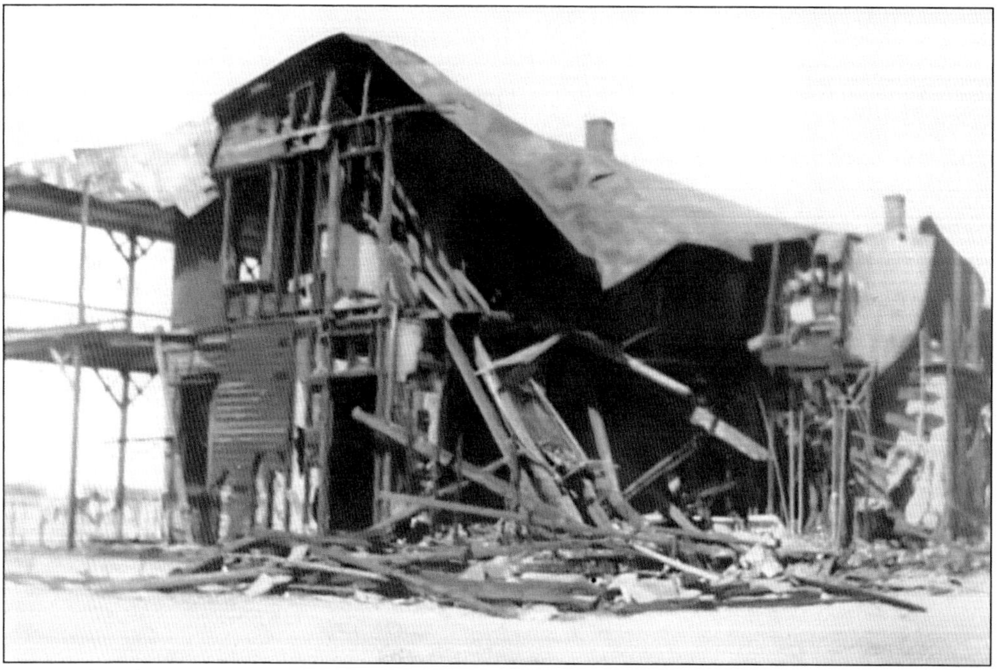

A 1912 fire destroyed about half of Boyne's Hotel and killed Alice Kennedy, a cook who had been employed for only two weeks. The hotel was rebuilt and operated until the early 1930s. The deteriorated building was condemned in 1946 and the property sold. The site later became John Anthony's On the Water and presently houses the Venetian Yacht Club.

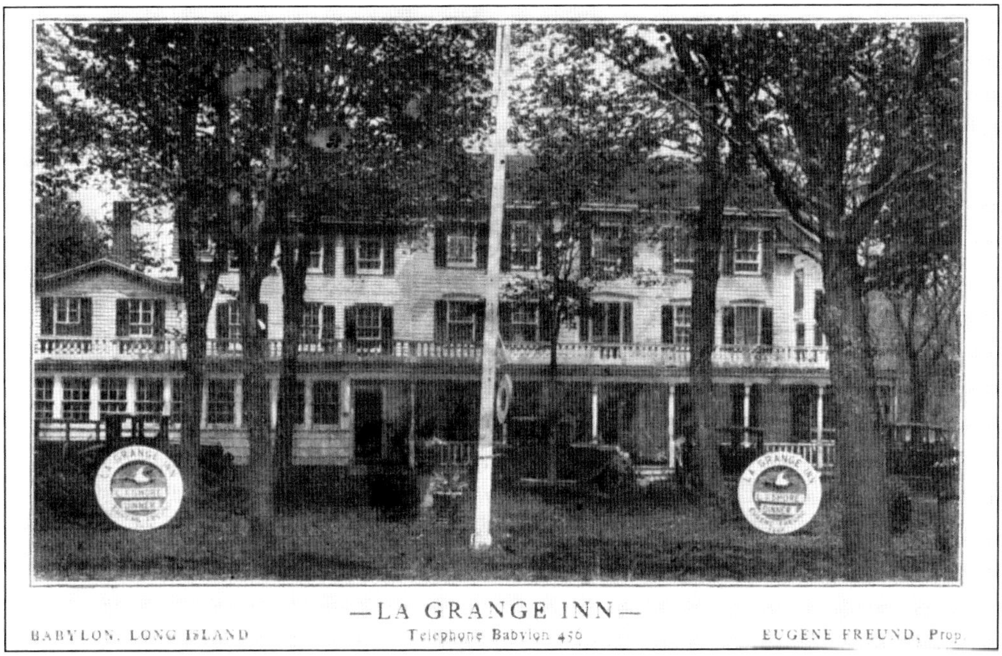

The Higbie family opened La Grange Inn shortly after the end of the Revolutionary War, named after the French estate of General Lafayette, who fought for the Colonies. Just east of Babylon, La Grange was a popular restaurant through the 20th century. By 2010, the property had been sold, and the historic inn was vulnerable to demolition. Through community efforts, including the West Islip Association and CVS Pharmacy, the building is being restored for community use.

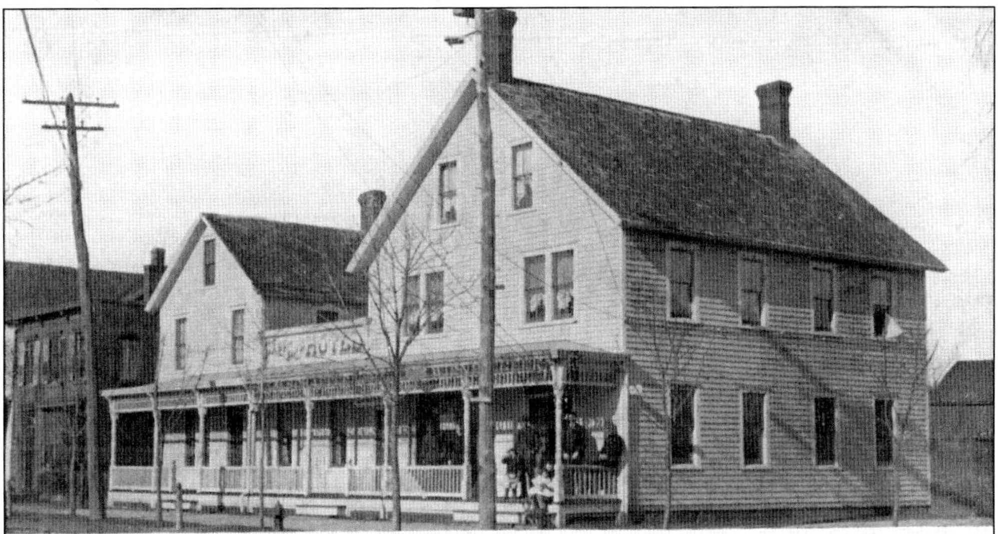

The East End Hotel, at the northwest corner of East Main and Cooper Streets, opened in the 1880s. Thomas F. Tierney assumed operation of the hotel in 1890 and continued for nearly 50 years. When the hotel was modernized in 1939, the *Babylon Leader* boasted that "the hostelry has sixteen master guest chambers" and a renovated restaurant for "anyone who desires real cuisine." The hotel burned down in 1982 and is the present site of the restaurant Cooper Street. (Edward Kauf.)

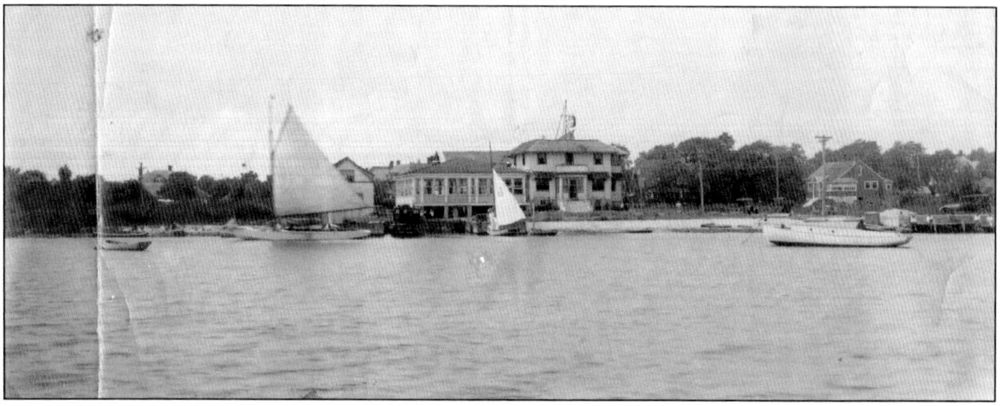

George Melcher's South Shore Inn, at Robbins and Fire Island Avenues overlooking Sumpwams Creek, opened on June 10–11, 1933. The *Babylon Leader* declared, "Every guest will receive gratis beef steak and the trimmings. . . . Let every Leader reader be among those present and enjoy the hospitality of one good, generous, whole souled host. A real prince of caterers and a true progressive forward marching man, deserving of support from every citizen who wishes Babylon to progress."

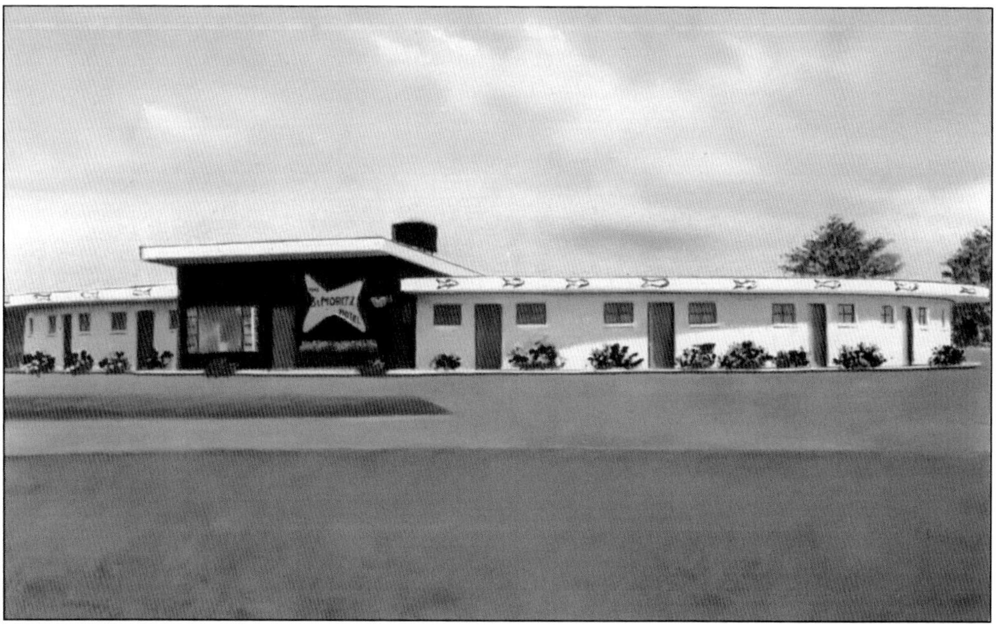

The St. Moritz, with a beautiful view of the Great South Bay, was built in 1953 and operated as a motel until 1965, when it became a rest home. The Lockwood family has owned it since 1979, and it is now an assisted living facility. The facility has maintained the same telephone number since 1953: MO9-3323.

Four

HOME SWEET HOME

RESIDENCES AND STREETS

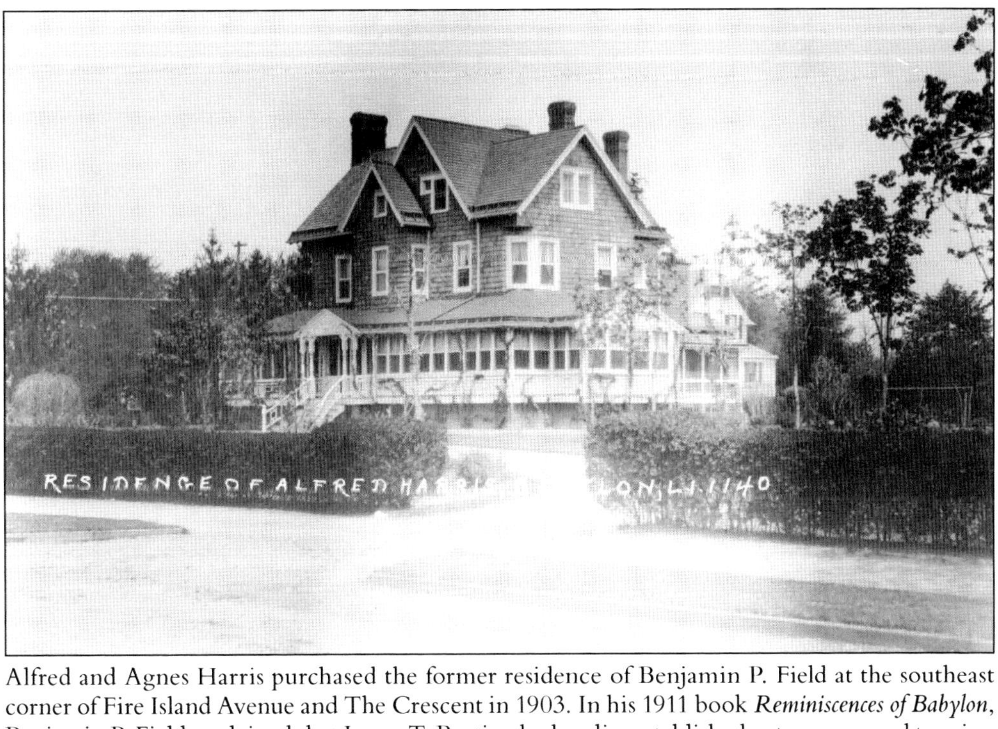

Alfred and Agnes Harris purchased the former residence of Benjamin P. Field at the southeast corner of Fire Island Avenue and The Crescent in 1903. In his 1911 book *Reminiscences of Babylon*, Benjamin P. Field explained that James T. Bertine had earlier established a steam saw and turning mill near the site of the former home.

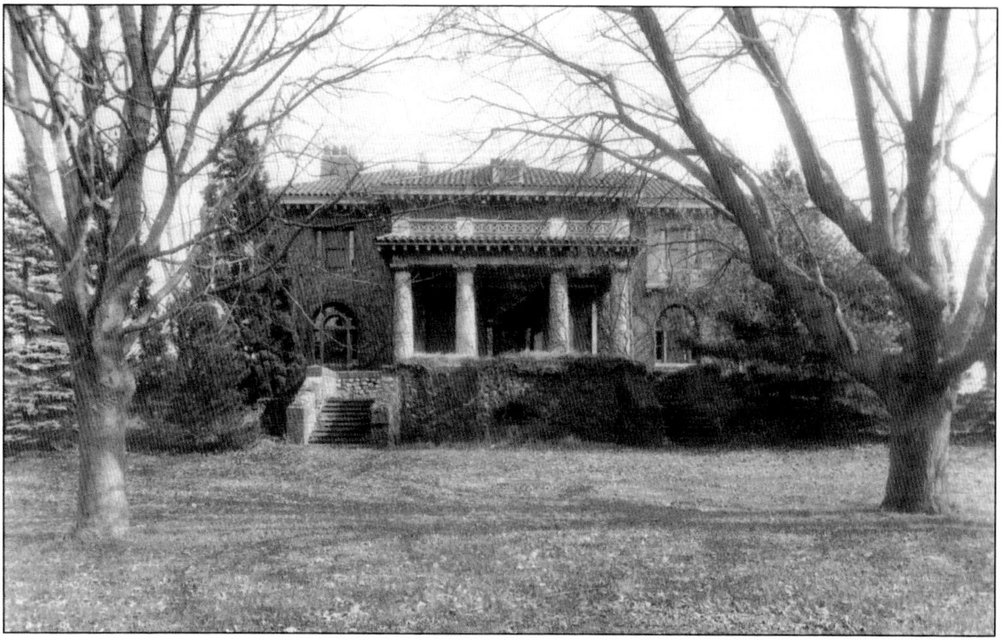

The residence of Jay Stanley Foster sat on 142 acres south of Montauk Highway, bounded by Carll's River and Little East Neck Road. In 1909, Foster built the 40-room mansion to share with his wife, Jennie Rice Morgan. Three generations of Fosters lived in Babylon, starting with William R. Foster, founder and president of the Bowery Savings Bank. W.R. Foster donated the property for the erection of the Methodist church on Deer Park Avenue. (TOB.)

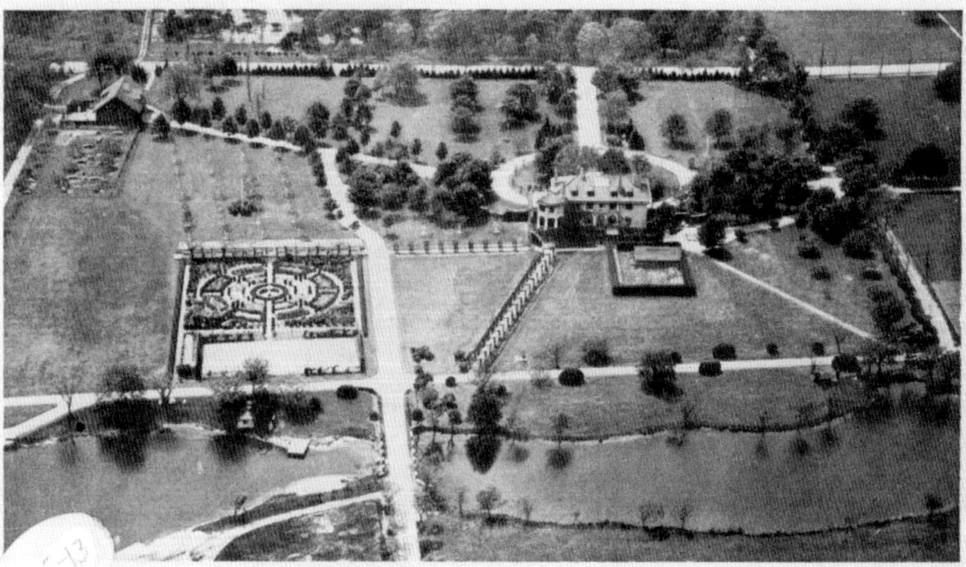

Airplane View of SAMPAWAM CLUB *and Grounds*

William R. Foster's son, John Strong Foster, and his grandson, Jay Stanley Foster, succeeded him as president of the Bowery Bank. After Jay Stanley Foster's death, the estate was sold to the Sampawam Club in 1929. The mansion was sold to the Babylon American Legion Post 94 in 1947 and used as their clubhouse until the late 1950s, when the post relocated to Grove Place.

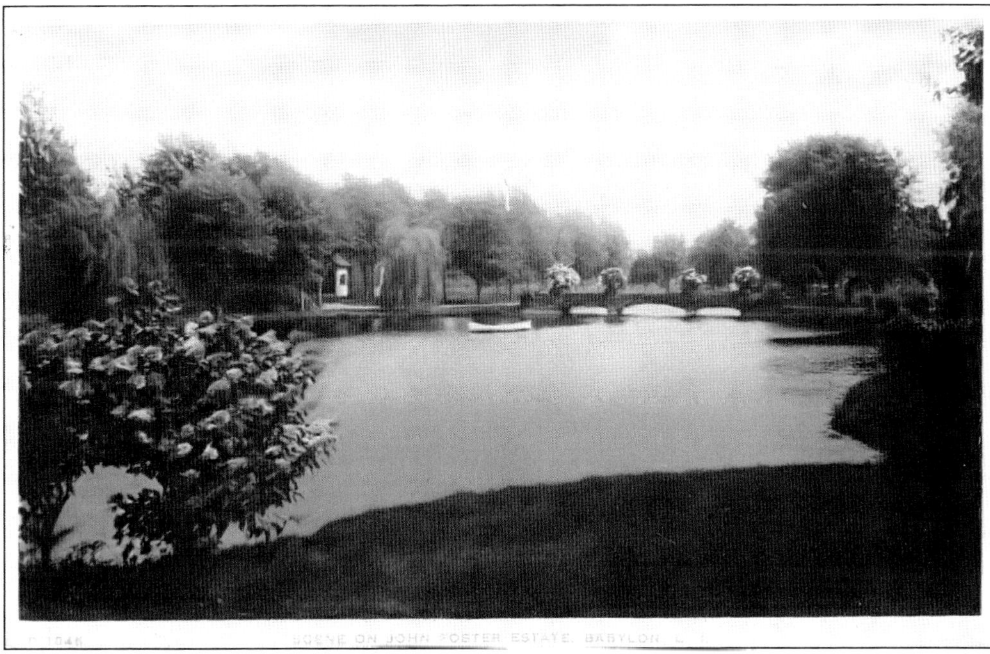

Eighteen acres of the estate were developed as Blue Harbor Colony. Promoting the prestige of the former banker's property, advertisements extolled the area's convenience: "within 35 miles of New York City . . . enjoy the use of the world's finest public and private ocean and bay beaches, golf courses, restaurants, riding and tennis clubs plus the neighborliness of the country's more noted families." (Edward Kauf.)

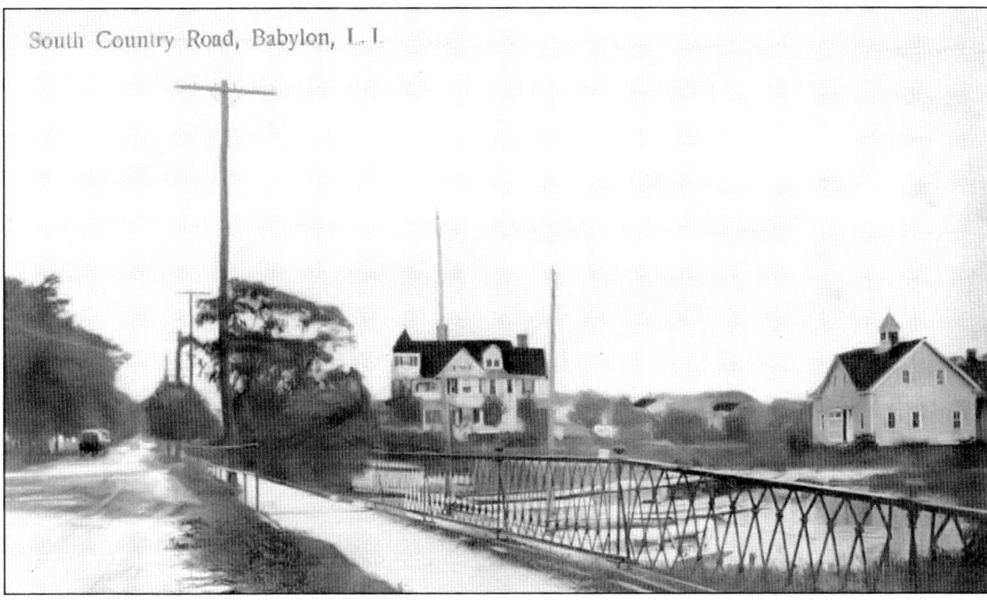

The Charles M. Bergen House is seen as it was originally situated on West Main Street. In 1990, the two-and-a-half-story Queen Anne–style home was moved a few hundred feet south on Thompson Avenue, on the site once occupied by the home of Robert Moses, to make way for the development of the Argyle Commons office complex. Bergen Avenue in West Babylon denoted the western border of Bergen's former farm on the south side of Montauk Highway.

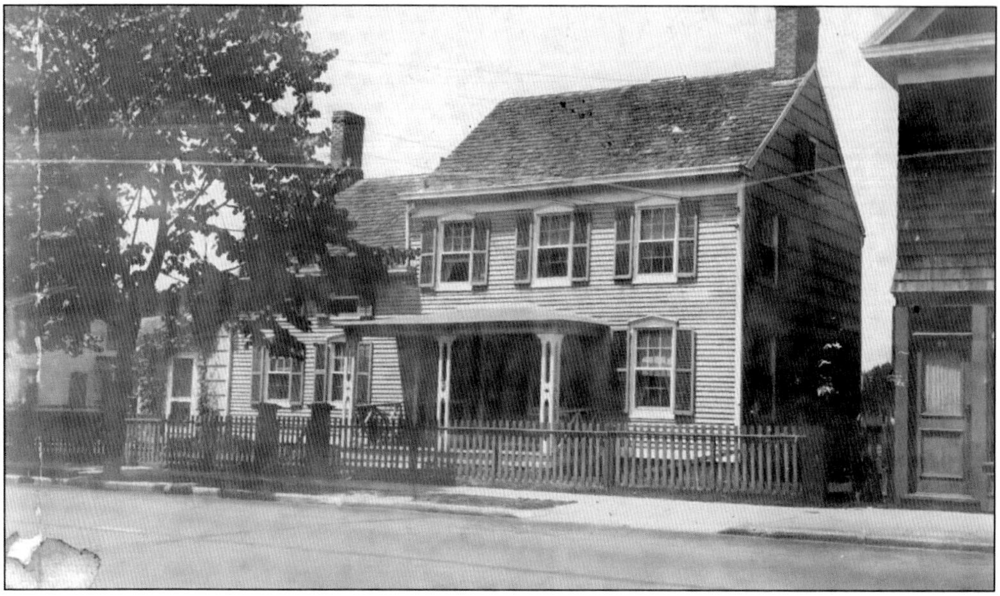

"Aunt Julia's" house was erected in 1826 by Selah Smith Carll and his wife, Julia, the daughter of West Islip judge Isaac Thompson. The familial "Aunt Julia" was used out of affection by local residents who admired her generosity. As a widow, Julia lived with her daughter Mary Ann, the second wife of Elbert Carll. The West Main Street building accommodated many doctors and lawyers over the years, most recently the late Patrick Kevin Brosnahan.

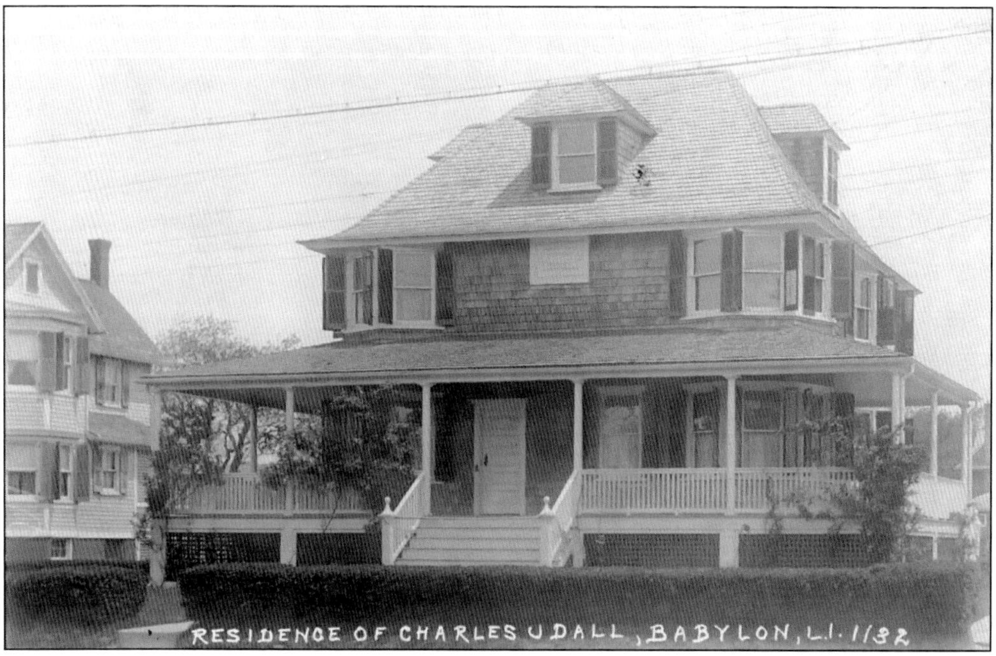

This South Carll Avenue home belonged to village trustee Charles H. Udall and his wife, Florence. In his younger days, Udall was a member of the US Life-Saving crew at Oak Island and worked with his father, Sylvester, in the oyster business. In 1917, he was appointed oyster commissioner by the Babylon Town Board to serve on the joint commission with the town of Islip.

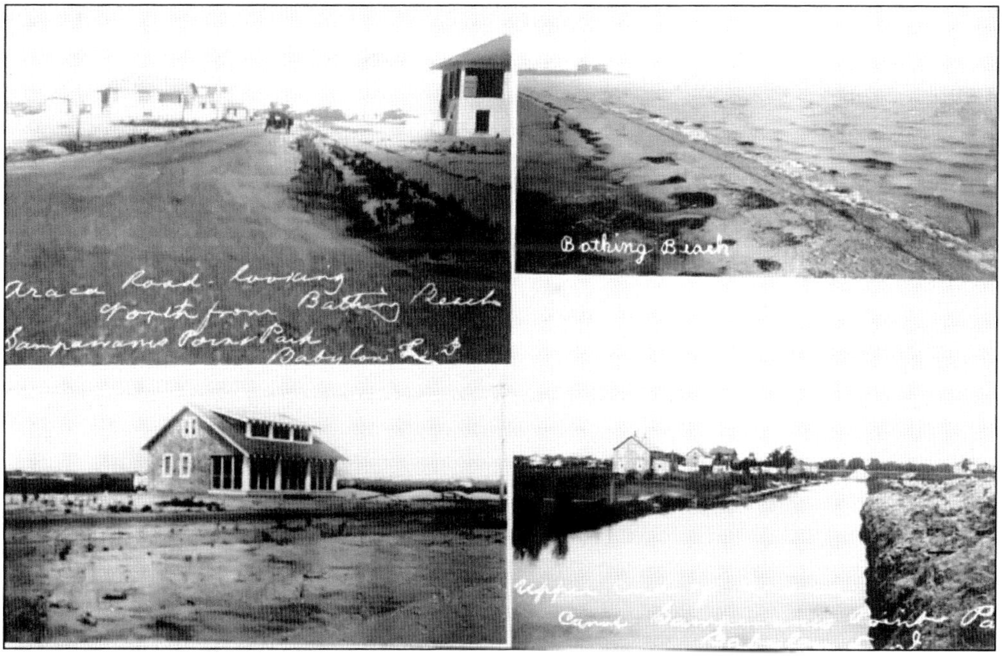

A visitor noted on this 1920s postcard of Araca Road and the Sumpwams Point Park residential development, "this is a picture of the place where we are . . . the canal goes right back of the house so you can row a boat right up here. We are a mile and a quarter from the village. The beach is only two minutes from the house at the end of this road."

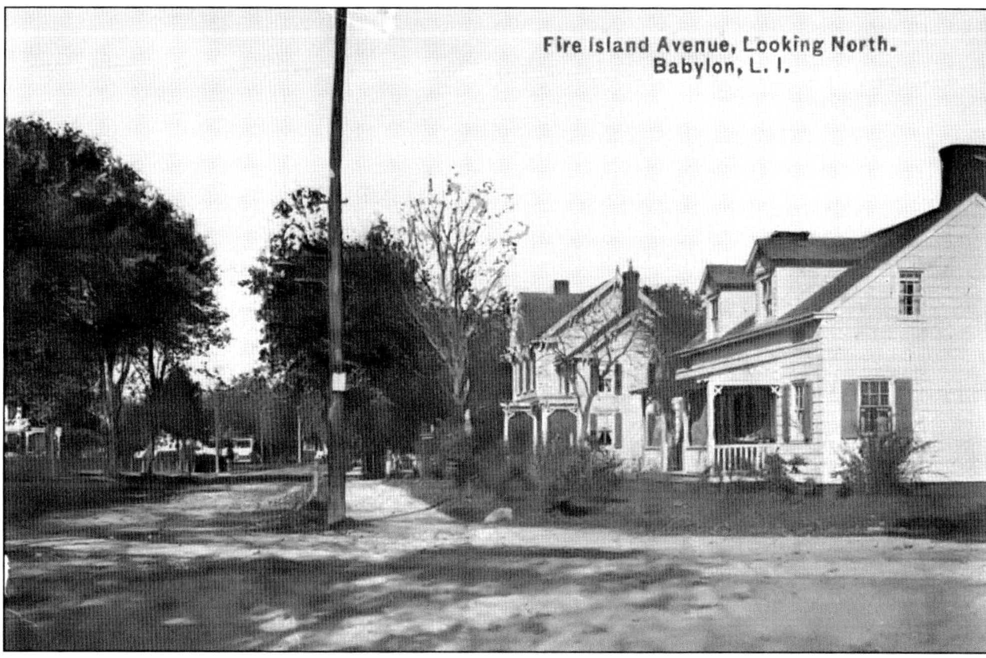

Fire Island Avenue stretches from the south side of Main Street to the Village Docks. It would seem that the street name refers to the fact that it led to the ferries that transported visitors to Fire Island. The sharp turns in Fire Island Avenue appear to have been made to circumvent some of the large private estates, including that of Judge John R. Reid.

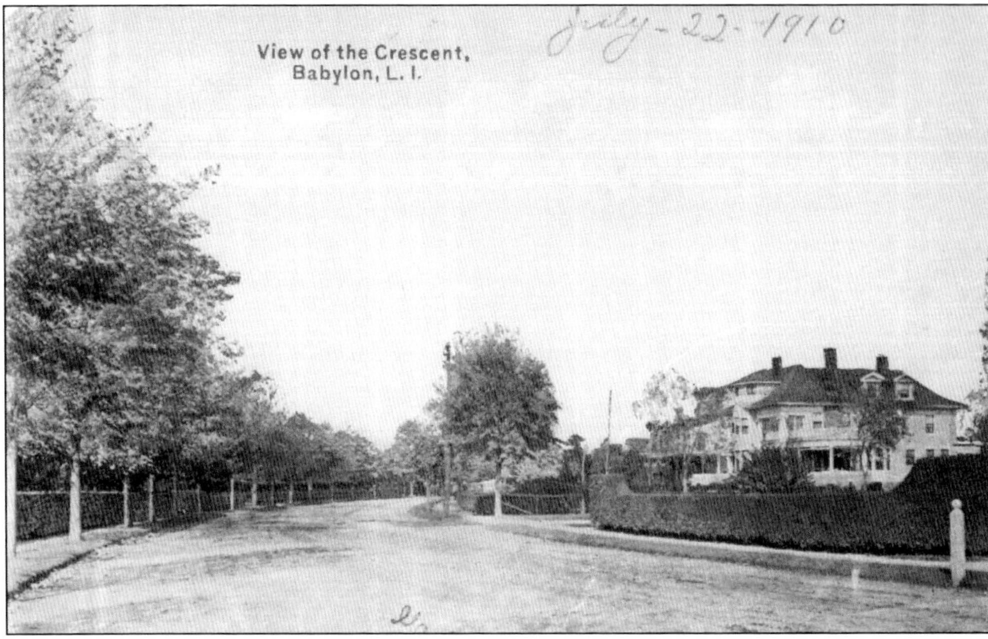

Developed around 1882 by the firm of Higbie and Robbins, The Crescent is comprised of two gentle curves extending south from Fire Island Avenue. Originally built as resort or vacation homes for well-to-do New York City residents, the houses and lots were some of the largest and grandest in Babylon.

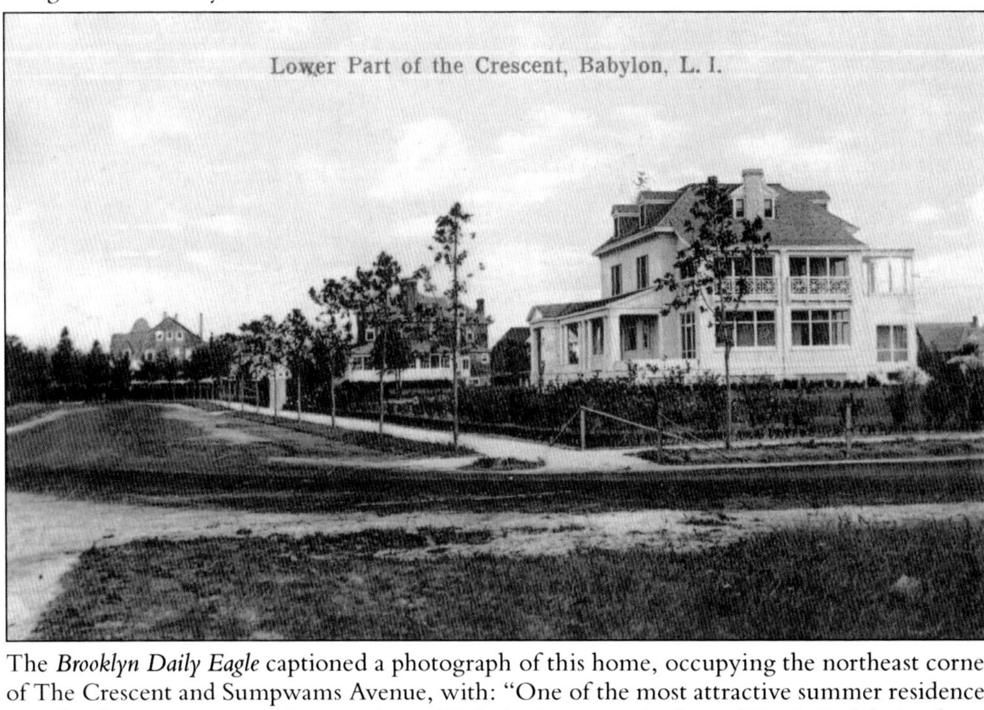

The *Brooklyn Daily Eagle* captioned a photograph of this home, occupying the northeast corner of The Crescent and Sumpwams Avenue, with: "One of the most attractive summer residences on The Crescent, one of the prettiest of Babylon's streets, is that of Dr. J. Ralph Jacoby of Manhattan. The building is of stucco and commands a view of the Great South Bay and of the East and West Creeks."

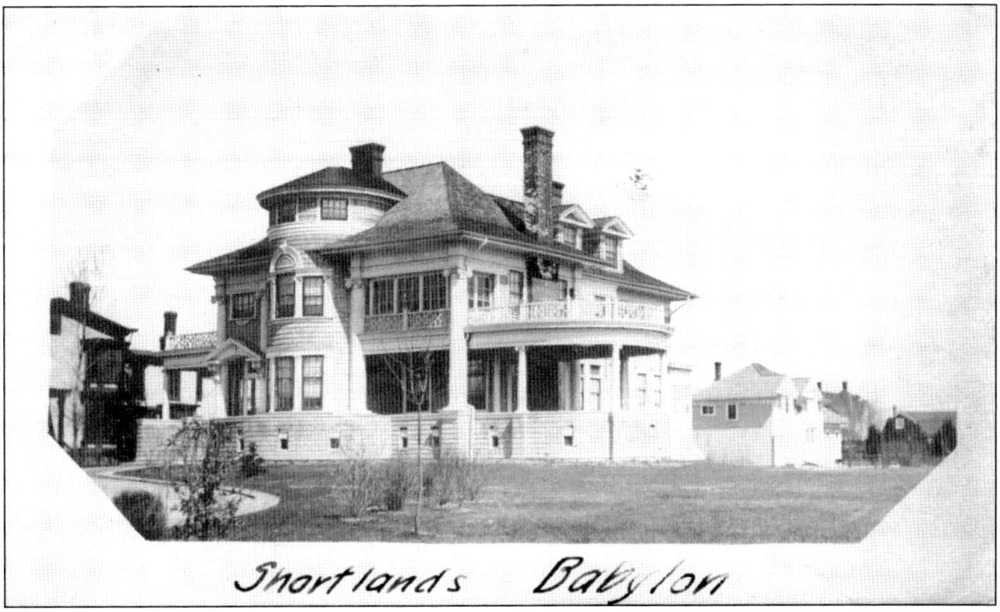

Shortlands was a summer residence on The Crescent and Robbins Avenue built for Brooklynite Thomas F. Shortland and his family. Shortland was a member of the firm of Shortlands Brothers, which was engaged in the business of loading, unloading, and transporting goods by barge or lighter, and was an active member of the Babylon Yacht Club.

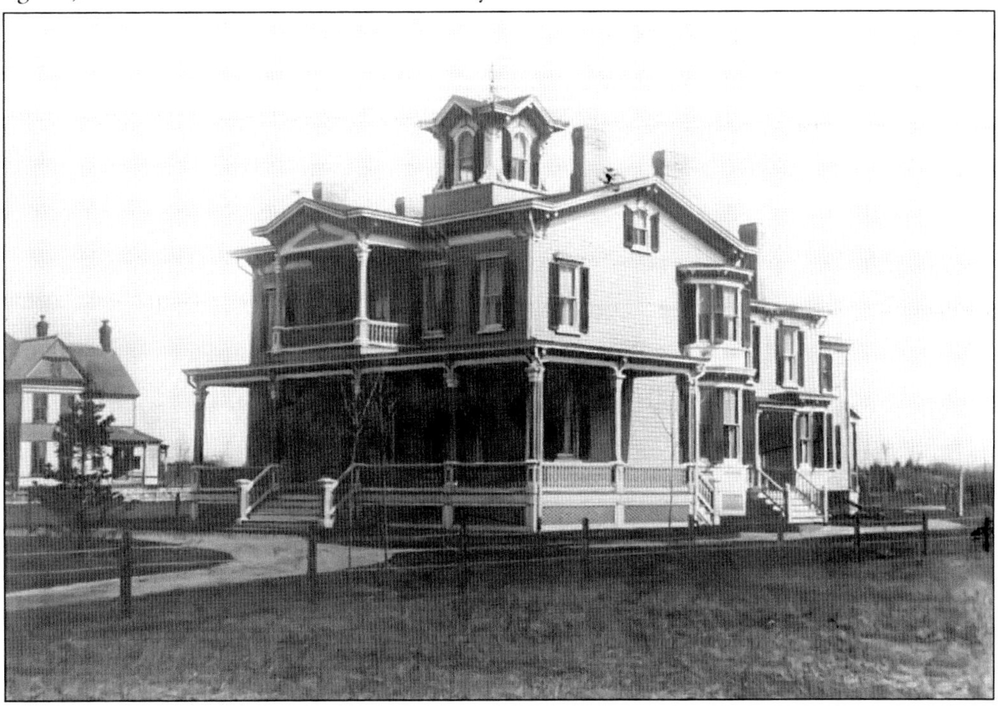

This Italianate residence was built in 1870 for local builder J. Sanford Udall on the northeast corner of Deer Park Avenue and George Street. In 1894, Udall hired Moses Drake's Sons of Bay Shore to move the house to The Crescent. The *South Side Signal* reported, "The house is large and the distance long, but the Messrs. Drake feel themselves fully equal to the undertaking."

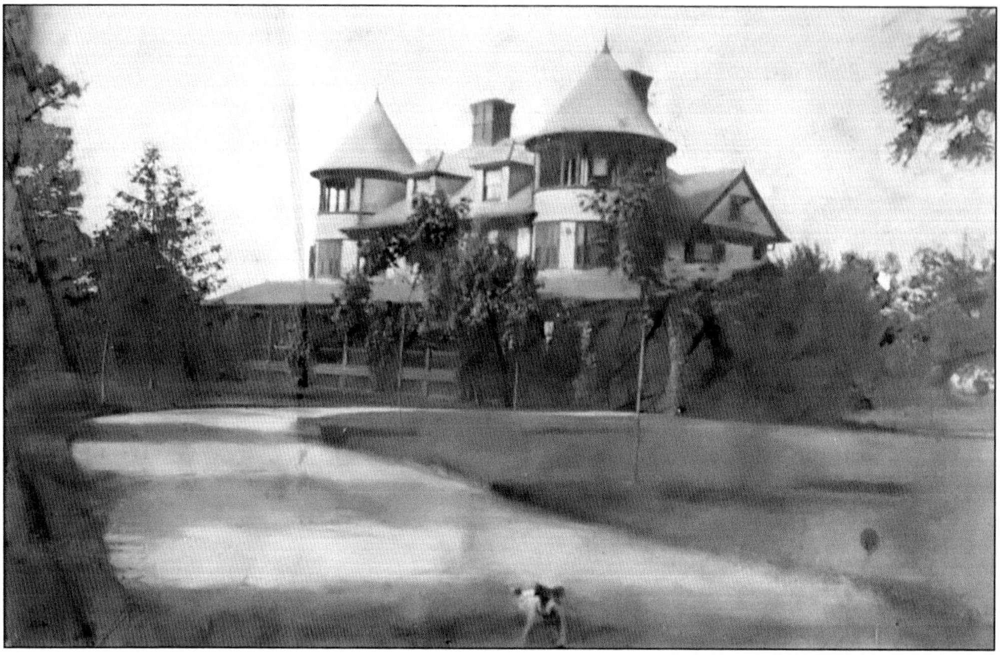

This residence of Judge John R. Reid was formerly located on present Reid Avenue. Reid was an editor of the *Suffolk Democrat* and later founded the *Babylon Budget* newspaper, printed from 1876 to 1881. A strong supporter of the Union during the Civil War, he was elected county and surrogate judge in 1869, a position that had not been held by a Democrat in nearly 50 years. After his 1902 death, his private library was reportedly worth $150,000.

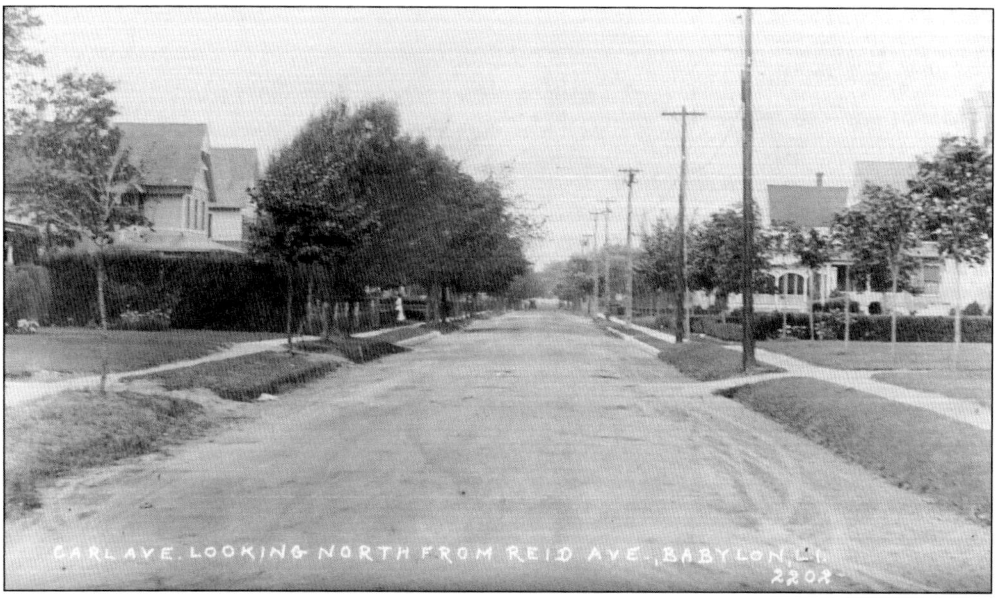

Carll Avenue is pictured looking north from Reid Avenue around 1910. Close to the village center, South Carll Avenue still features many of the large frame houses made popular during the resort era of the early 1900s. Amusing to some contemporary residents, many of these great houses were called "cottages" in the late 1800s and early 1900s, referring to their seasonal use by many New York City visitors.

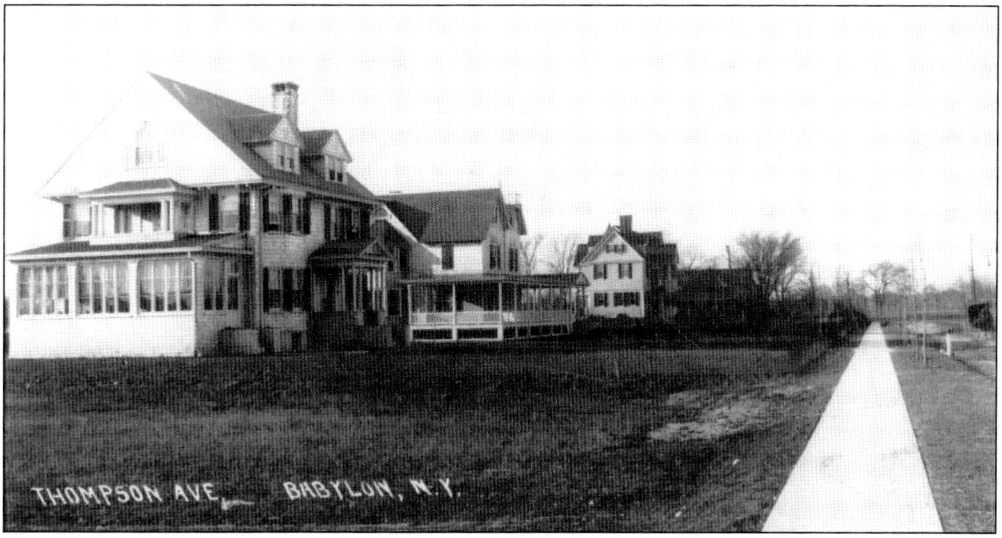

Thompson Avenue is seen facing north toward Montauk Highway. The house at far left was built for James B. Lowerre and his family. In 1895, the *South Side Signal* touted the quality of Lowerre's merchandise: "One of the handsomest lady's wheels [bicycles] we have seen this season is one of the Remington make . . . purchased of James B. Lowerre, the Main street dealer in high grade wheels."

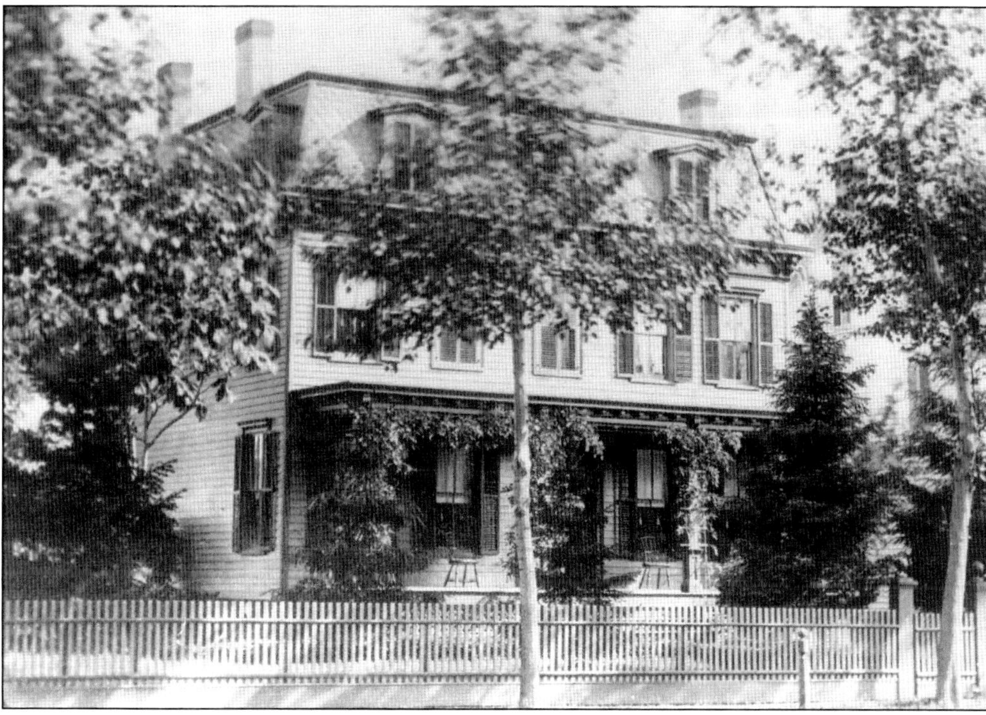

This was the Main Street residence of *Signal* founder and editor Henry Livingston. The Livingston home was next door to the newspaper office building, which was published in Babylon from 1869 to 1920. Henry Livingston left an indelible mark on the Babylon community. He served as the first chief of the Babylon Fire Department, was grand master of Babylon Masonic Lodge No. 793, and built the first summer cottage on Oak Island. (TOB.)

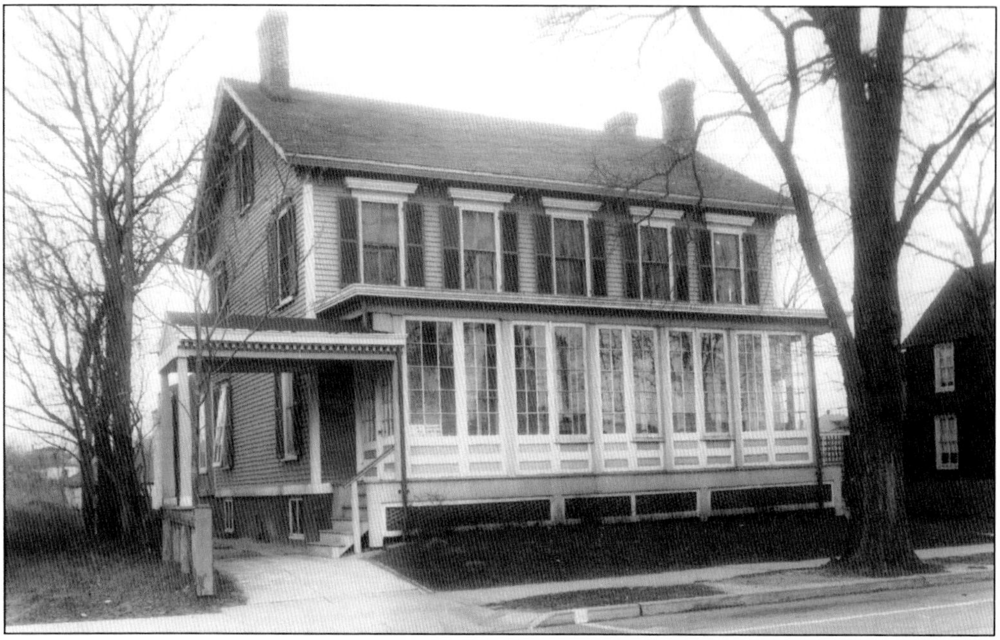

The former East Main Street home of Leopold Henry Fishel is pictured in 1937. An Austrian immigrant, Fishel settled in Babylon soon after his arrival at the age of 16. He owned and operated Fishel Dry Goods in the old Sumpwams Hotel building for many years. Fishel was also a founder of the Babylon Electric Light Company and a director of the Babylon National Bank and Sumpwams Water Company. (TOB.)

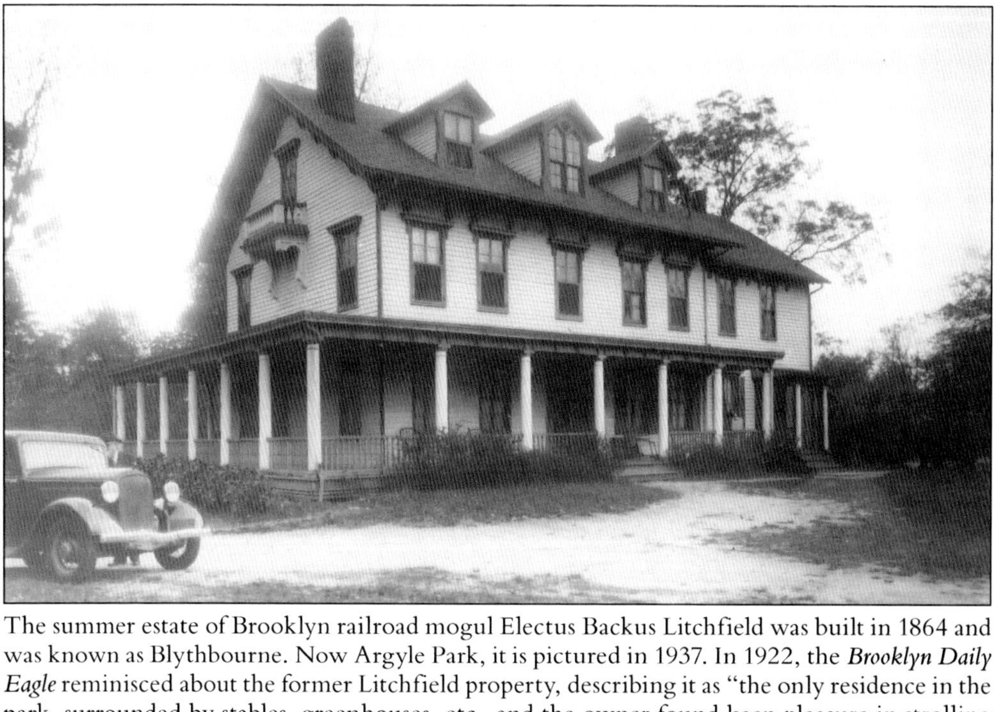

The summer estate of Brooklyn railroad mogul Electus Backus Litchfield was built in 1864 and was known as Blythbourne. Now Argyle Park, it is pictured in 1937. In 1922, the *Brooklyn Daily Eagle* reminisced about the former Litchfield property, describing it as "the only residence in the park, surrounded by stables, greenhouses, etc., and the owner found keen pleasure in strolling and driving along its wooded roads and footpaths." (TOB.)

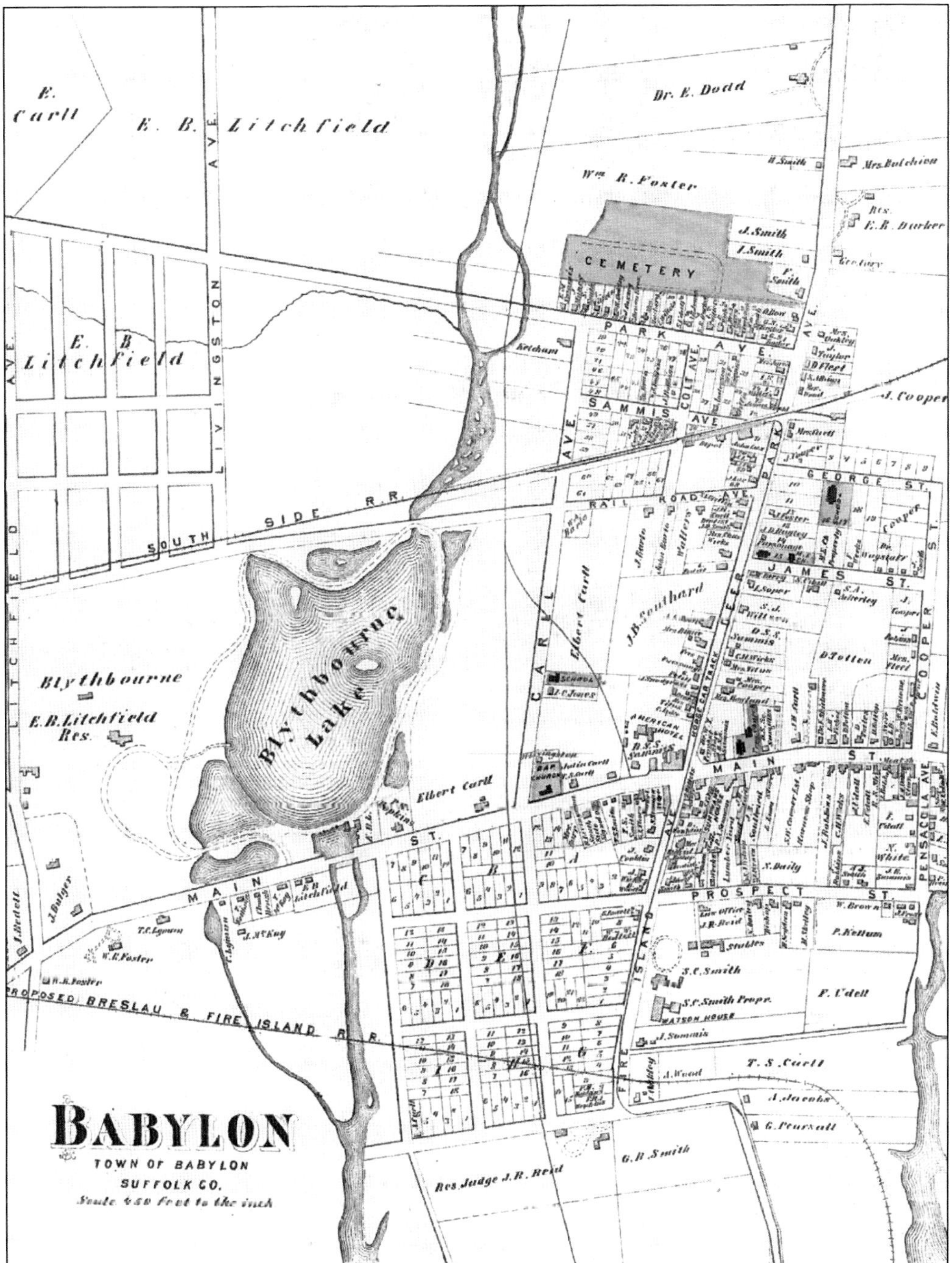

E.B. Litchfield's estate, Blythbourne, is depicted here on the west side of its namesake lake in the 1873 *Atlas of Long Island, New York*. The railroad is identified as South Side Railroad, later acquired by the Long Island Rail Road. The proposed Breslau & Fire Island Railroad was drawn on the south side of Main Street toward the Babylon docks. The American House compound is shown at the northwest corner of Deer Park Avenue and Main Street. (TOB.)

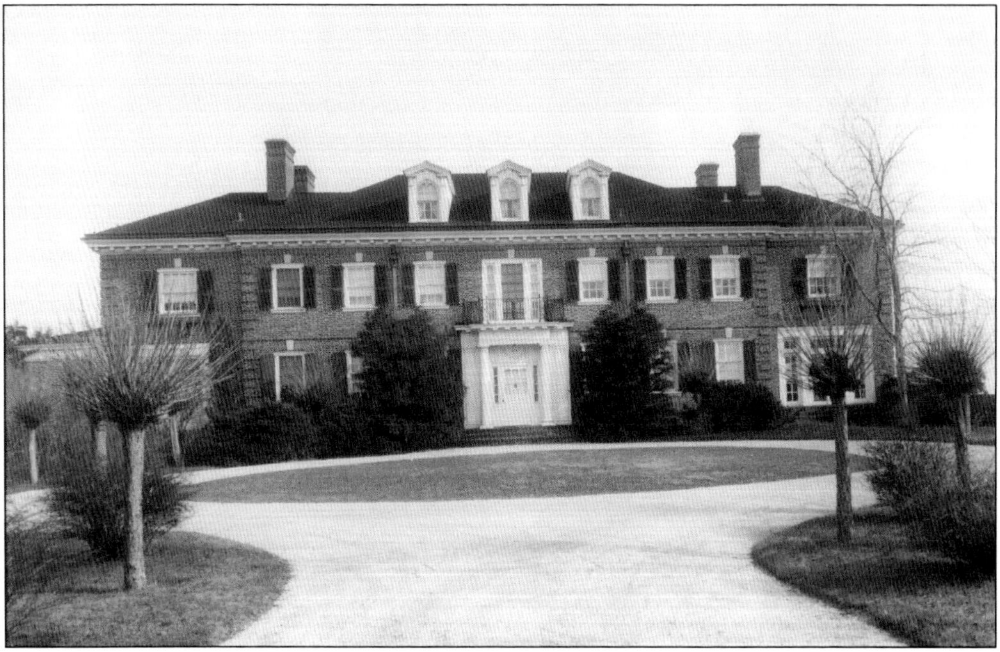

The 17-room Georgian Colonial residence of artist Edward Trenchard and his wife, Mary, was designed by architects Nelson and Van Wangeren of New York City and constructed by the E.W. Howell Company on Little East Neck Road in 1910. The property was formerly part of the estate of Jacob M. Bergen, a Brooklyn merchandise broker. Today, the former Trenchard home is the Long Island Yacht Club. (TOB.)

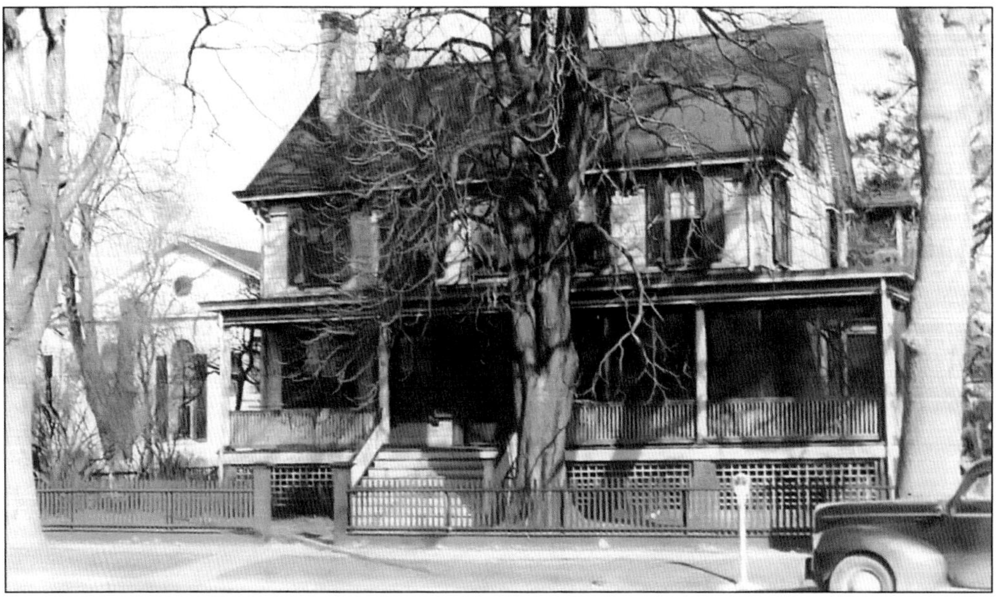

The former David S.S. Sammis home was on the east side of the Presbyterian church on East Main Street. Built near the close of the Revolutionary War in 1783, the Sammis house was erected as the Presbyterian congregation's second house of worship. Sammis was first married to Antoinette Wheeler, with whom he had one daughter. After Antoinette's death, Sammis married her sister Emeline, and they had one son and seven daughters.

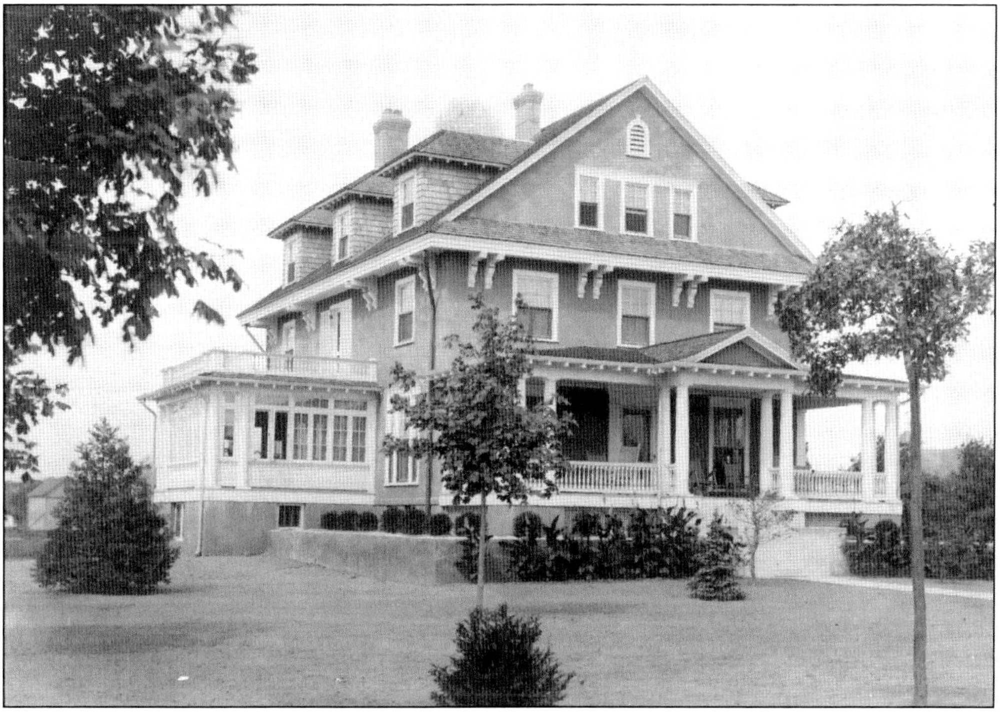

The Thompson Avenue residence of Charles Searle is pictured soon after its construction in 1911. A native of England, Searle married Babylon native Frances Barto and made his fortune as a cotton broker. Searle was active in the Babylon Yacht Club, serving as commodore, and built the third residence on Oak Island in 1883.

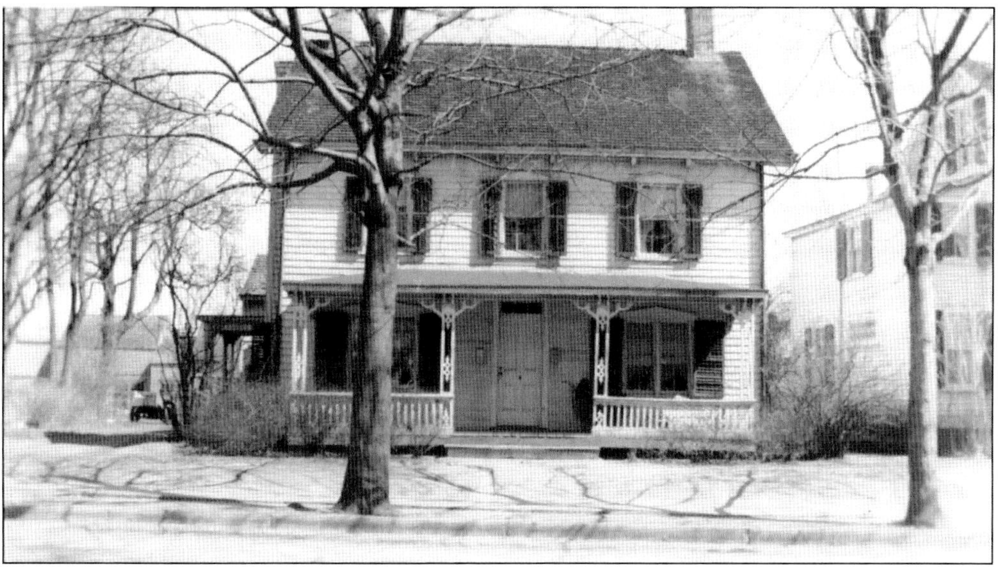

This Fire Island Avenue home belonged to Henry Placide, who was described by the *New York Times* as "one of the greatest favorites of the American stage . . . to which thousands owe some of the sweetest pleasures of their lives." The *South Side Signal* declared his talents "devoted to the drama, with the almost matchless delineation of the characters he assumed . . . never surpassed, if equaled, on the American stage, and have long since become a part of history." (TOB.)

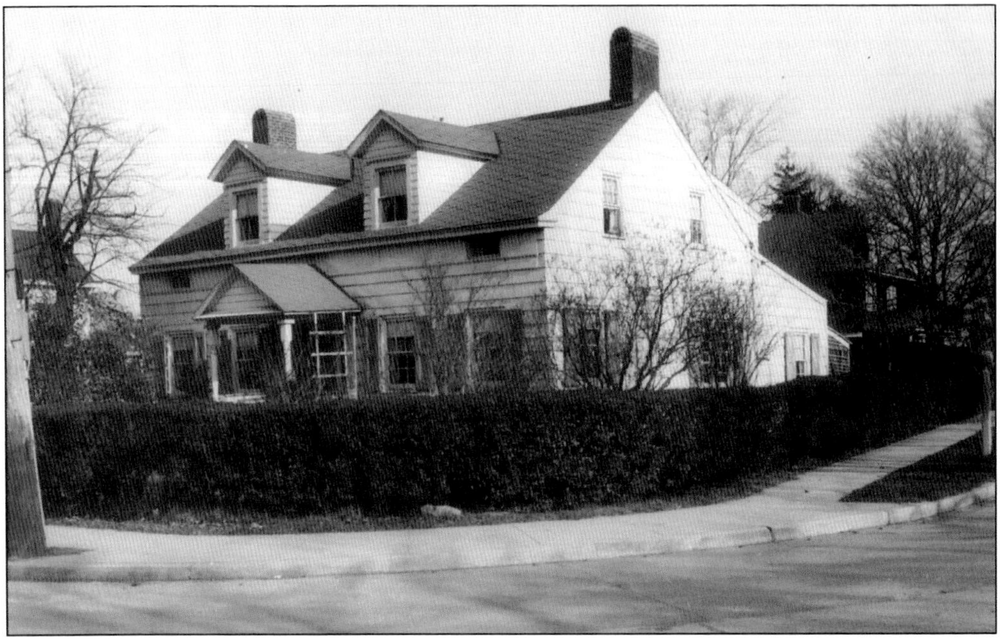

The former home of Henry Oakley (1824–1929) stood at Fire Island Avenue and The Crescent. Described in his *New York Times* obituary as "one of the last of the old-time whaling masters of Long Island," Oakley was on the crew of the whaler *Monmouth*, which was decorated for bravery by the British parliament for the rescue of 100 lives from the British ship *Meridian* in 1854. Oakley also commanded the US sloop-of-war *John Adams* during the Civil War. (TOB.)

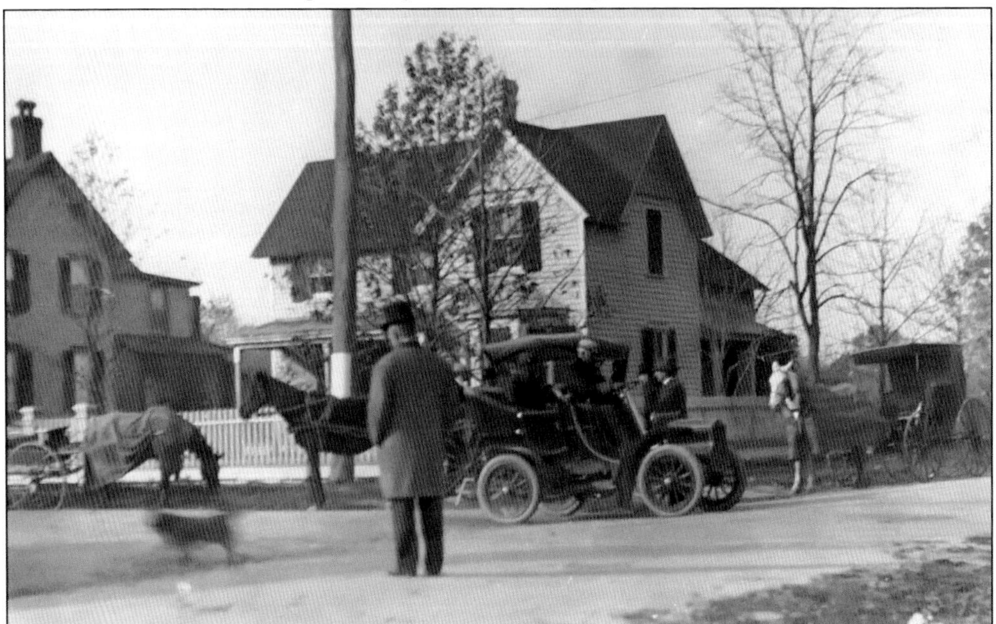

A flurry of activity, automobiles, and horse carriages passes the home of Ed and Beatrice Smith on Simon Street. The transition from horse power to mechanical engine did not occur overnight. For decades, local streets were occupied by both beast and machine, a potentially dangerous situation for all.

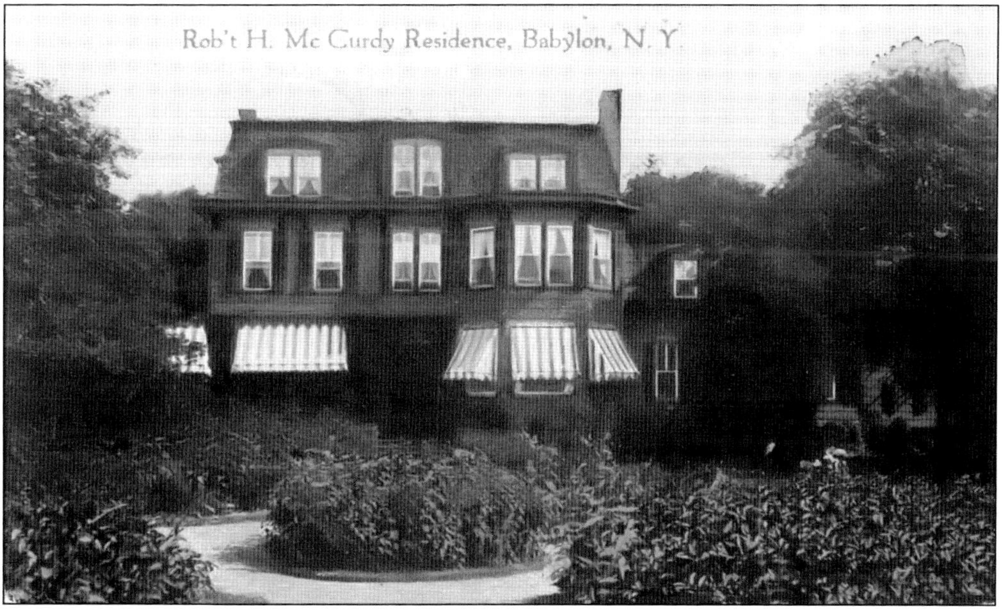

The social boundaries of Babylon extended to parts of West Islip, as indicated on many early 1900s postcards. The West Islip country estate of Robert H. McCurdy, general manager of the Mutual Life Insurance Company of New York, was built in 1879 on Montauk Highway between Eaton and Sequams Lanes. After the death of his wife, Mary, in 1924, McCurdy sold the 90-acre estate, described by the *New York Times* as "one of the show places on the south shore of Long Island."

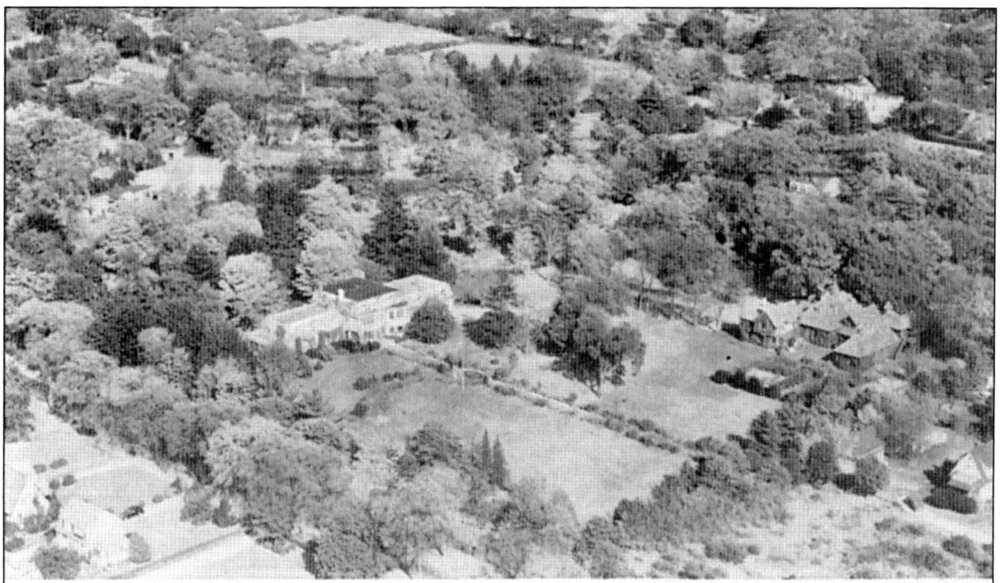

In 1925, ten acres of the old McCurdy estate were purchased by the Community Service Society of New York through a bequest from the late Emily Howland Bourne. Deeply interested in social services, Bourne provided $300,000 for the purchase of a rest and recuperation home for nurses, whom she observed worked hard for modest salaries without the means to pay for retreats. By 1960, as nurses' working conditions improved and fewer found use for the property, the house and property were sold.

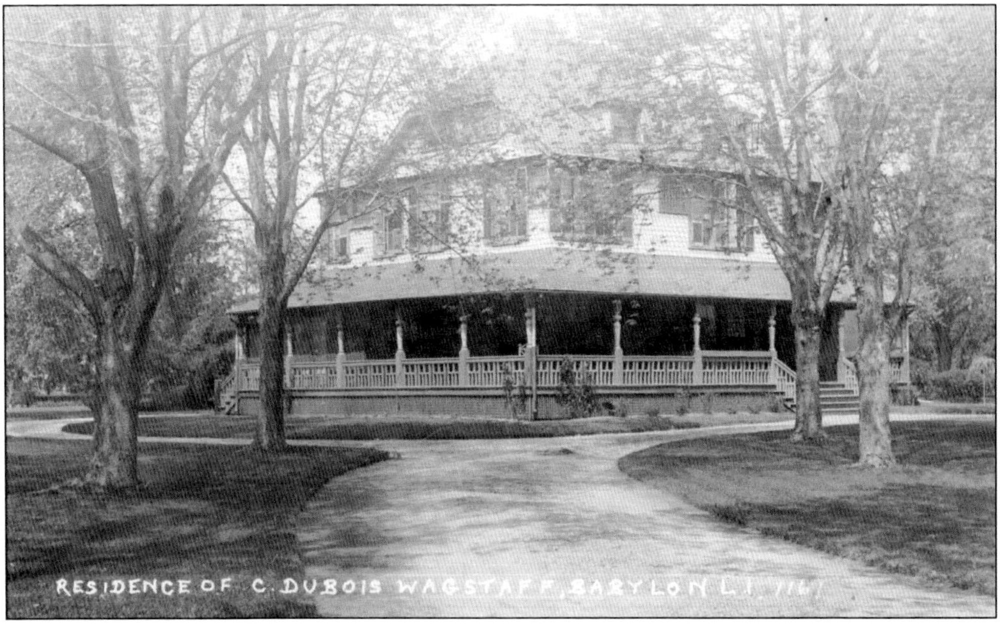

All four children of Dr. Alfred and Sarah DuBois Wagstaff built homes on their expansive West Islip estate. Their second son, Cornelius DuBois Wagstaff, divided his time between New York City and his country estate, where he bred field dogs at his Tahlulah Kennels. Cornelius was one of the 18 charter members of the Westminster Kennel Club. In the first Westminster show in 1877, he exhibited an Irish water spaniel and an Irish setter.

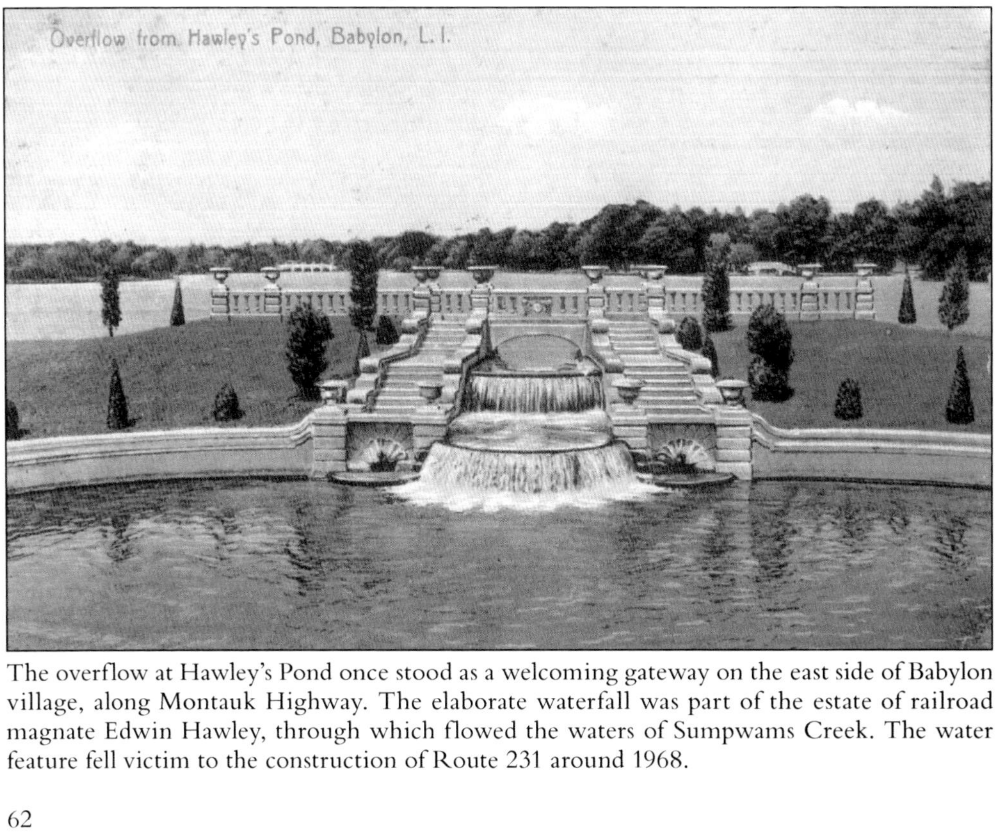

The overflow at Hawley's Pond once stood as a welcoming gateway on the east side of Babylon village, along Montauk Highway. The elaborate waterfall was part of the estate of railroad magnate Edwin Hawley, through which flowed the waters of Sumpwams Creek. The water feature fell victim to the construction of Route 231 around 1968.

Five

Argyle Park
Jay Stanley Foster's Lasting Gift

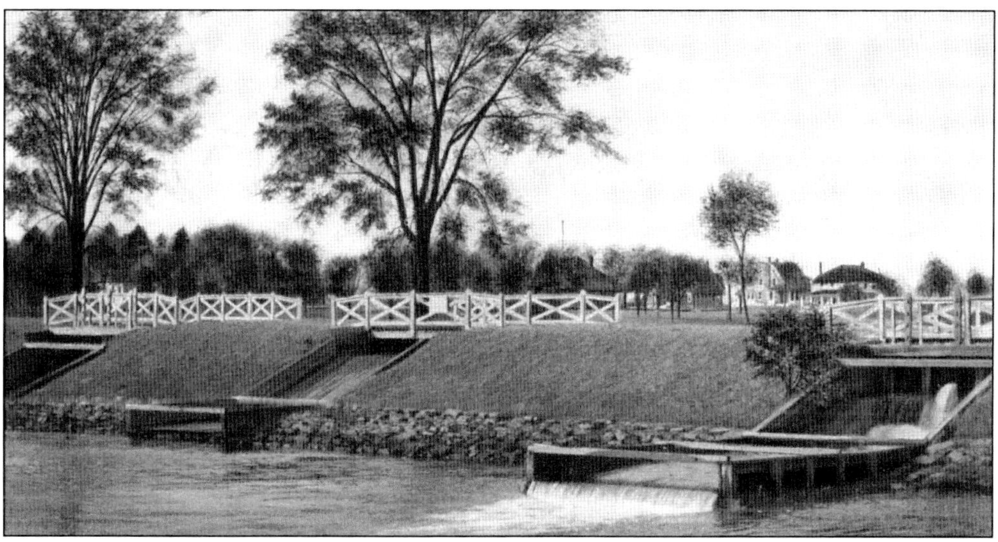

Village sage Benjamin P. Field recalled Argyle Lake as the former site of the Isaac Willets mill: "In those, the clanging of machinery and the music of the paper mill wheels, could be heard both day and night with ceaseless hum, until . . . Sunday morning. Strangers now passing . . . to admire the cascade overflowing from the beautiful 'Argyle' lake, would not dream that this quiet spot was once the scene of such busy activity."

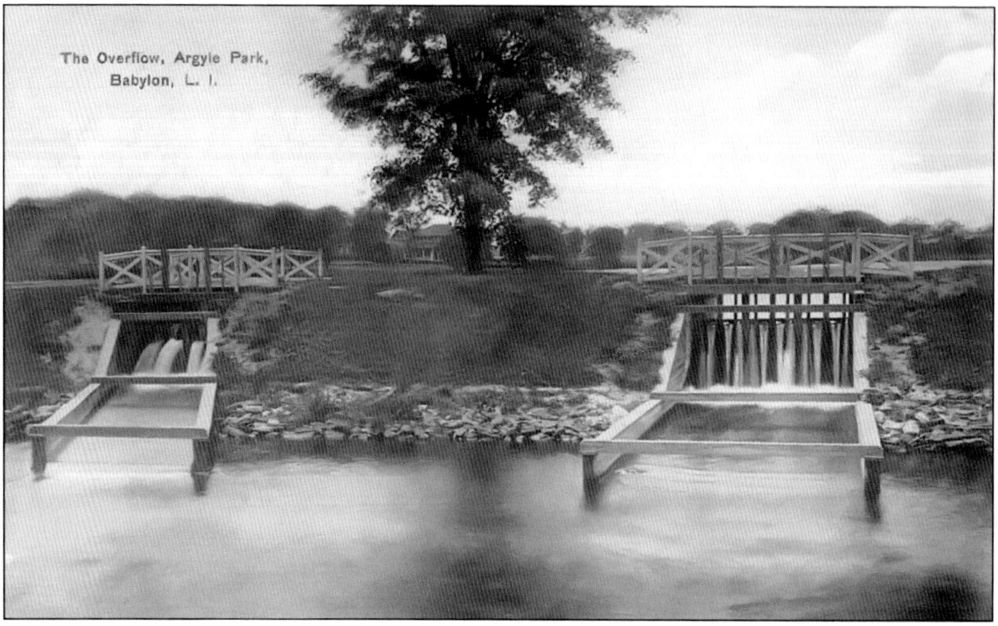

This view shows the overflow after demolition of the Argyle Hotel, which stood a mere 22 years. The March 5, 1904, *South Side Signal* reported: "Caretaker Peter Jommes . . . received orders . . . to begin the total destruction of the hotel property, and forty carpenters and laborers were immediately set at work on the job of demolishing the building. Over 100 men . . . are doing their best to get the building off the site before the end of the month."

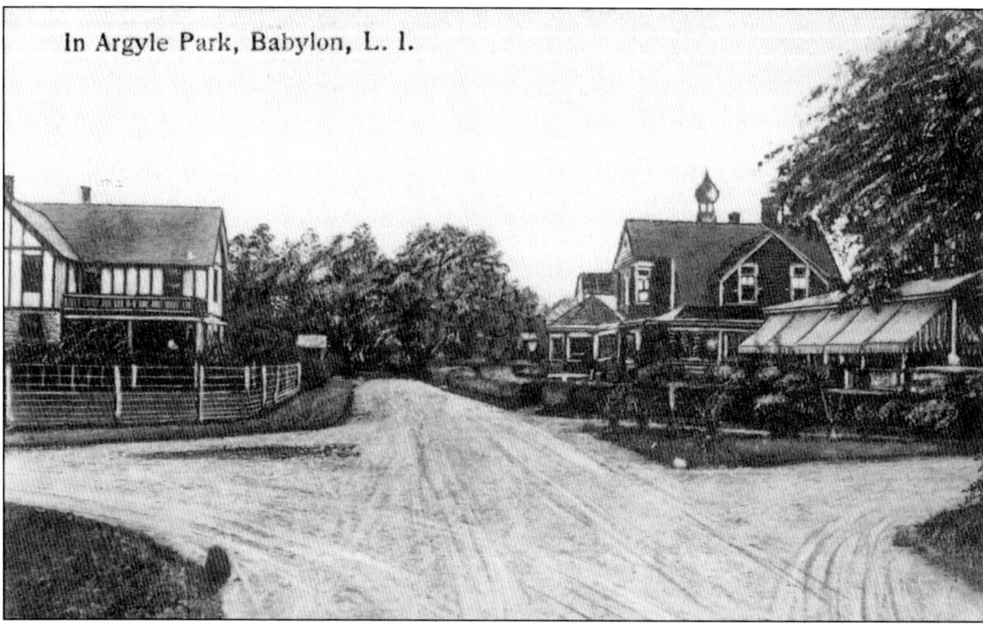

The *Signal* further reported that "Some of the principal drives in the park will be changed so as to allow room for convenient cottage sites. Then the erection of twenty cottages of attractive design, which will average a cost new of about $3500, will be built from the hotel lumber." The paper anticipated that each cottage, fully furnished and equipped with new plumbing and lighting systems, would be "offered for sale or rented to desirable tenants."

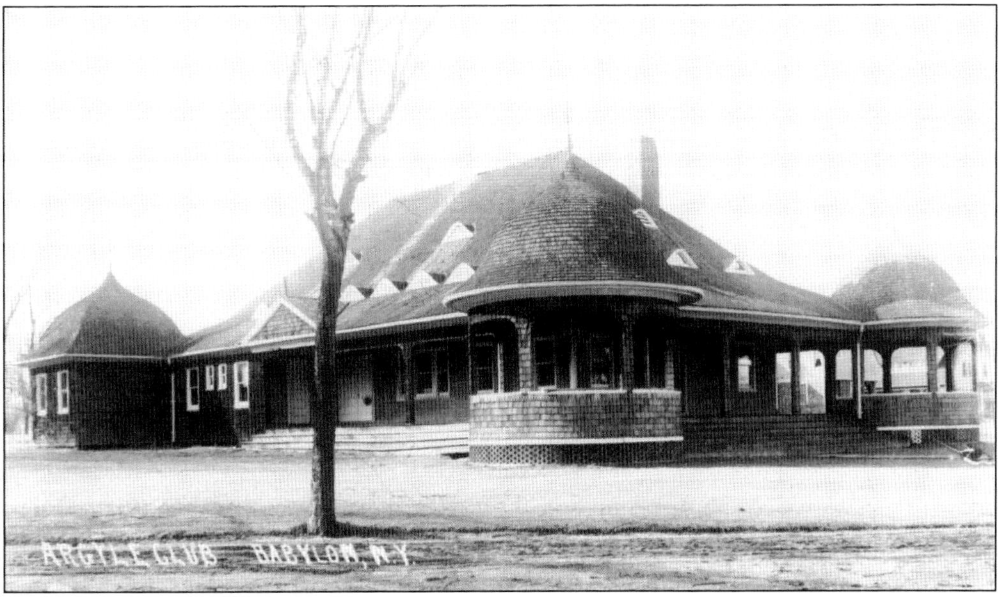

Pictured is the Argyle Club. William Ziegler, owner of the former hotel and managing agent of the Realty Trust Company, asserted plans to retain ownership of the lake "and ten feet of land surrounding it, granting to dwellers in the park boating privileges. The casino will remain on its present site." The *Signal* explained that "The hotel was not very successful from a financial standpoint, despite the fact that every effort was made to make it popular." (Herbert Ketcham.)

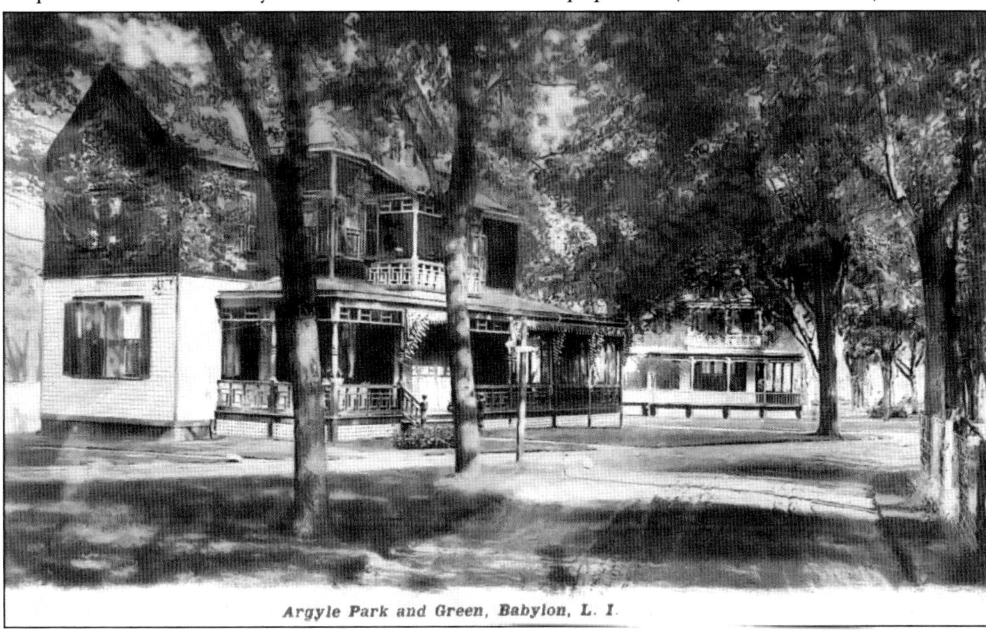

A 1906 real estate advertisement professed, "A Country Home at Babylon, Long Island. . . . We want the 'hard-to-please' man—the man who has looked everywhere for a country home and can't be satisfied." Duckworth Realty offered 24 newly completed homes, "delightfully situated on Argyle Lake. Every kind of house from the small, cozy summer cottage to the more pretentious all-year-round homestead. All modern improvements, best transportation, magnificent surroundings, every attraction, yet cheap."

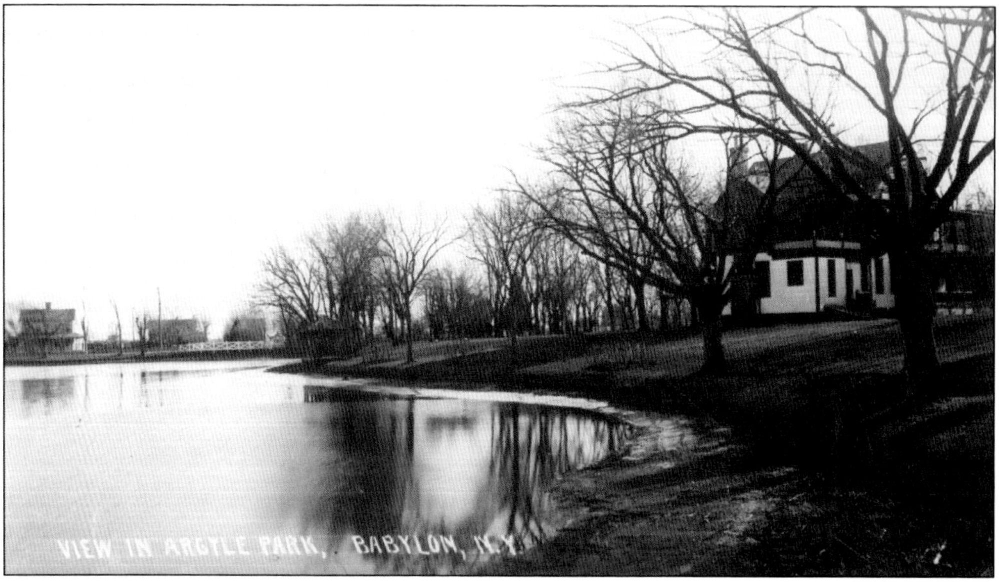

In December 1921, the *New York Times* reported that local real estate broker "Jeremiah Robbins, representing an unknown client, has purchased from the estate of William Ziegler the three lakes and yacht harbor at Argyle Park, Babylon, L.I., which the purchaser is to present to the village of Babylon to be used as a park." The property is described as "one of the most attractive lake propositions on the south shore of Long Island, beautifully landscaped and surrounded by handsome houses."

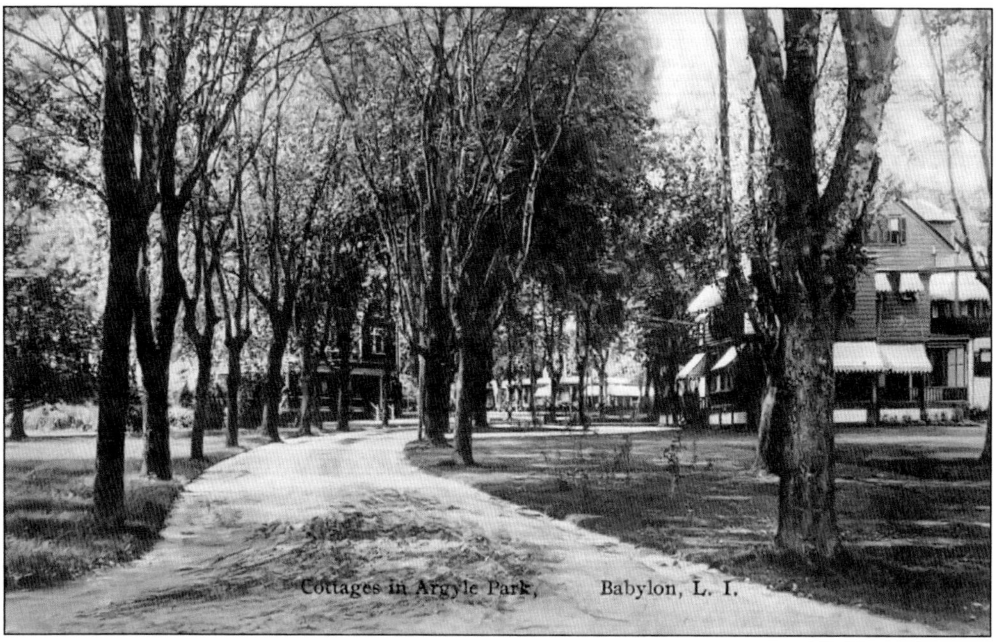

A few weeks later, the *Suffolk County News* of January 6, 1922, revealed that "J. Stanley Foster, who owns a large estate in Babylon and is President of the Bowery Bank in Manhattan, and a director of the Babylon National Bank, is the donor of the Argyle Lake property, which was presented anonymously to Babylon village several weeks ago. . . . The identity of the donor was made known when the deed of gift was presented to the village."

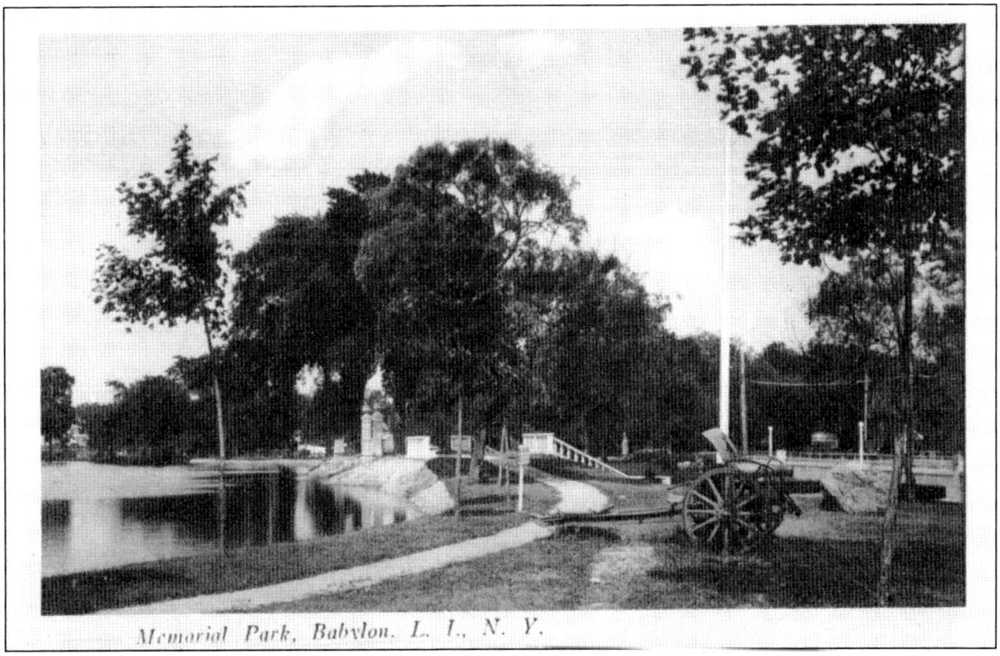

On December 2, 1922, the Babylon Village Board passed a resolution officially designating the lake and commons as "Babylon Memorial Park." The name referenced Foster's desire that the beautiful land be a passive public park and stand as a memorial to local residents who had served admirably in World War I.

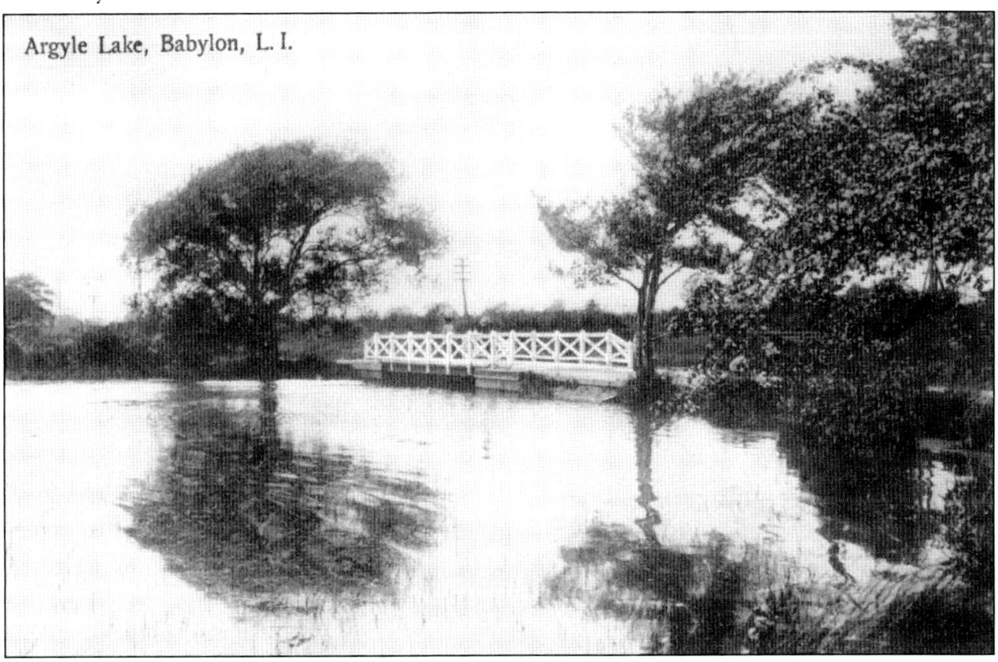

Around 1904, Foster joined the National Guard, 7th Regiment of New York. When the United States joined World War I, he volunteered for the Army Air Service and was made a captain adjutant, the officer in charge of his aviation division. Foster served about one year at Fort Waco, Texas, before he was honorably discharged for health reasons.

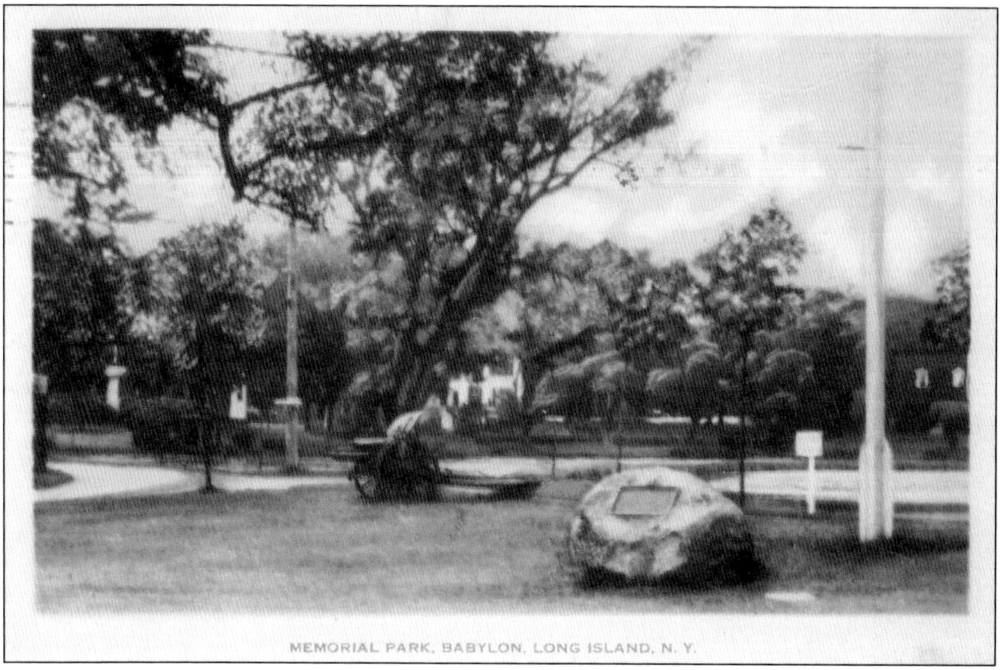

This stone monument was erected to World War I veterans. In July 1924, the Babylon Village Board accepted an offer of $15,000 from Foster for purchase of a 264-by-100-foot plot at the northwest corner of Main Street and Carll Avenue, "with the understanding that this plot will be purchased and used as a site for a municipal building and fire house with provision for an ambulance." The board voted unanimously to accept the offer, with sincere thanks.

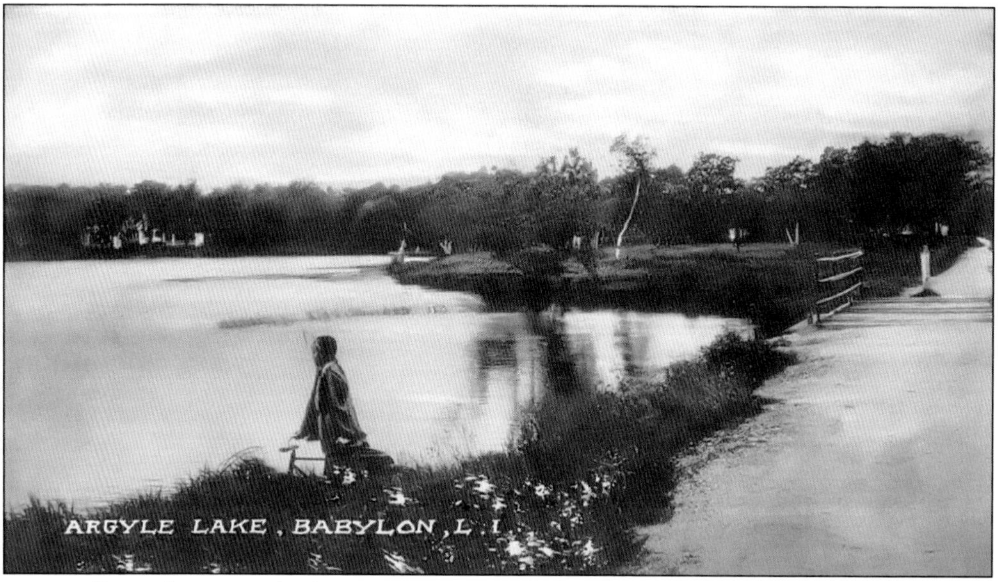

Long suffering from poor health, Foster died on August 14, 1925, aged 48. The *Babylon Leader* declared, "Foster extended man a helping hand where it was never known to the public, befriending many whom he thought needed aid." His generous donation of the Memorial Park "will ever stand as a monument to his liberality." Locally, "it was the first time the flag had flown at half-mast to show respect to the memory of a private citizen." (Steve Loudon.)

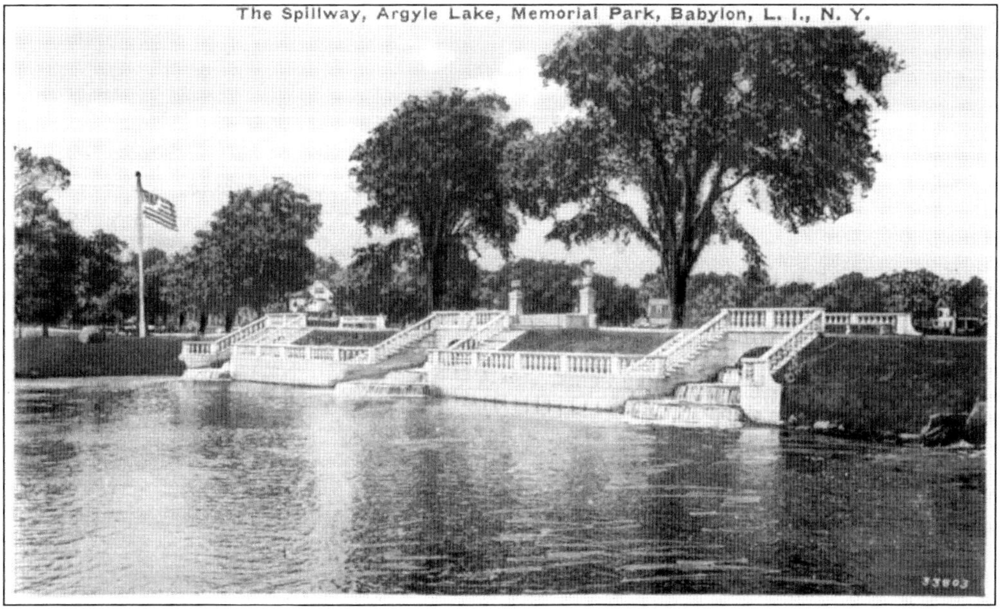

In June 1928, less than three years after Foster's passing, his sister Caroline Foster Savidge proposed to pay for the construction of decorative flumes at the south end of Argyle Lake in honor of her brother at the site of his munificent bequest. Again, the village board voted unanimously to accept the offer "with a resolution of appreciation." Preliminary estimates for the flagstone-and-concrete terrace were announced as "not less than $25,000."

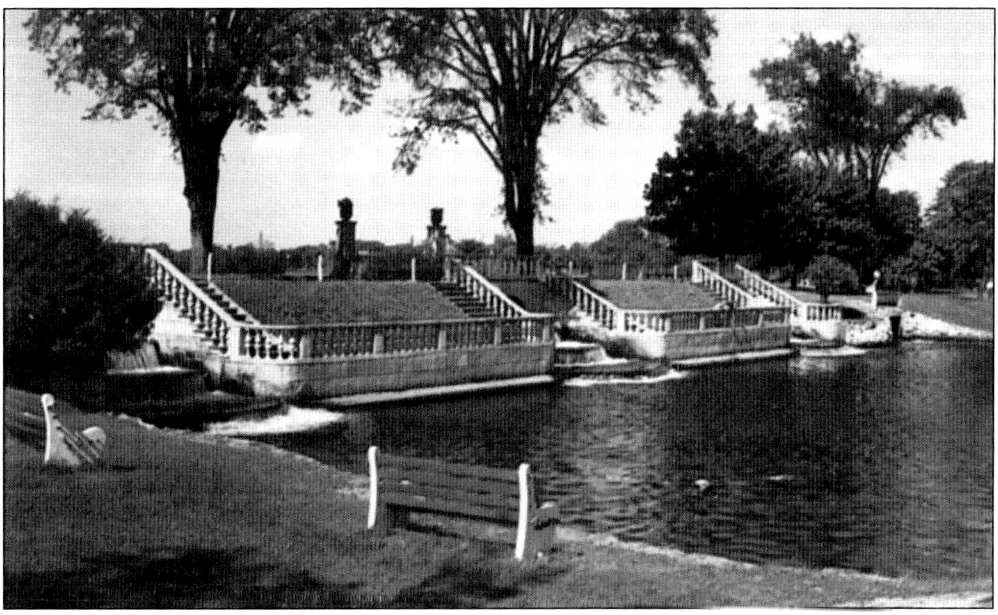

The ornate flagstone-and-concrete terrace and triple waterfall were designed by noted New York City architect and Babylon resident John H. Phillips. The center bench, flanked by planter pillars, was inscribed "Babylon Memorial Park, presented to the Village of Babylon by J. Stanley Foster, Esq." The Foster memorial was formally dedicated on Armistice Day (now Veterans Day) 1928. Marchers paraded to Babylon Cemetery and laid a wreath on Foster's grave, then processed to the park.

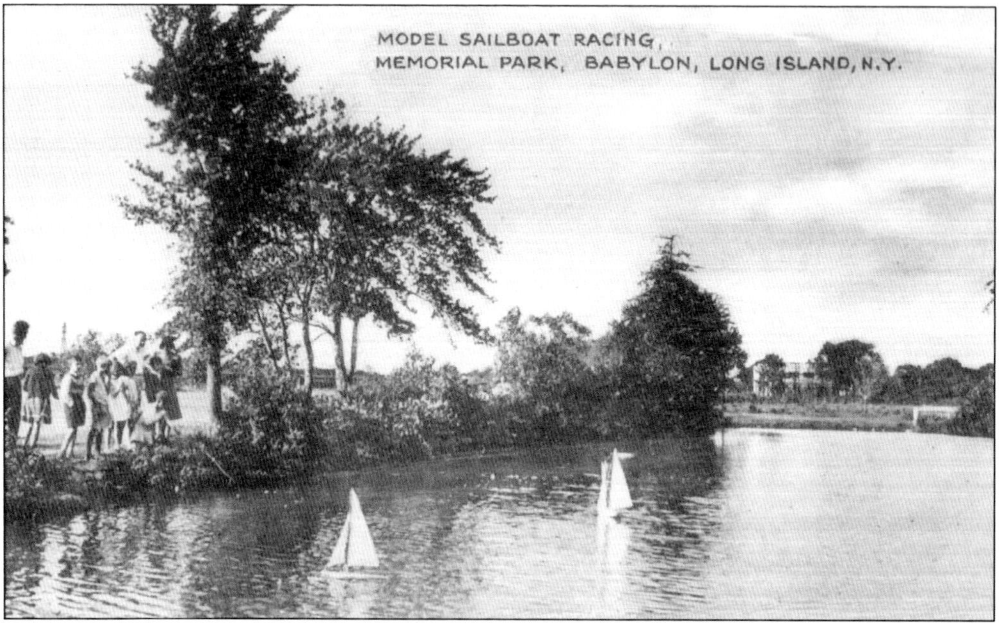

The lake was once a favorite haunt for ice skaters. This is now prohibited for safety, but it remains popular for fishing—licensed, as required. In 1935, the Long Island State Parks Commission exhibited a wooden, nine-foot, 250-pound, remote-controlled model of the aircraft carrier *Saratoga* on the lake at Argyle Park. The trial appearance was described as a "reenactment of historic naval encounters . . . for the edification of visitors to [the Long Island State Parks Commission's] extensive park system."

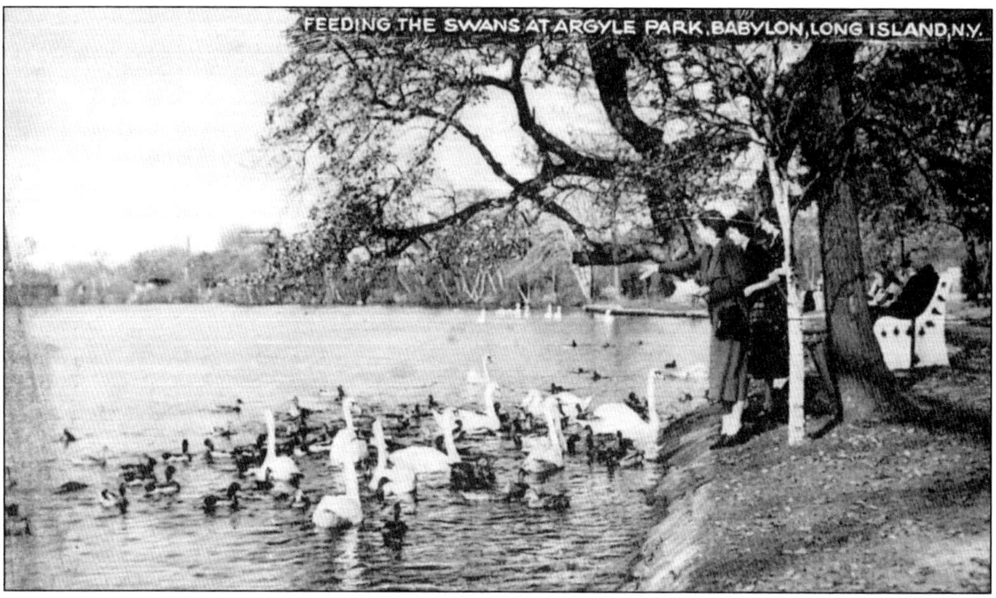

The park is host year-round to photogenic bridal parties, playful children, joggers, dog-walkers, and migrant birds. Each September, the Babylon Beautification Society, founded in 1975, hosts the popular Country Fair in and around the park. In 2002, a memorial garden was dedicated at Argyle Park to the 11 Babylon residents who lost their lives in the September 11, 2001, attacks. A Cuban Giants memorial was dedicated at the northwest corner of the park in 2010.

Six

Mind Your Business
Downtown and Local Commerce

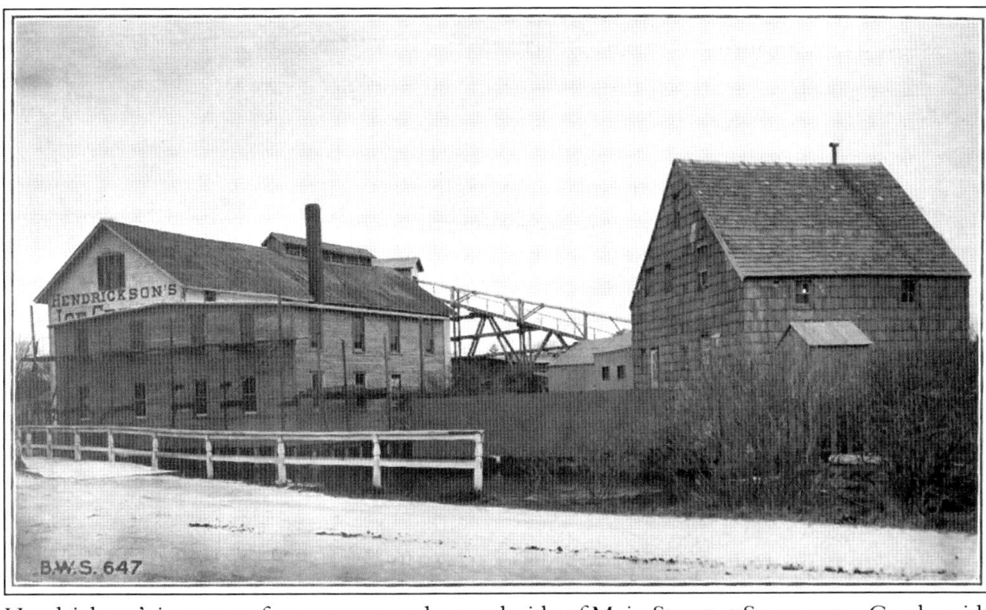

Hendrickson's ice cream factory was on the north side of Main Street at Sumpwams Creek, aside the old mill. In the summer of 1909, the *South Side Signal* reported that the factory was producing "nearly 2,000 quarts a day . . . [workers] labor hard to supply the public with what has long since become a necessity rather than a luxury." The following year, Edwin Hawley reclaimed the property to build his decorative overflow, and the factory relocated to John Street. (TOB.)

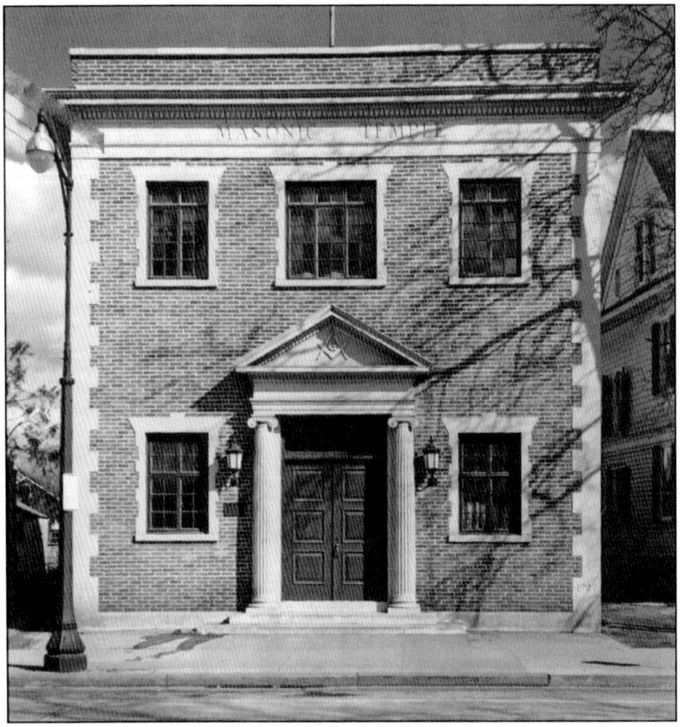

Babylon Masonic Lodge No. 793 officially formed on June 10, 1887. The lodge was headquartered in various locations, including the third floor of the Dowden Brothers building. In 1910, the Masons settled in this Deer Park Avenue building, which had been a headquarters for the *South Side Signal*, just north of the Methodist church. The Masons built and relocated to their current lodge on West Main Street in 1958. (Masons.)

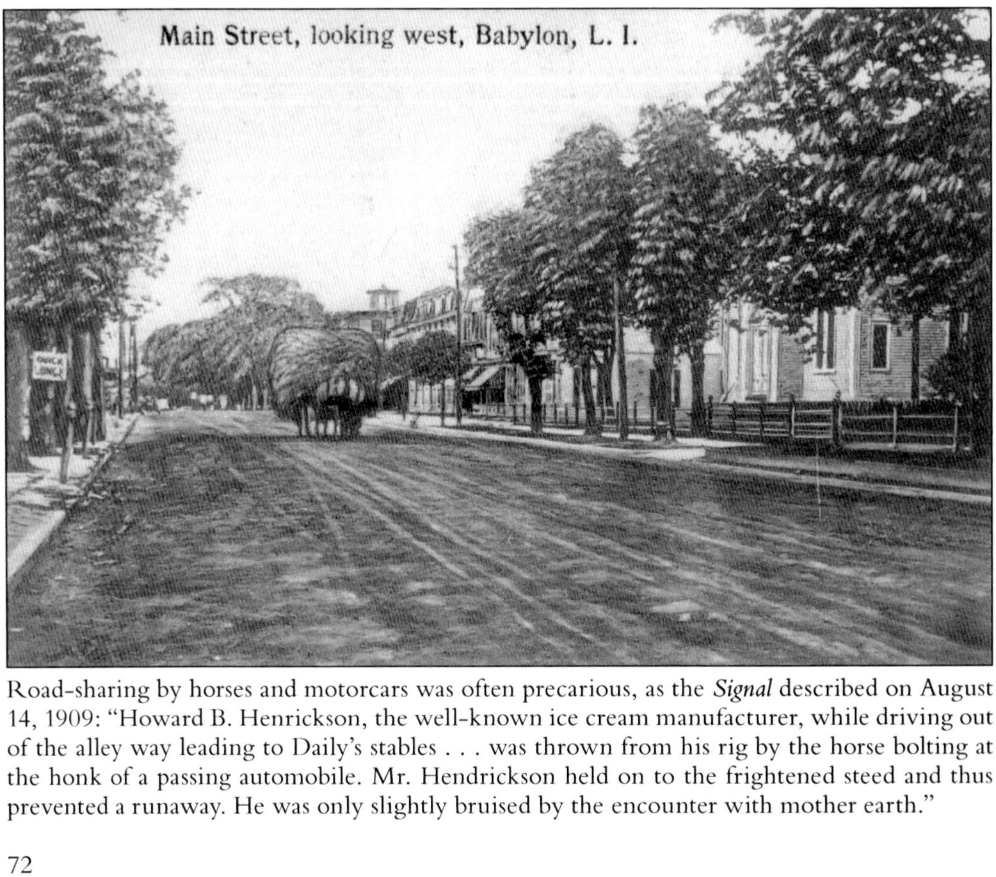

Road-sharing by horses and motorcars was often precarious, as the *Signal* described on August 14, 1909: "Howard B. Henrickson, the well-known ice cream manufacturer, while driving out of the alley way leading to Daily's stables . . . was thrown from his rig by the horse bolting at the honk of a passing automobile. Mr. Hendrickson held on to the frightened steed and thus prevented a runaway. He was only slightly bruised by the encounter with mother earth."

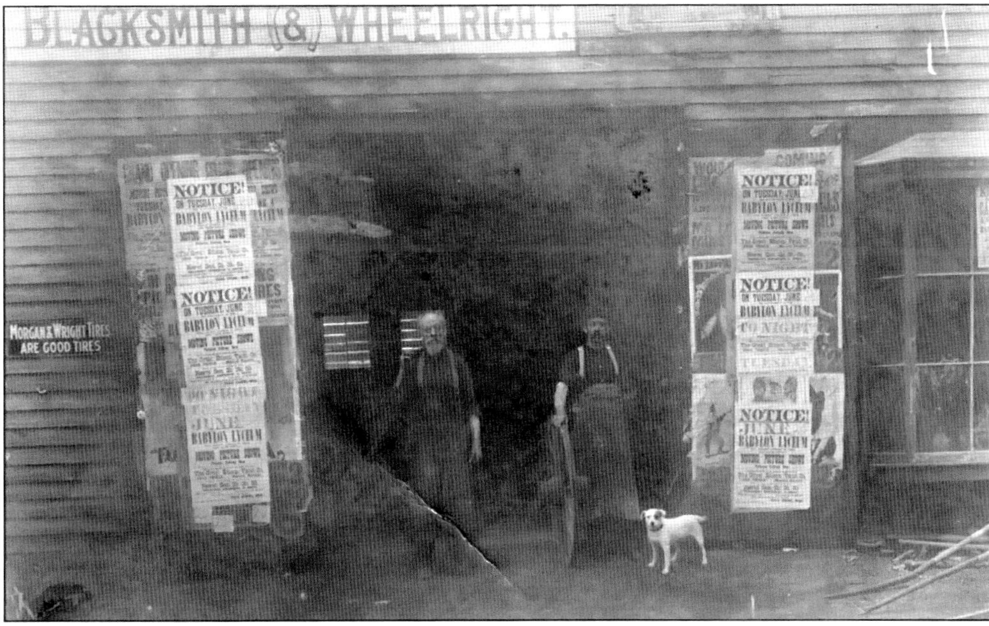

Local blacksmiths in the 19th century included Charles Bruene, Augustus A. Cornelius, Samuel Maginnes, Treadwell Smith, William H. Terry, and Andrew Titus. Cornelius operated a shop on the west side of Deer Park Avenue until the property was purchased in the 1890s by Terry, who constructed a three-story building. The first floor was Terry's blacksmithing, with John Hilton's wheelwright shop in the rear. Andrew J. Week's carriage factory was on the second floor, and Joseph Covert's upholstery and painting shop was on the third.

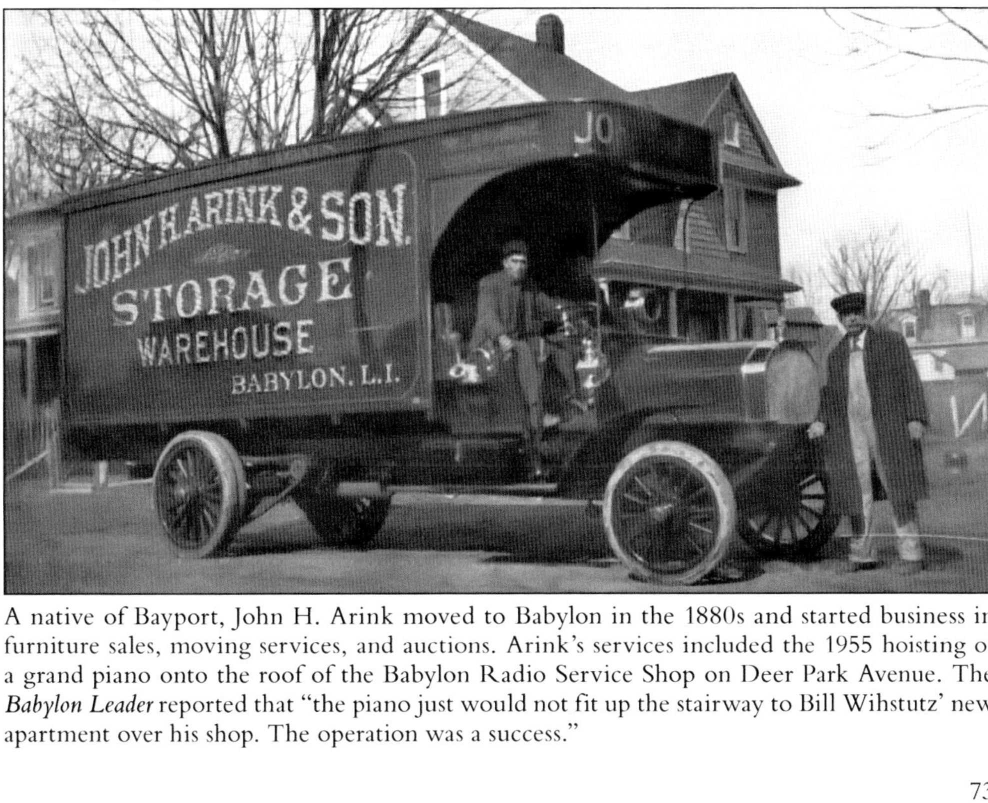

A native of Bayport, John H. Arink moved to Babylon in the 1880s and started business in furniture sales, moving services, and auctions. Arink's services included the 1955 hoisting of a grand piano onto the roof of the Babylon Radio Service Shop on Deer Park Avenue. The *Babylon Leader* reported that "the piano just would not fit up the stairway to Bill Wihstutz' new apartment over his shop. The operation was a success."

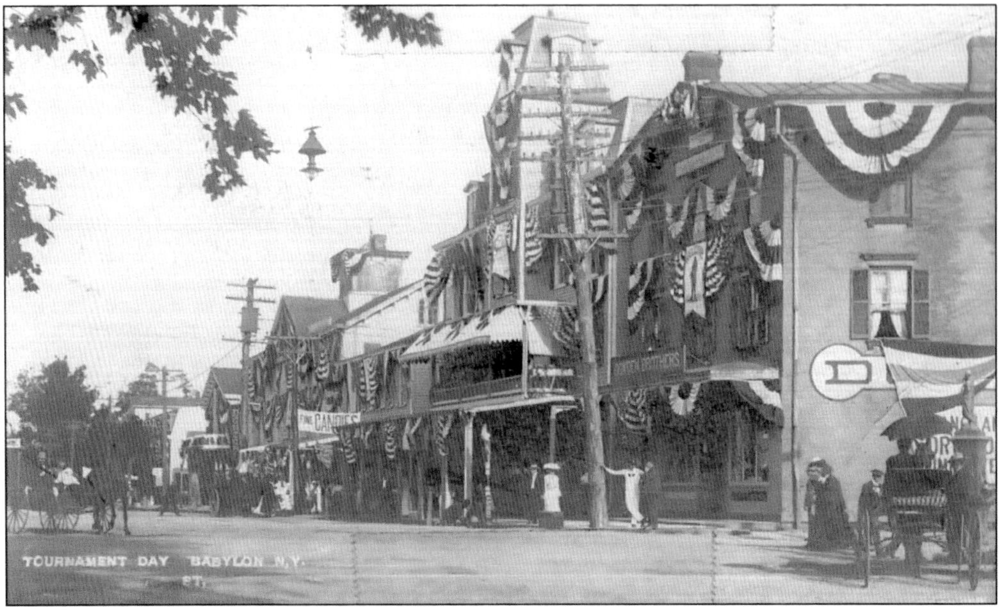

F. Augustine Dowden and Thomas Edward Dowden of Cold Spring Harbor opened a general store at the southeast corner of Main Street and Fire Island Avenue around 1876, offering groceries, housewares, hardware, and alcoholic beverages "for family and medicinal purposes." Dowden Brothers operated until 1919, including Augustine's stint as postmaster, when the siblings retired. Known as the Willet's Building, it was previously the dry goods store of Marcus F. Ketcham and Theodore N. Hawkins.

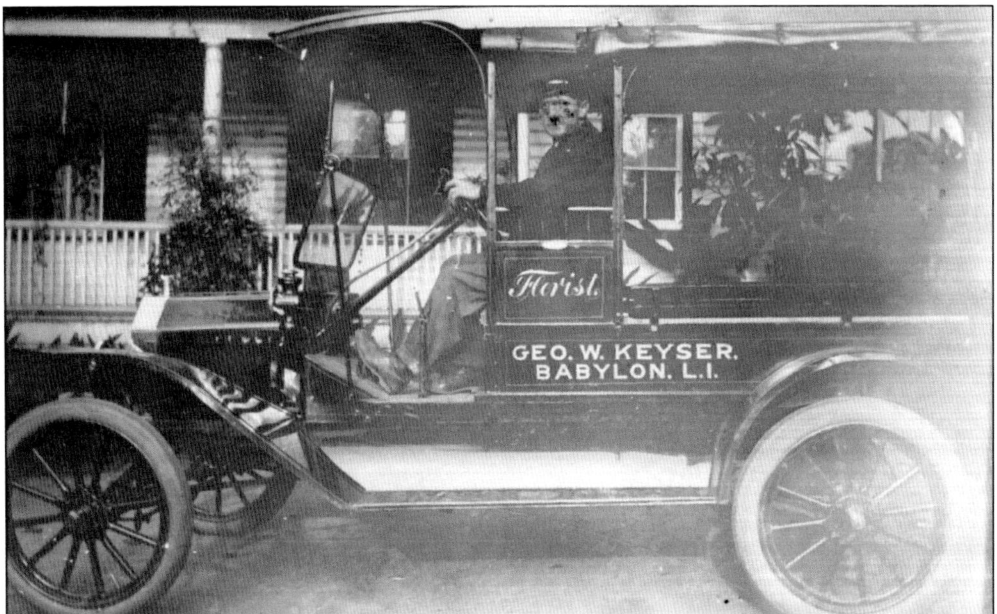

Queens County resident George W. Keyser married Minnie Voss at her parents' Babylon home in 1896. Three years later, he purchased a Park Avenue plot from his in-laws for his floral business. In 1914, the *South Side Signal* touted Keyser's Park Avenue greenhouses as "a trip to a city of flowers . . . under 25,000 feet of glass." The florist later relocated to Little East Neck Road, where the flourishing operation continues.

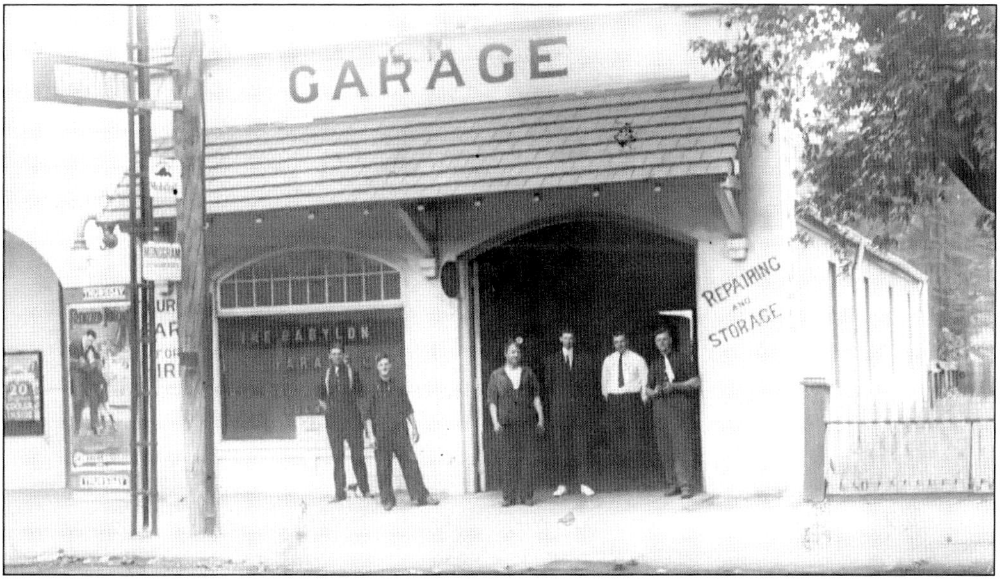

A corner of the original Babylon Theatre is seen at the far left of this c. 1913 postcard of the Babylon Garage, operated by Thomas B. Sprague on Deer Park Avenue. Sprague was later associated with the Sprague and Duryea garage and the Reo Service Station. A 1916 advertisement for the service station declared, "The automobile has become a very important factor in the development of Long Island."

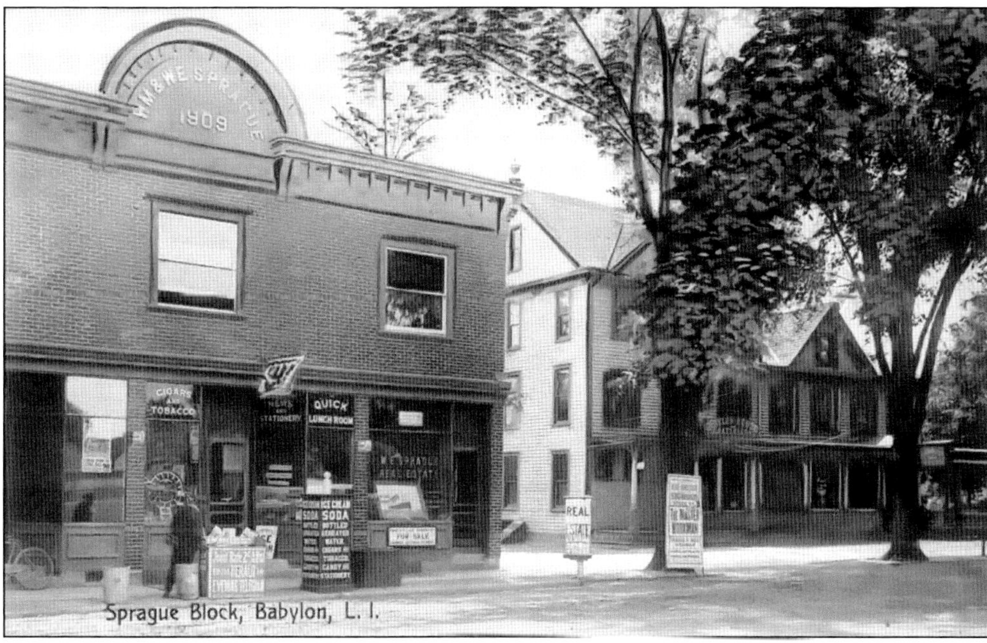

The Sprague Building stood on the south side of Railroad Avenue. The old Babylon House is pictured at right. Commercial occupants in the 1910s included insurance agent William H. Suydam, Sumpwams Point Park real estate agents Babylon and Shore of Bay Land Company, carpenter and builder Henry W. Lange, the Babylon Republican Club, and Isadore Goldberger's lunch room. Goldberger was an uncle of comedian Rodney Dangerfield, who was born in 1921 at Goldberger's Railroad Avenue home.

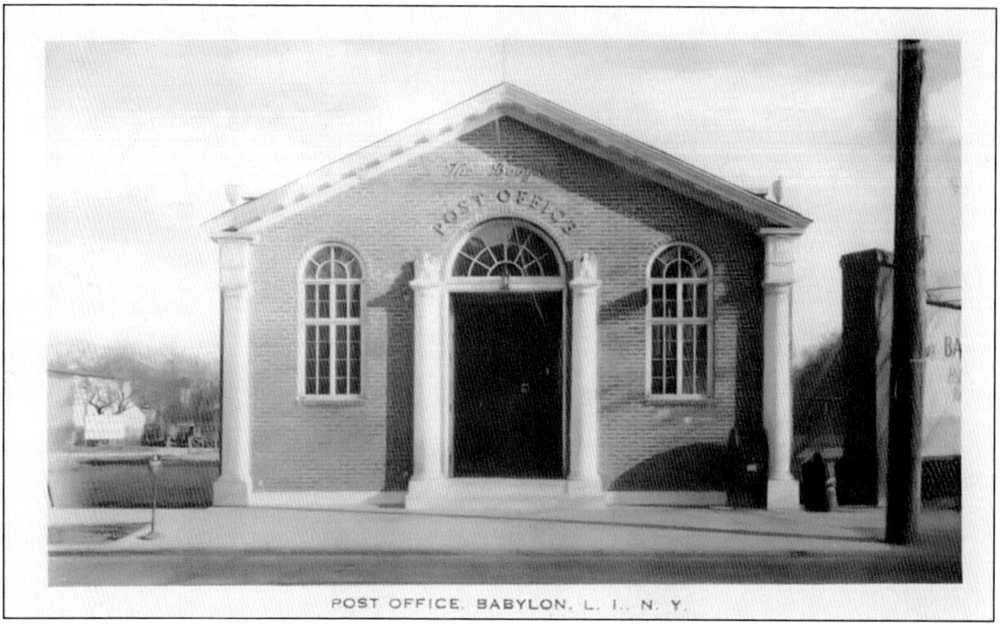

The first post office was established in 1803 under Postmaster Abraham G. Thompson. Originally named Huntington South, it was renamed Babylon in 1830. The pictured post office on the south side of West Main Street was built in the 1920s and is presently the Post Office Café. The current post office, on Cooper Street, was dedicated in 2006 to Jacob Samuel Fletcher, an Army soldier and native Babylonian who was killed in Iraq in 2003.

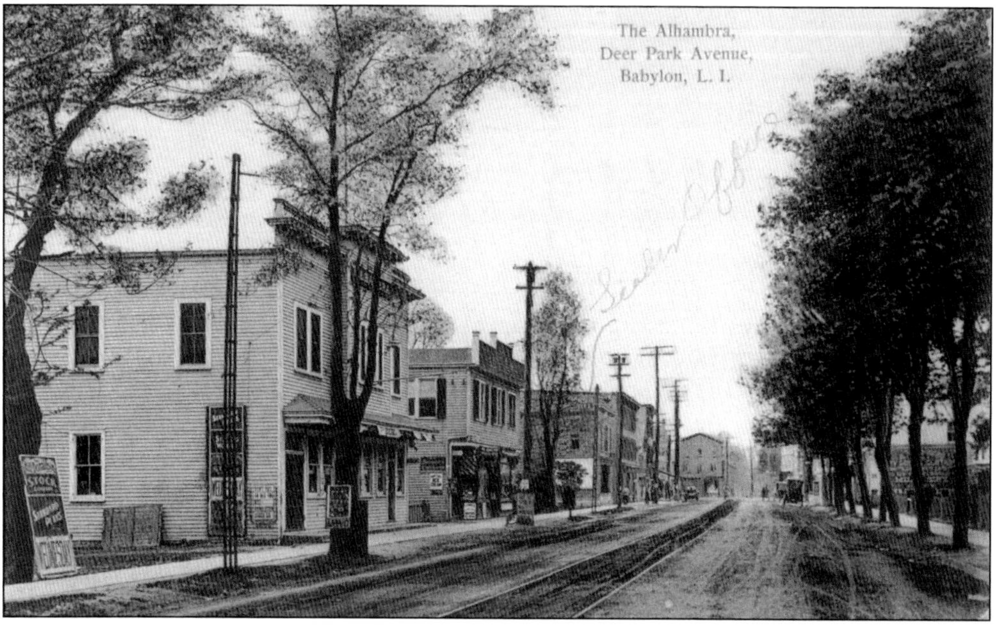

Benjamin F. Saxton opened the Alhambra Opera House on Deer Park Avenue in 1909. The first floor offered billiards and bowling, while the second floor was billed as an "amusement hall." Events for the week of January 22, 1910, included moving pictures and illustrated songs, roller-skating, a basketball game between the Halcyon and Far Rockaway athletic clubs, and two stage performances. The theater closed in February 1914 and was sold to the Sampawams Odd Fellows Lodge.

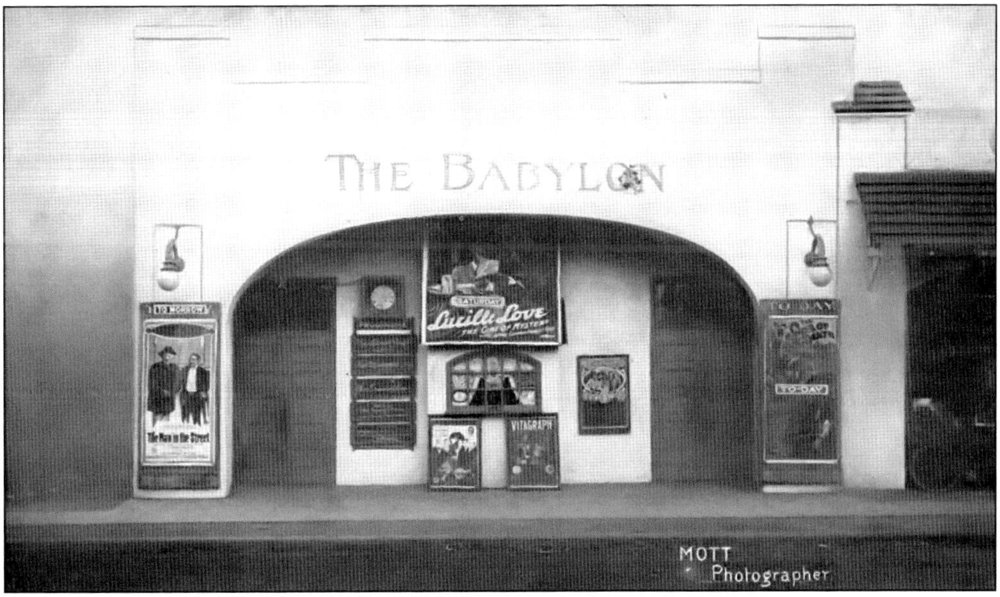

The Babylon Theatre, a 500-seat movie house owned by Graham M. Polley on Deer Park Avenue opposite Railroad Avenue, opened on April 5, 1913, with two performances of *The Dawning*. In 1919, the village board voted unanimously to prohibit showing movies on Sundays. By 1923, local opinions changed, and voters overturned the Sunday movie ban 758 to 307. However, this theater closed in 1922 after declining attendance and the impending opening of the Capitol Theatre.

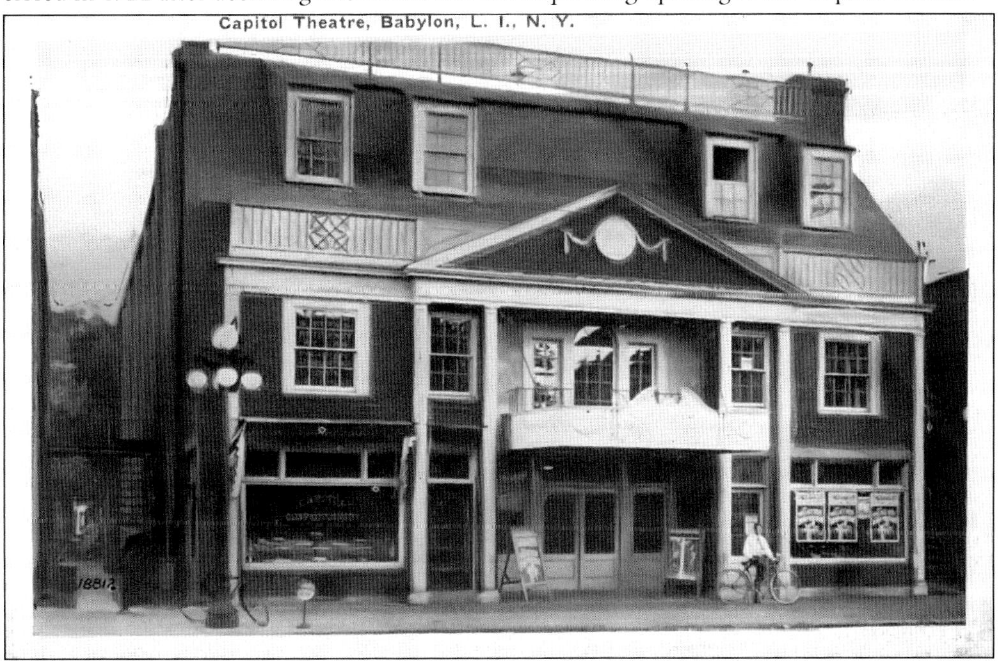

The Capitol Theatre, on West Main Street, opened in 1923. The Colonial Revival picture house, designed by John H. Philips with seating for over 1,000, suffered a fire in 1944 and again on April 5, 1955, allegedly caused by faulty wiring in the stage curtain mechanics. The renovated and air-conditioned theater, designed by Maurice P. Sornik, reopened three months later with a modern facade. The Babylon cinema was in continual use until 2014 and is expected to reopen in 2017.

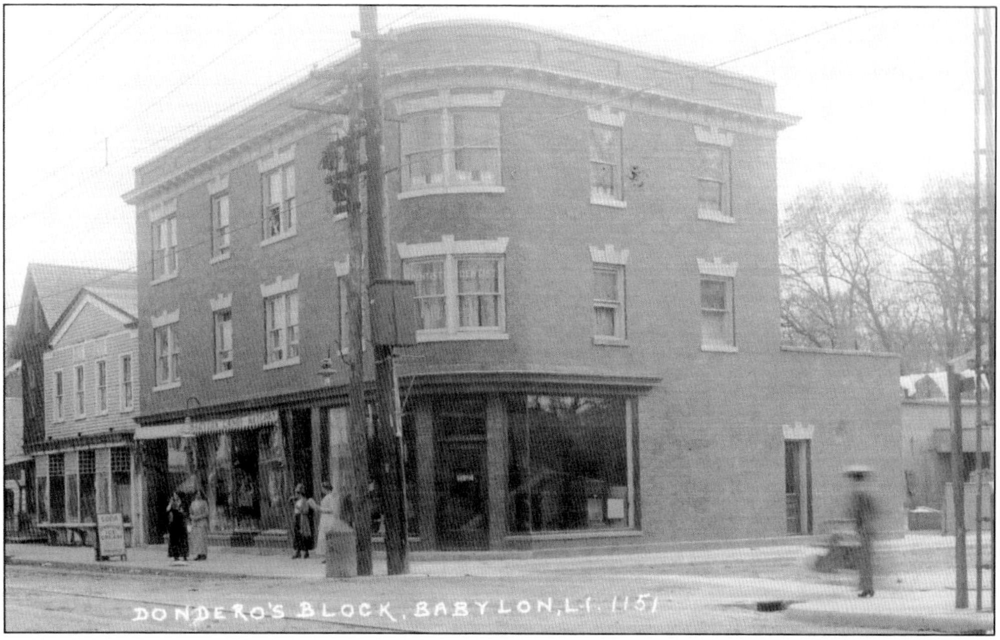

The Dondero building, at the southwest corner of Deer Park Avenue and Grove Place, was home to a variety of confectioneries. In 1906, New York City baker E. West advertised that he was "prepared to furnish bread, cake, pies, etc., to those who should call upon him." In 1911, Greek confectioners Stopluus and Contoulus opened a candy shop. That same year, Dr. A.C. St. Amand opened a "dental parlor" on the second floor.

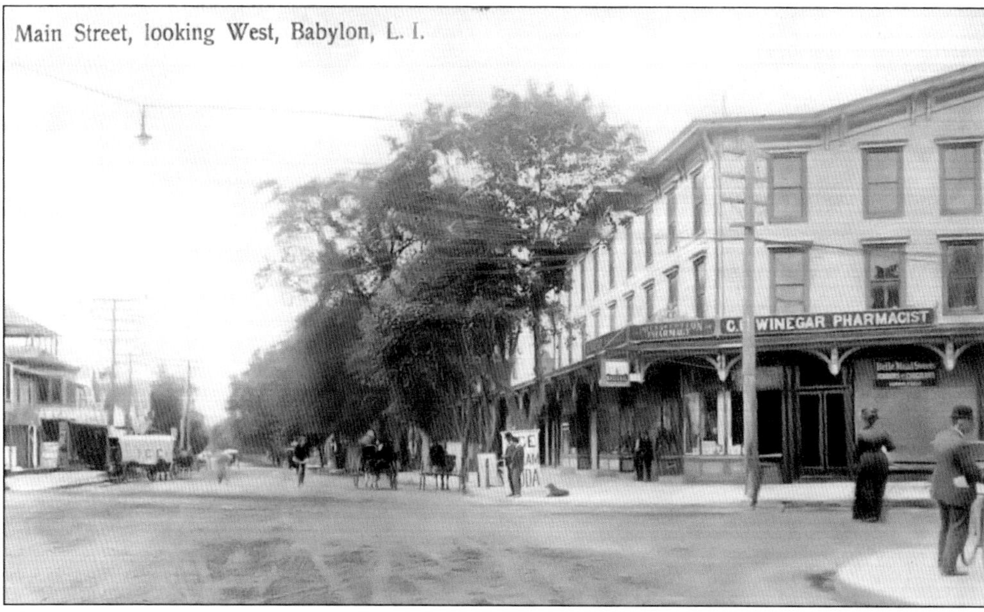

The northwest corner of Deer Park Avenue and Main Street was home to a series of druggists, pictured around 1910. Oswego County native Dr. Madison W. Beecher opened the first drugstore on that corner around 1884. Following his death in 1894, the business was purchased by Henry M. Burtis, a graduate of the Brooklyn College of Pharmacy. Philip W. Link succeeded Burtis in 1900 and sold to Edward C. Reiss the following year.

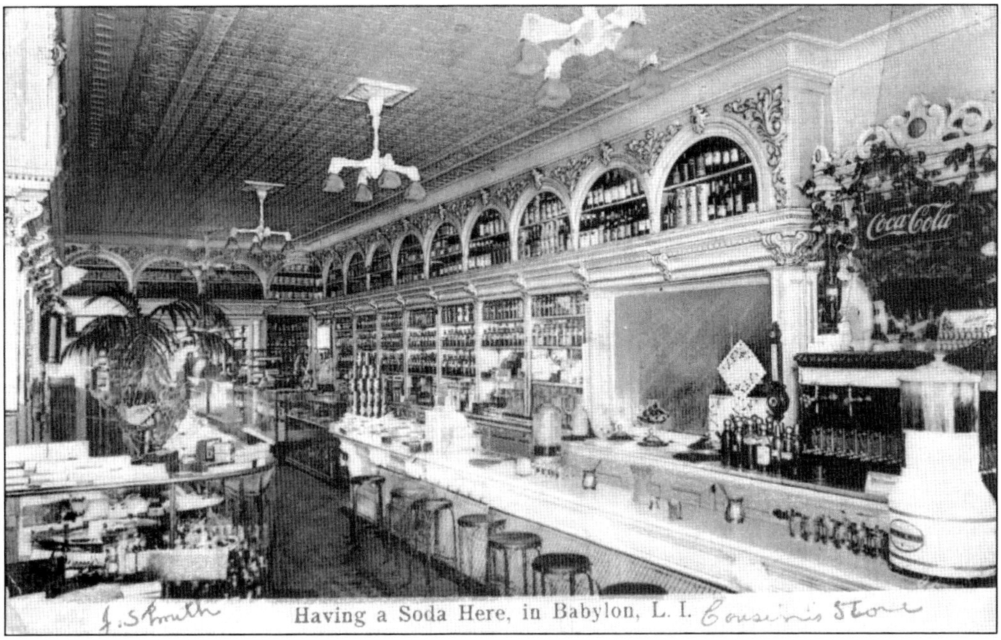

An ornate ice cream parlor and soda fountain is pictured around 1910 on Deer Park Avenue. It was later part of F.A. Griffith's Drug Store. Soda fountains were popular features of many local retailers. Edward C. Reiss opened his Main Street pharmacy in 1901. The adjoining Reiss' Annex had an ice cream parlor, confectionery, and stationery store. In 1907, New Rochelle pharmacist Charles E. Winegar purchased and renovated the old pharmacy, including installation of a new $2,000 soda fountain.

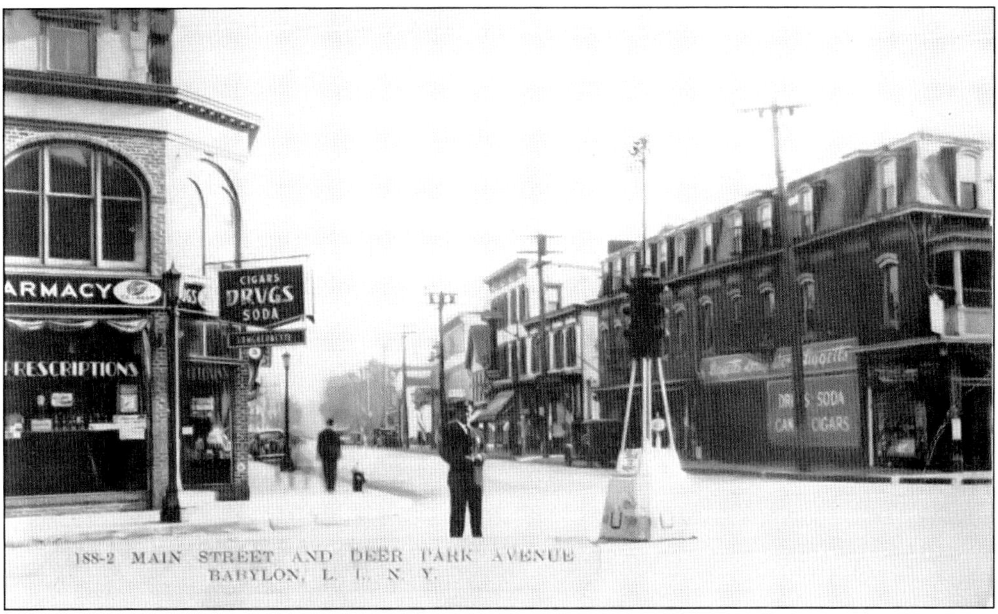

This c. 1920 scene looks north on Deer Park Avenue from Main Street. In addition to his pharmaceutical duties, C.E. Winegar was the local enrolling officer for the US Merchant Marine and would "give applicants for this service full particulars by calling at his drug store." In 1919, Winegar sold to James G. Brown, who operated a Rexall drugstore, the last pharmacy on that corner.

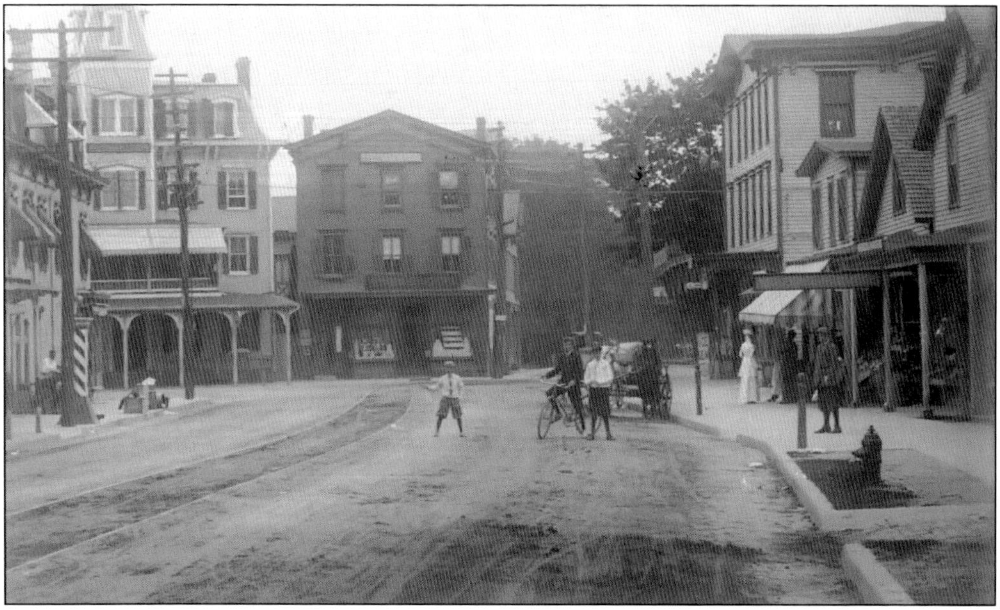

By the early 1870s, Babylon was home to at least three druggists. The first may have been Dr. Egbert Jarvis, who opened his drugstore on Deer Park Avenue in 1869. After Dr. Jarvis died in 1871, his widow Elizabeth Soper Jarvis continued the business until the late 1880s. Daniel J. Runyon opened a drugstore around 1873 and operated for about a decade. Conveniently, Dr. J.O. Smith, the "popular Babylon dentist," opened a branch in Runyon's store.

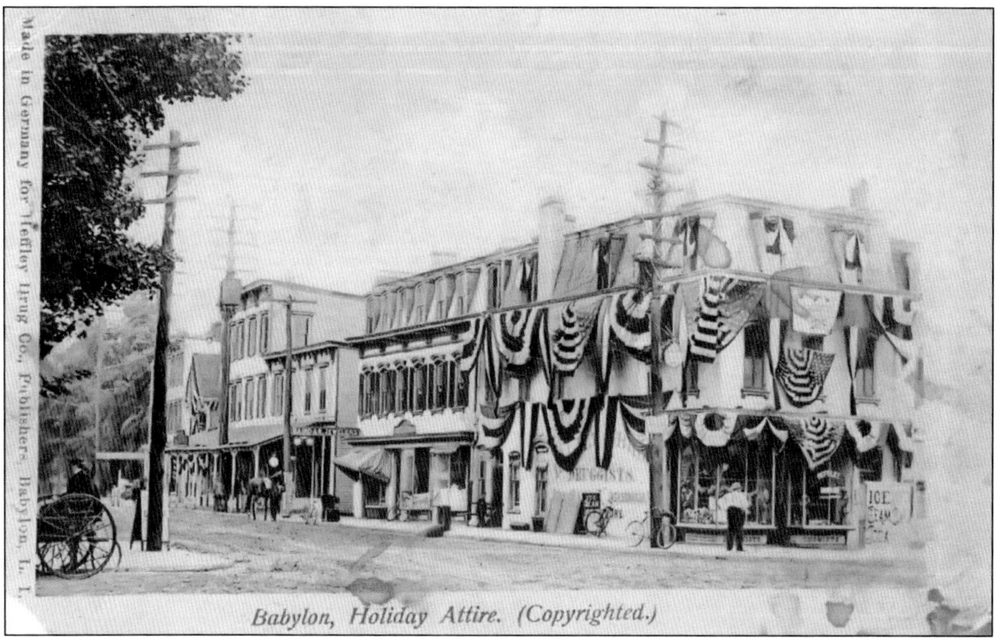

Civil War veteran surgeon Dr. William Y. Provost purchased the northeast corner of Deer Park Avenue and Main Street from D.S.S. Sammis in 1872, the year following the relocation of the Nathaniel Conklin House. Provost had this impressive three-story building constructed by G.S. Taylor for his use as a drugstore. By the early 1880s, Provost was appointed health officer for the town of Babylon, and sold the business to succeeding pharmacists.

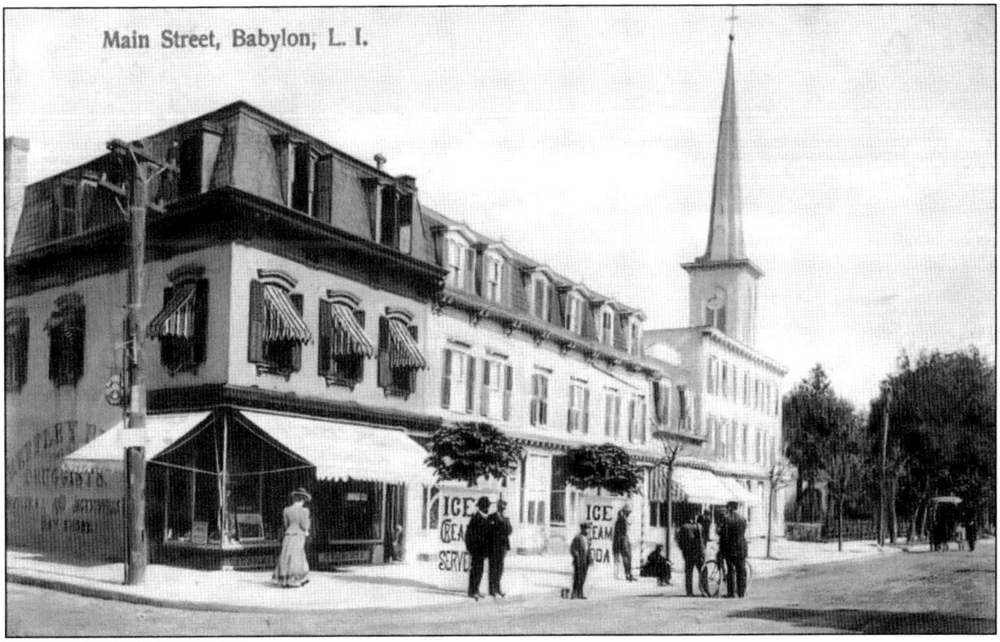

Theodore C. Fletcher operated the "brick drug store on the corner" until 1898, when he was appointed village postmaster. He sold to Heffley Brothers of Northport, which operated a series of stores, including those in Bay Shore and Hicksville. In 1911, Charles C. Heffley sold the business to Harry G. Salmon and Eugene P. Smith, who continued operation under the syndicate name of Heffley Drugs, as seen painted on the side of the building in many historic images.

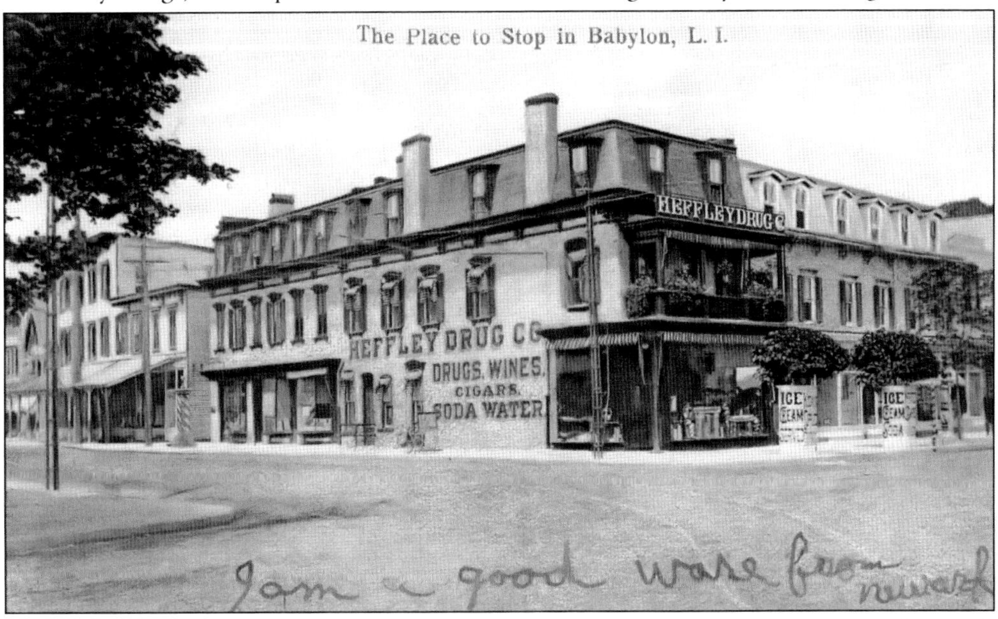

Smith and Salmon sold to Harvey Weinschenk in 1915. Active in the community, Weinschenk served as president of the Bank of Babylon and sold the pharmacy to Liggett's drugstores in 1928. The Liggett-Rexall chain operated the store until the mid-1900s. The building later housed Town and Country Paint and Wallpaper. Current occupants are the children's store Bubble, Ooh La La boutique, and Juice 'N Blendz.

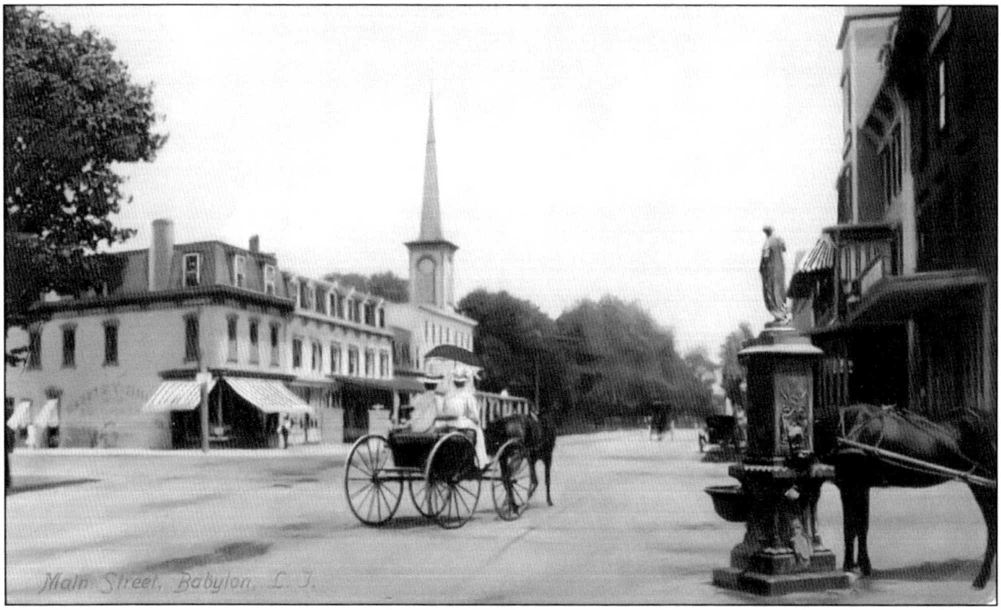

In 1897, the Babylon Woman's Exchange donated a public drinking fountain, with three levels of basins for humans, horses, and dogs, at the southwest corner of Main Street and Fire Island Avenue. The beautiful font was short-lived. In 1916, officials forced the fountain dry, fearing public drinking spaces a danger to public health by spreading disease. The following year, plans were made for the erection of a village flagpole at the corner.

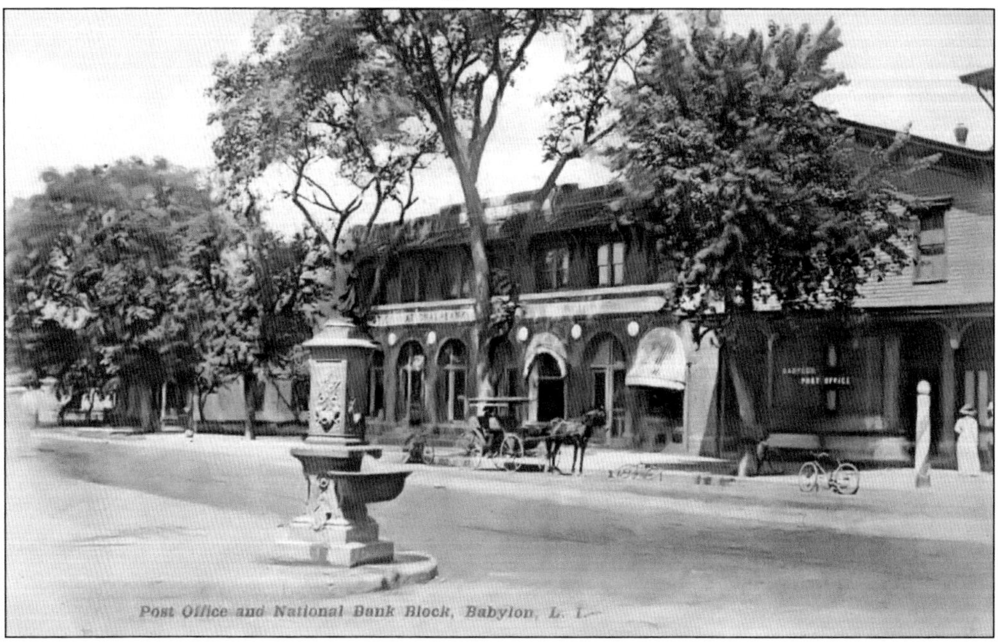

Village officials had begun removal of the fountain when a trolley car on slippery rails crashed into the monument. One resident quipped she "didn't know a trolley car would get up spunk enough to do it." Though destroyed, the fountain lived on in community memory. On Memorial Day 2011, the Historic Fountain Reconstruction Committee dedicated a replica of the original fountain in front of the village historical society, 114 years after the original dedication.

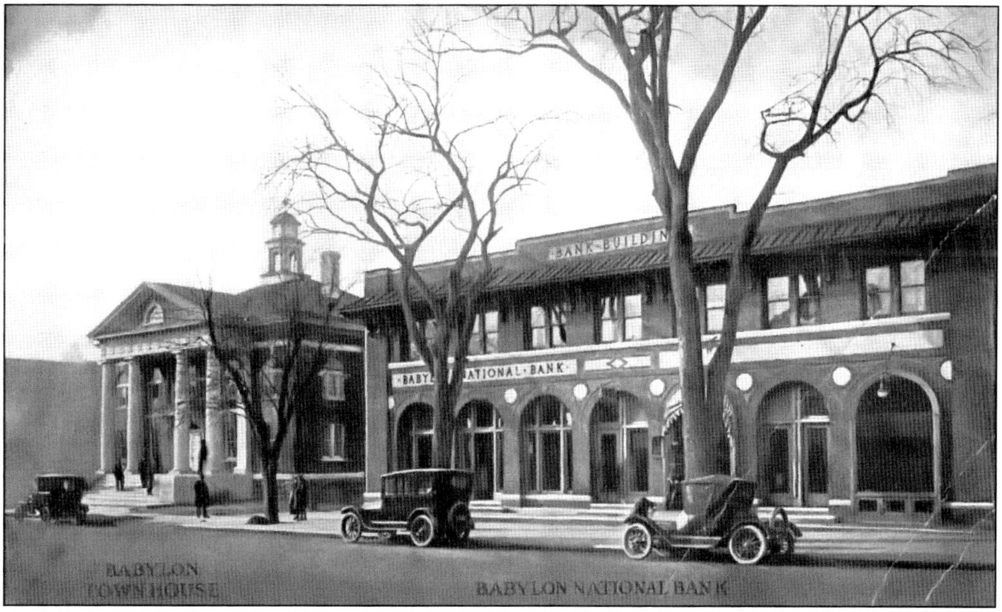

Organized by local businessmen, the Babylon National Bank opened on West Main Street on May 8, 1893. The *South Side Signal* reported the bank was "conveniently arranged light and airy," with a handsomely carved counter topped by a brass railing. A week before, the four-ton safe arrived at the railroad depot and was "moved without accident and in very good time." The first deposit was made by "Charles S. Hendrickson, who tossed a copper cent into the money chest."

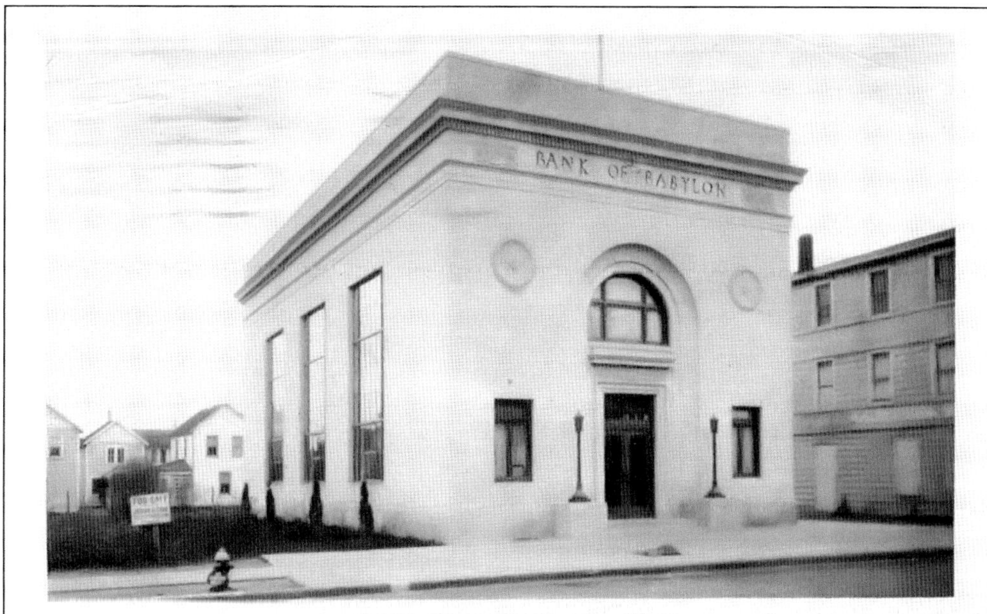

BANK OF BABYLON. L. I., N. Y

The Bank of Babylon, the second bank to open in the village of Babylon and the fifth in the town of Babylon, first opened on June 2, 1913, on the east side of Deer Park Avenue. To accommodate increased business, the Bank of Babylon built this stately edifice, which opened on March 31, 1923, on the west side of the street. In 2012, the bank was renovated and now houses the restaurant Monsoon.

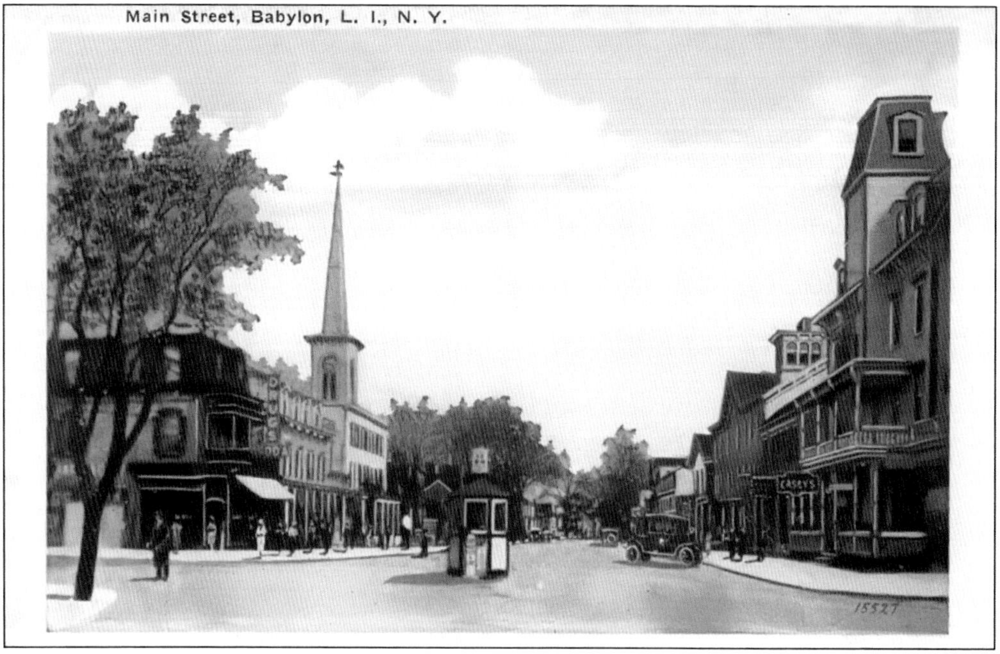

Main Street is seen looking east from Deer Park Avenue. The prominent Presbyterian steeple soars above the trees and Dr. Provost's drugstore building stands steadfast, much as they appear today. Prior to the installation of a traffic light, local police assisted traffic flow from a police booth in the intersection. (TOB.)

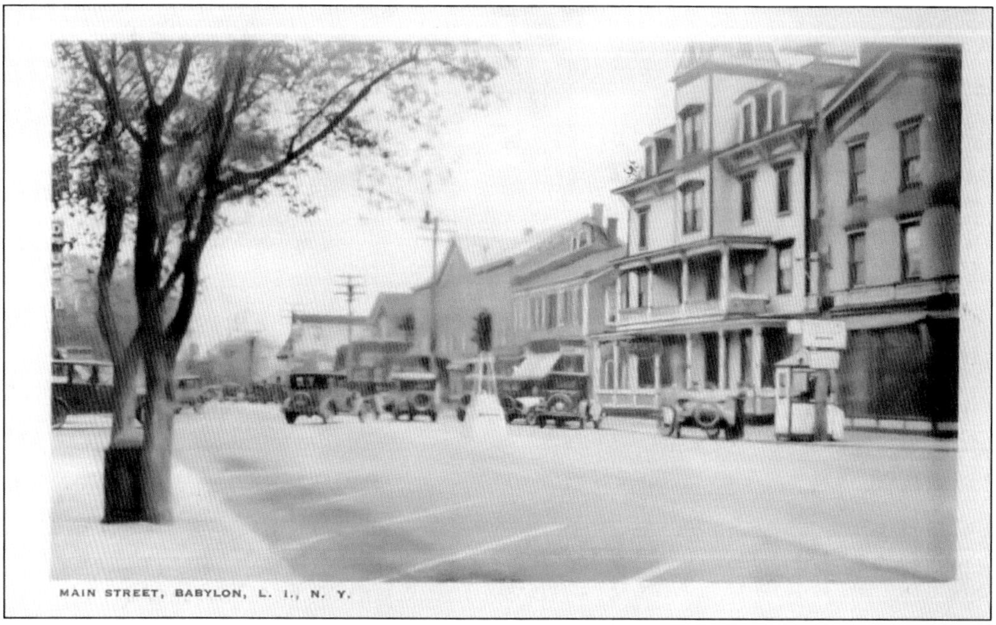

On the south side of Main Street are Casey's Hotel, formerly the Sherman House, and the old Dowden Brothers building. A few doors east of Casey's was the old Sumpwams Hotel, later the Fishel Building. Today, the southeast corner of Main Street and Fire Island Avenue has been entirely redeveloped and includes the Norton and Siegel insurance company, which dates to 1892, and Plesser's Appliances, in business for nearly a century.

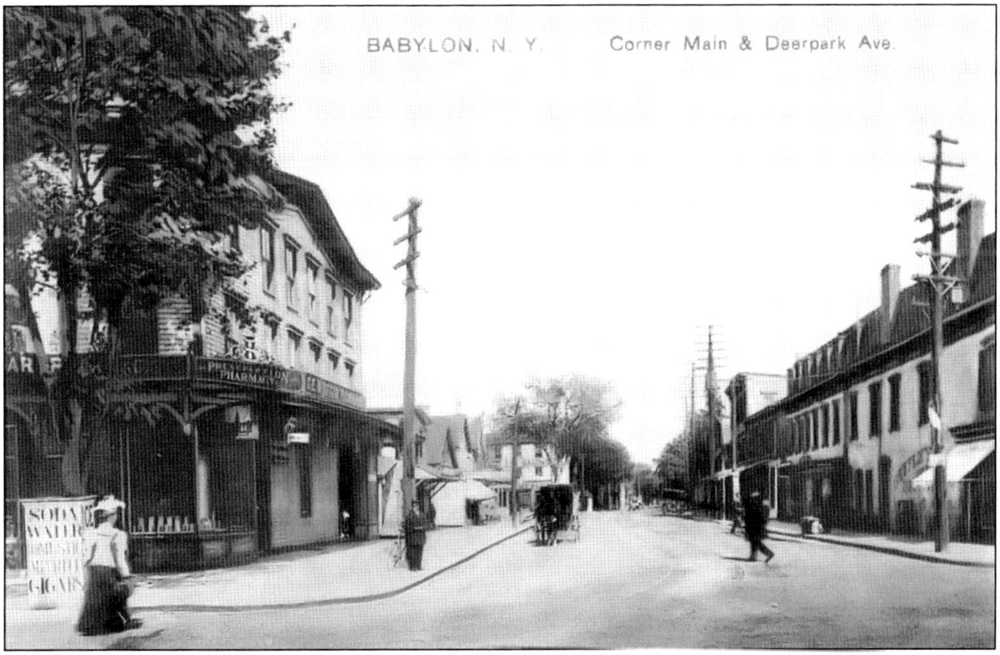

Deer Park Avenue is seen looking north from Main Street. Depicted about two decades apart, in the 1900s and 1920s, the business district is remarkably transformed. Above, a woman is dressed in a long skirt and wide hat while a horse walks toward Winegar's pharmacy, and a horse-drawn carriage travels south. Below, the A.J. Weeks carriage manufactory and W.H. Terry horse shoeing can be seen in the background. In the more modern postcard, skirts are shorter, hats are smaller, and motor cars line the street. The old Bank of Babylon building is topped with a flag.

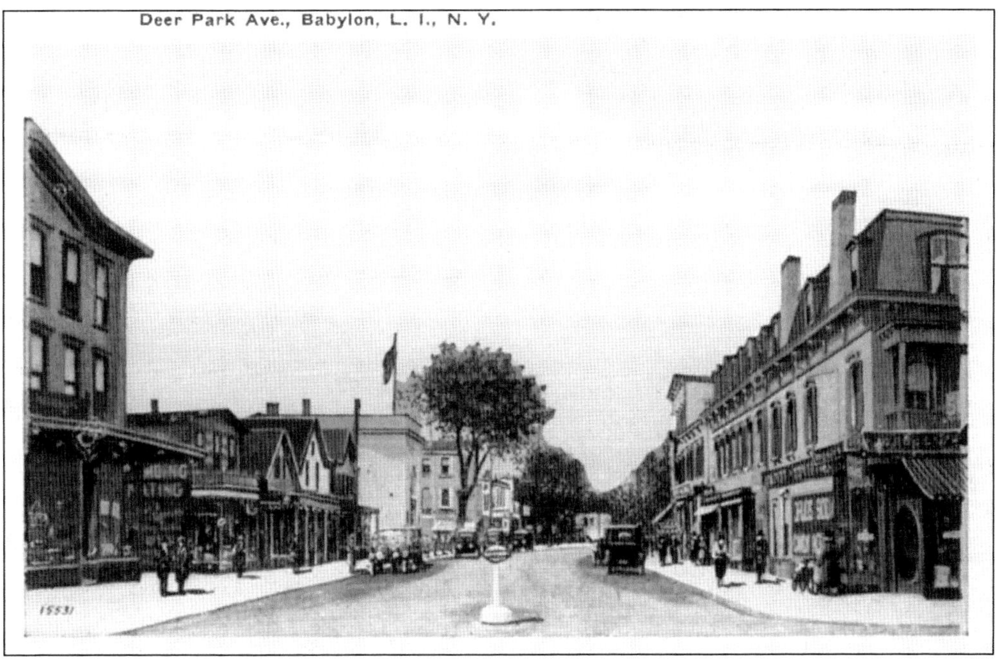

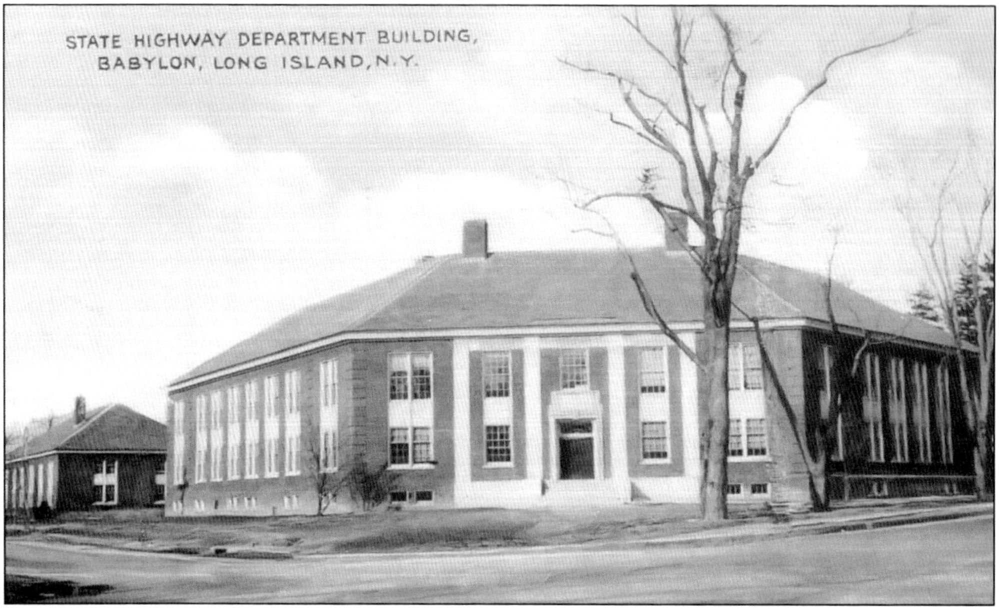

The massive New York State Public Works building for Long Island District 10 was constructed in 1940 at Little East Neck Road and Main Street. When it outgrew its previous headquarters, there was concern that the department would relocate, taking away over 200 local jobs. Guaranteeing retention of those jobs, Babylon village, led by Mayor Cadman H. Frederick, purchased the new building site and gifted it to the State of New York. The building is presently owned by Greenman-Pedersen Inc.

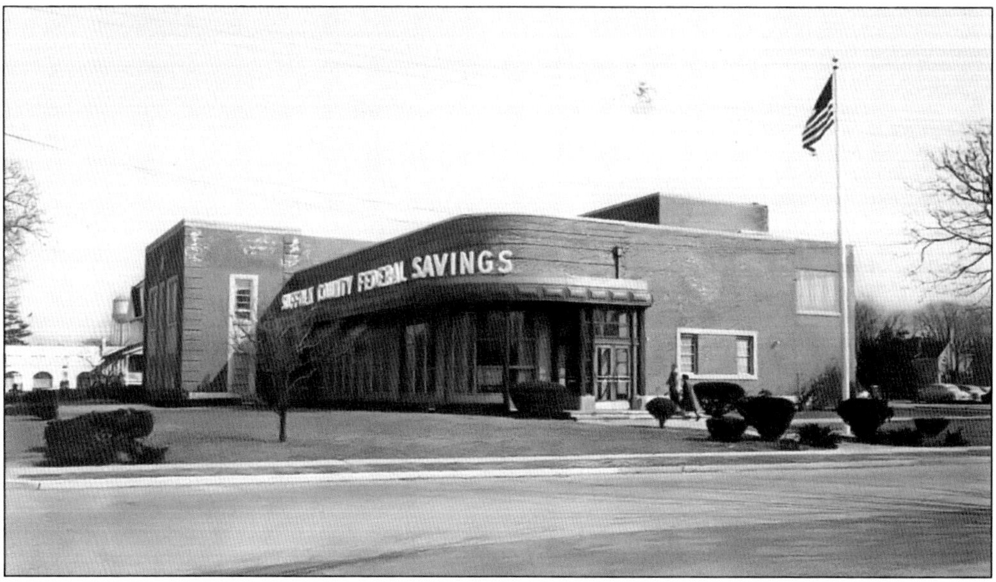

Organized by Cadman H. Frederick in 1935, the Suffolk Federal Savings and Loan Association took occupancy of its new building on Thompson Avenue and Main Street in December 1951. The opening of the $250,000 building was attended by 12,000 people and declared by the *Babylon Leader* a "new landmark . . . which enhances the already attractive western approach to the business district." A Long Island mural adorns the lobby showing 1950s local landmarks. Astoria Bank has occupied the building since 1998.

Seven

Community Service
Dedicated Public Service Groups

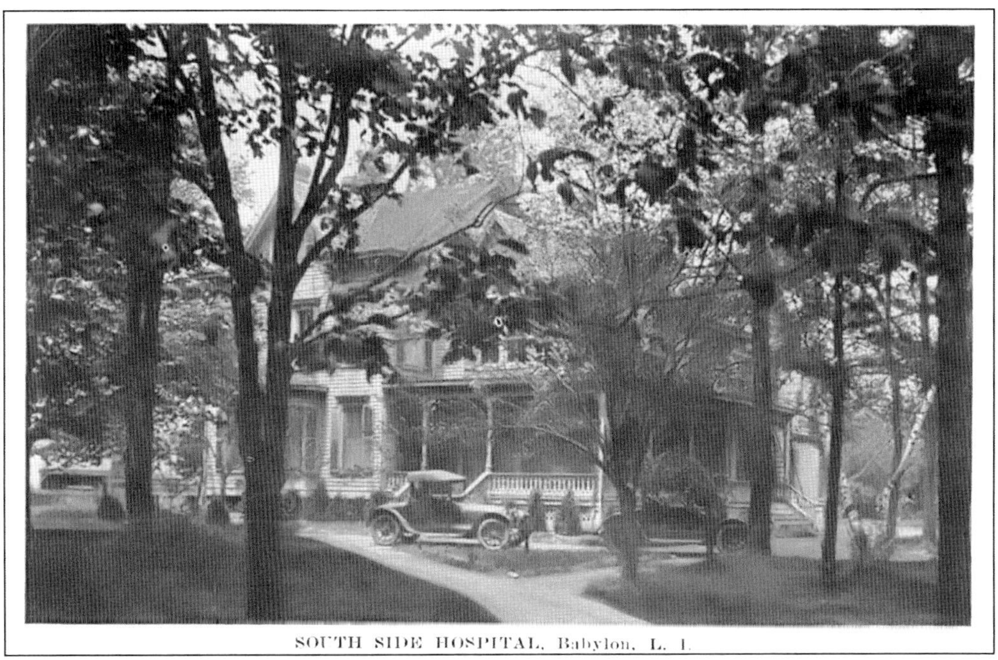

Southside Hospital opened in 1911 on the northeast corner of Cooper and George Streets, the current site of the Babylon Post Office. Chartered by the state in 1913, it was the first community hospital in Suffolk County, converted from the James B. Cooper residence, built around 1873. The building had previously served as a boardinghouse and a day school. The hospital was relocated to Bay Shore in 1923, and the building was razed around 1931. (TOB.)

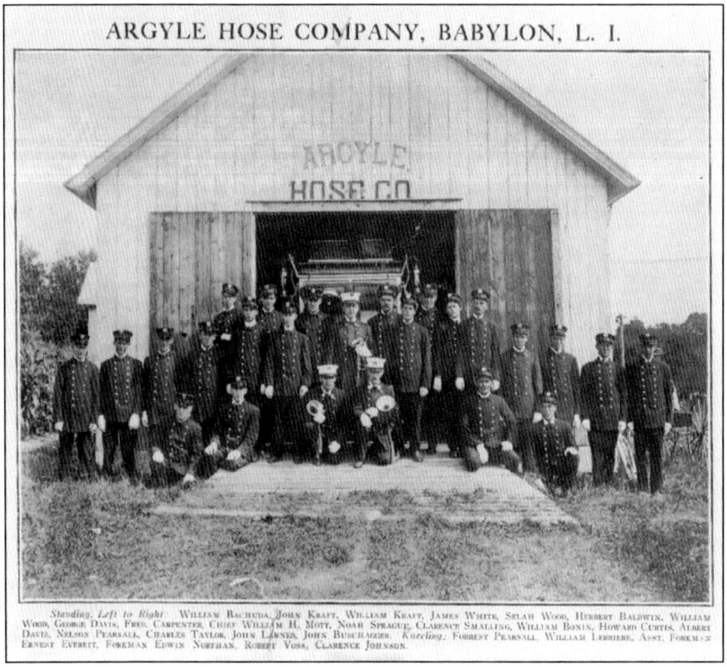

After years of attempts to organize and several buildings lost to fire, Hook & Ladder Company No. 1 formed on December 1, 1877. In 1881, the H&L Company and the newly formed Eagle Hose Company, renamed Storm Engine Company No. 1, merged as one department and by acclamation elected Henry Livingston its first chief. The first firehouse was erected on Grove Place to house equipment. In 1926, department headquarters were relocated to the municipal building on Carll Avenue.

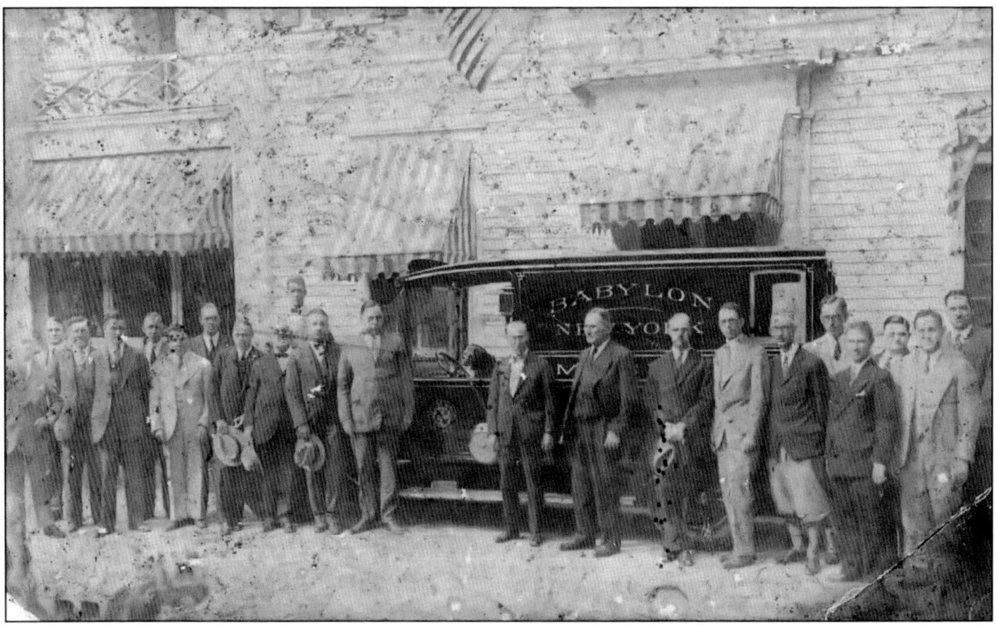

The department grew to include Phoenix Hose Company No. 1 (1882), Sumpwams Hose Company No. 2 (1895), Argyle Hose Company No. 3 (1899), Electric Hose Company No. 4 (1902), Fire Patrol Company No. 1 (1931), Drum Corps (1958), Rescue Squad (1960), Drill Team (1971), and Marine Unit (2005). In 1928, the Babylon Exchange Club donated the first ambulance, pictured in front of Martin Zonner's restaurant.

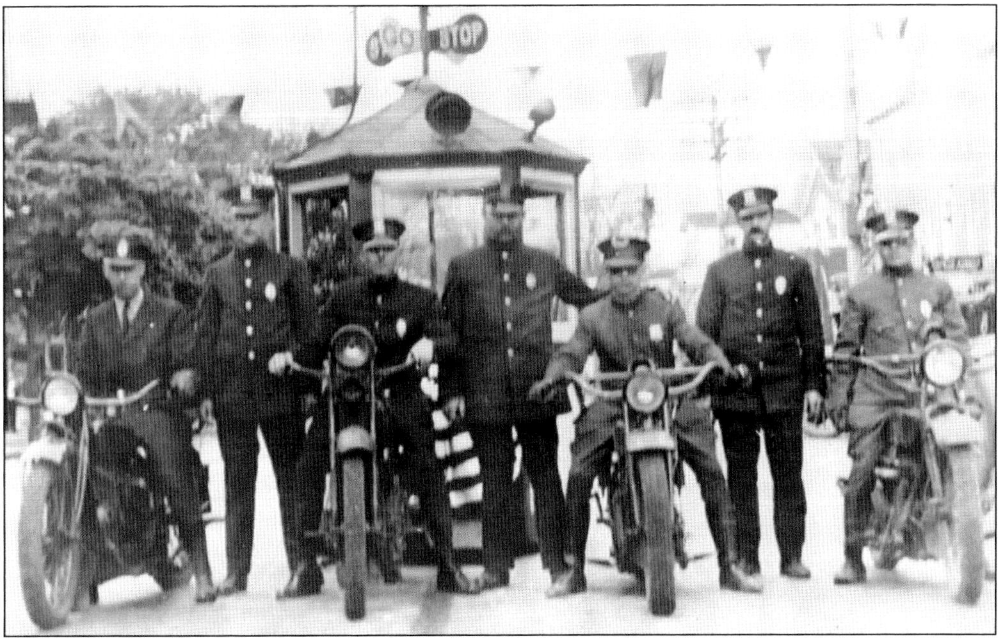

In 1894, the year after village incorporation, Oscar Balchen was appointed the first village constable, with a $35 monthly salary. The village purchased the first police motorcycle in 1922. Members of the Babylon village and Babylon town departments pose in front of the police booth on Main Street at Deer Park Avenue on May 20, 1925, when the village celebrated the electrification of the Long Island Rail Road to Babylon.

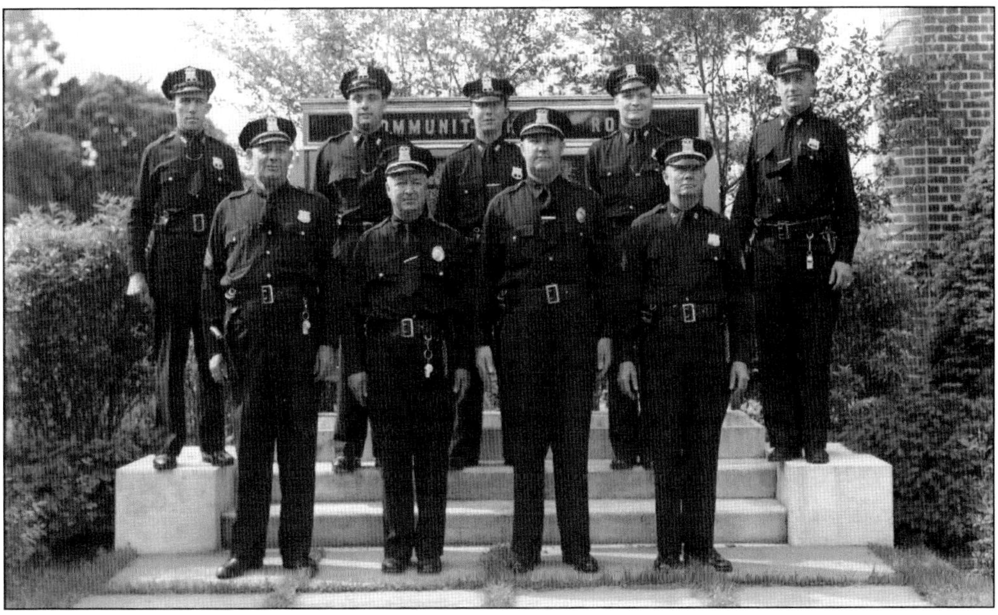

The village police department is pictured at village hall in 1948. The first village jail was built around 1882 behind the old fire headquarters on the south side of Grove Place and was referred to as the Babylon Lockup. In 1918, the three jail cells were relocated to the basement of the Babylon Town House on West Main Street and used until 1958. The cells are now exhibited in the Town of Babylon History Museum on West Main Street.

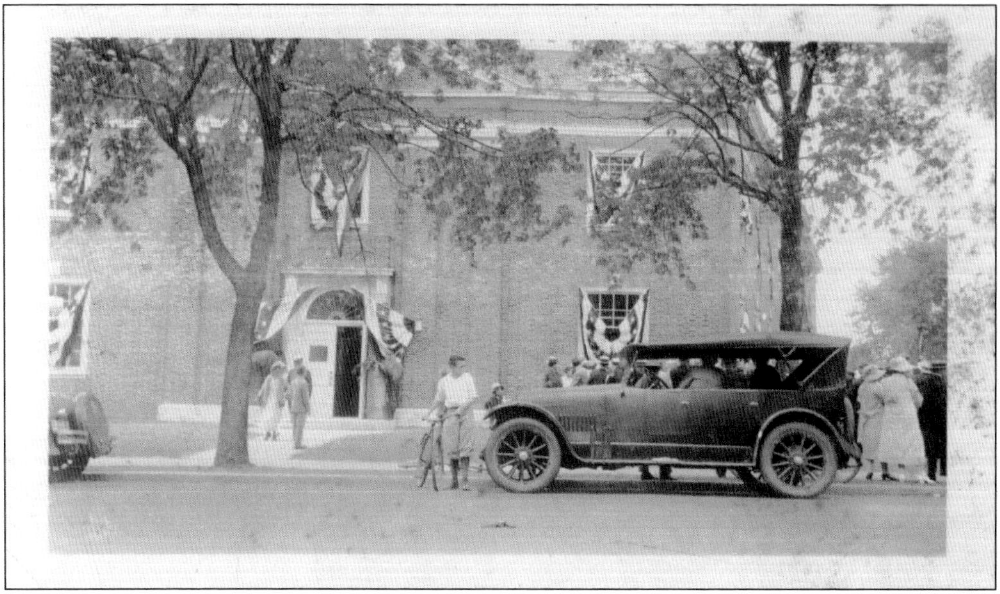

In 1924, village residents defeated proposals for a village municipal building fronting 71 feet on the east side of Deer Park Avenue. The action prompted Jay Stanley Foster to offer the community $15,000 toward the purchase of a larger property at the northwest corner of Main Street and Carll Avenue. The village accepted Foster's generous gift, and residents subsequently voted 577 to 124 to bond $90,000 for building construction.

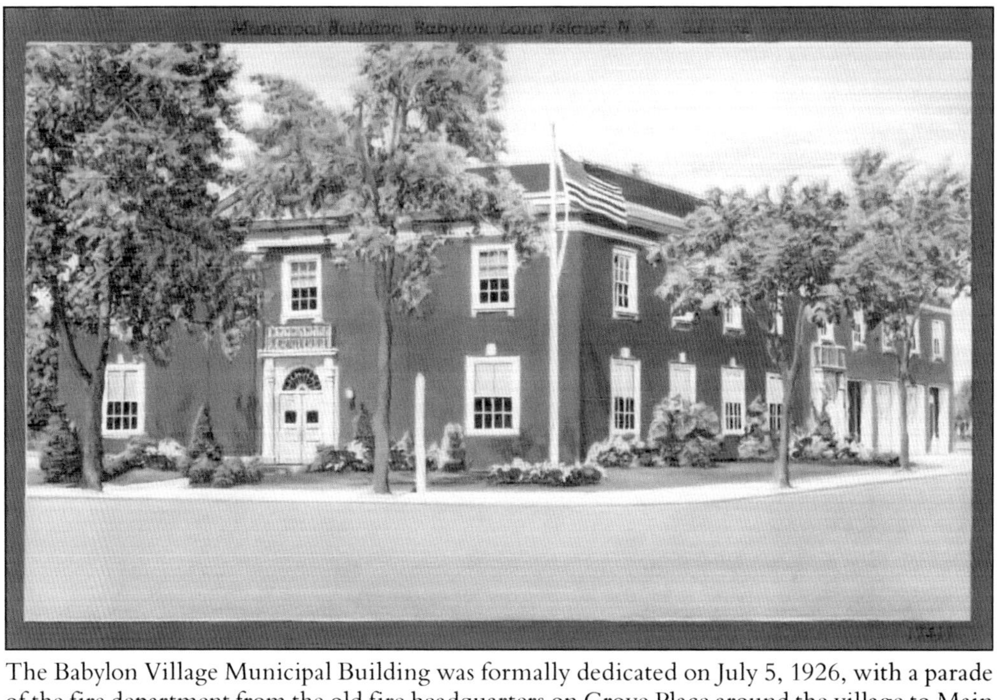

The Babylon Village Municipal Building was formally dedicated on July 5, 1926, with a parade of the fire department from the old fire headquarters on Grove Place around the village to Main Street. The cornerstone was laid by village president Robert N. Overton. The dedication was followed by a spirited game between Joseph Keenan's All Stars and the Babylon baseball team and a fireworks display.

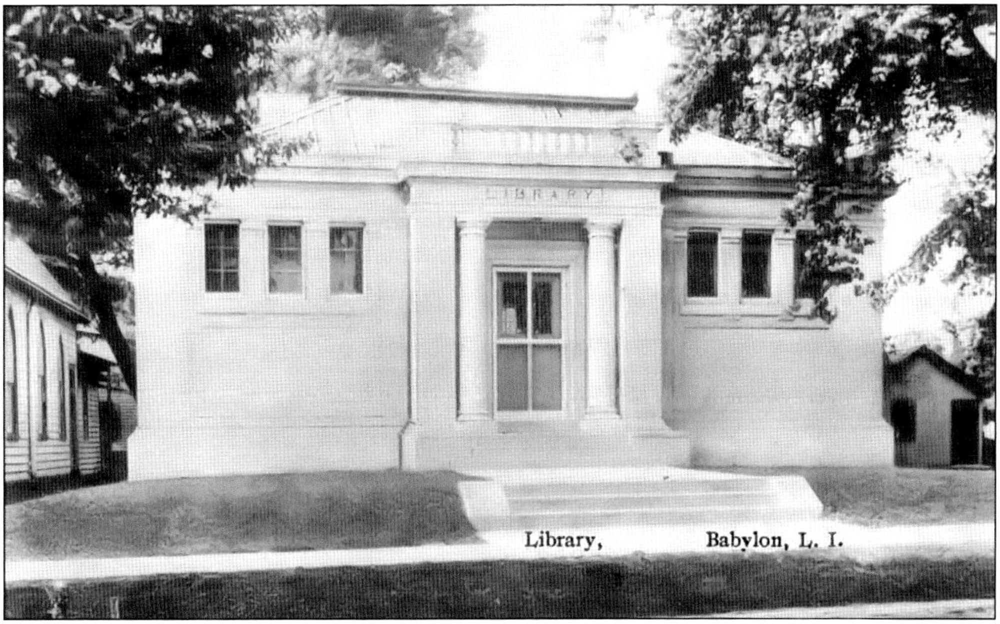

The first local library was the Babylon Book Circle, a private circulating collection started by Adelaide Arnold, Loreign Reed, and Louise Sammis in 1887, for 25 members at $3 per year. Eventually, the circle rented office space. On April 30, 1895, the privately funded Babylon Library Association was incorporated by community members Eva L. Diossy, James W. Eaton, Lillian Fishel, Lulu Fishel, Washington F. Norton, Minnie L. Reid, Antoinette Sammis, and Sarah E. Sammis.

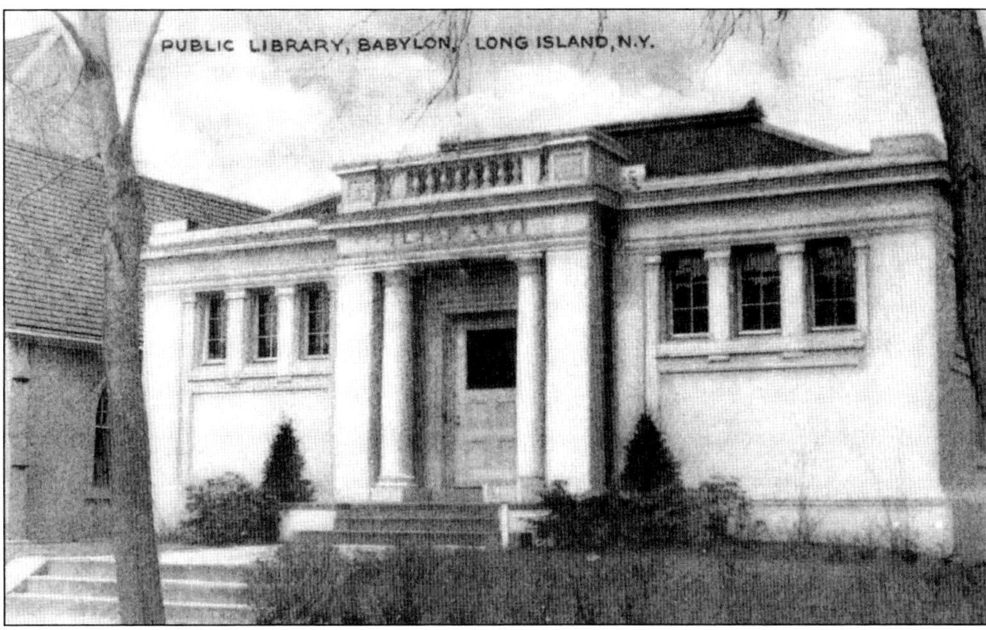

For years, the Babylon Library Association raised funds for a permanent building. In 1909, siblings Elbert Carll Livingston and Julia Livingston donated property on Main Street near Carll Avenue. The library, designed by A.D. Pickering and constructed by the E.W. Howell Company, was dedicated on October 23, 1911. This site was used until a larger library was built on South Carll Avenue and dedicated on October 23, 1968, the 57th anniversary of the first library building.

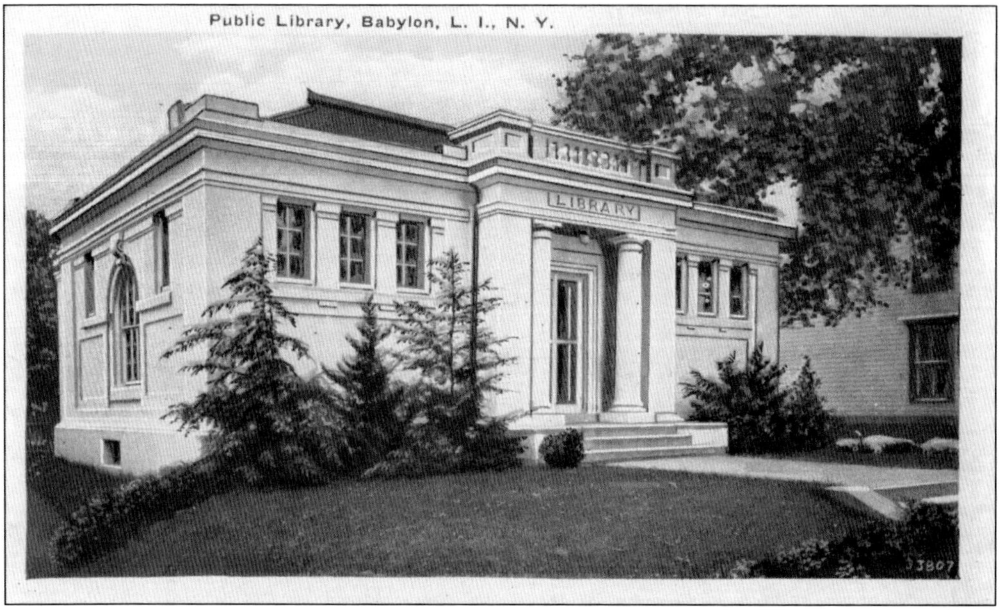

In 1970, the village took over the old library for use by the building department. Led by former village historian Stuart M. Aldrich, a movement was started for the building to be used by the Village of Babylon Historical and Preservation Society as a museum. The historical society museum opened in 1974, where it still thrives. The building was listed in the National Register of Historic Places in 2015.

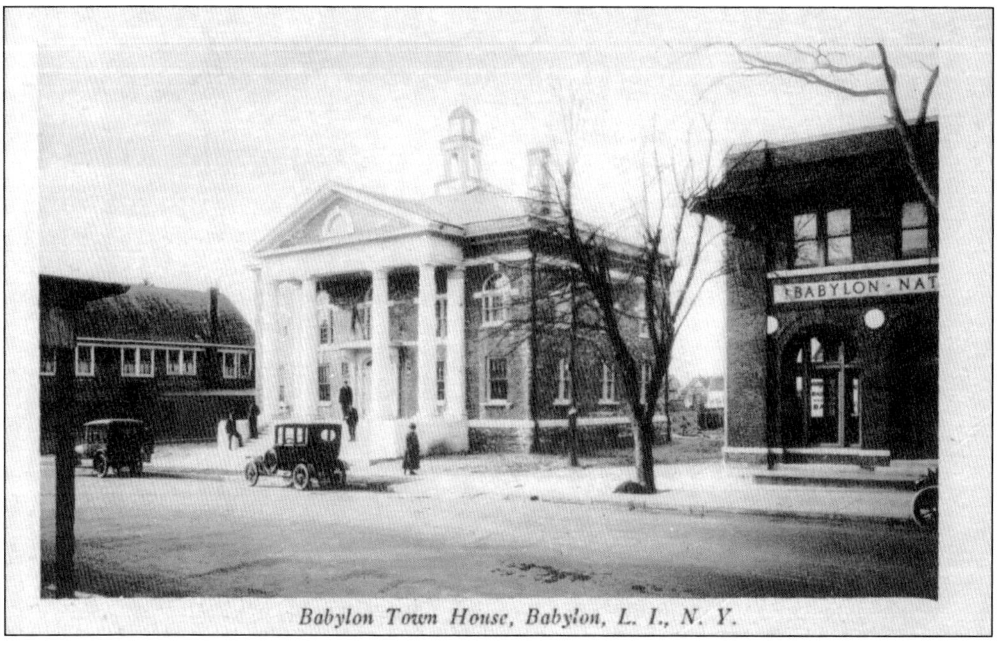

The town of Babylon built its first town hall in 1917, forty-five years after separating from the town of Huntington. Residents had deliberated for years about the expense and location of a town hall. Debates were quelled when the family of David S.S. Sammis donated the property for a town hall in honor of their esteemed loved one. The Sammis property, on Main Street and Cottage Row, was the former site of the American House.

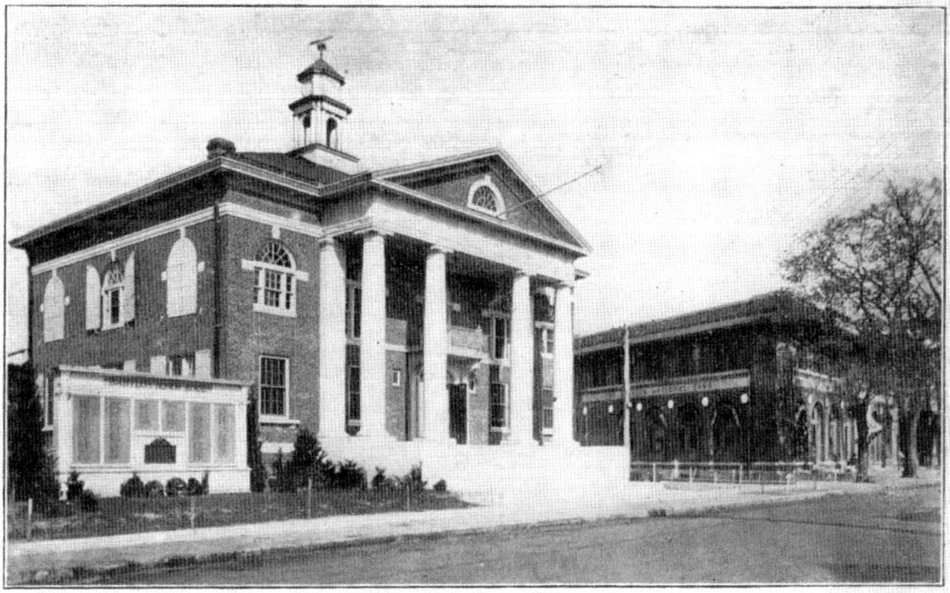

BABYLON TOWN HALL, BABYLON, L. I.

The building served as the seat of town government until 1958, when a more centralized town hall was built on Sunrise Highway in North Lindenhurst. The building was then used as a department of motor vehicles and designated as a district courthouse in 1964. By 1979, the court relocated, and the building was sold to local photographer William Higgins.

Town Hall, Babylon, L. I., N. Y.

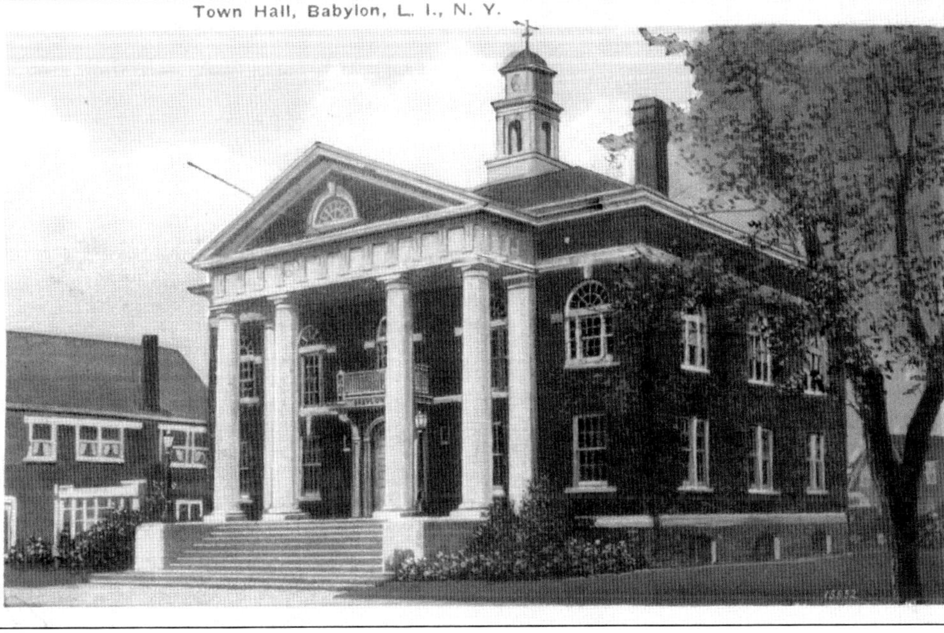

In 2004, the Town of Babylon reacquired the building, and it was listed in the National Register of Historic Places the following year. The Old Town Hall was dedicated as the Town of Babylon History Museum on June 11, 2010, honoring the 100th anniversary of the electric trolley line between Babylon and Amityville. The museum shares local history through photographs and exhibits, including the jail cells from the former Town of Babylon Police Department.

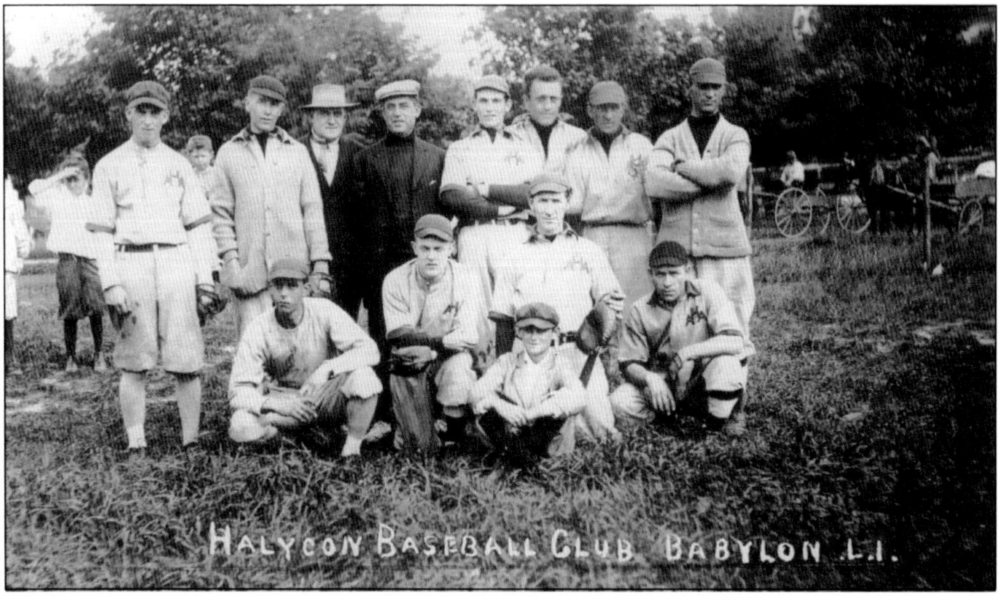

Named for their meeting hall, the Halcyon Athletic Association organized in 1903. The *South Side Signal* reported that "the initiation fee was placed at $1.00, and monthly dues 50¢. The club has a membership of 65. Gymnastic apparatus is now being installed and the hall is being put into shape. A basket ball team will be organized, which will no doubt arrange for games with outside clubs in the not remote future." The group also formed a racing yacht club.

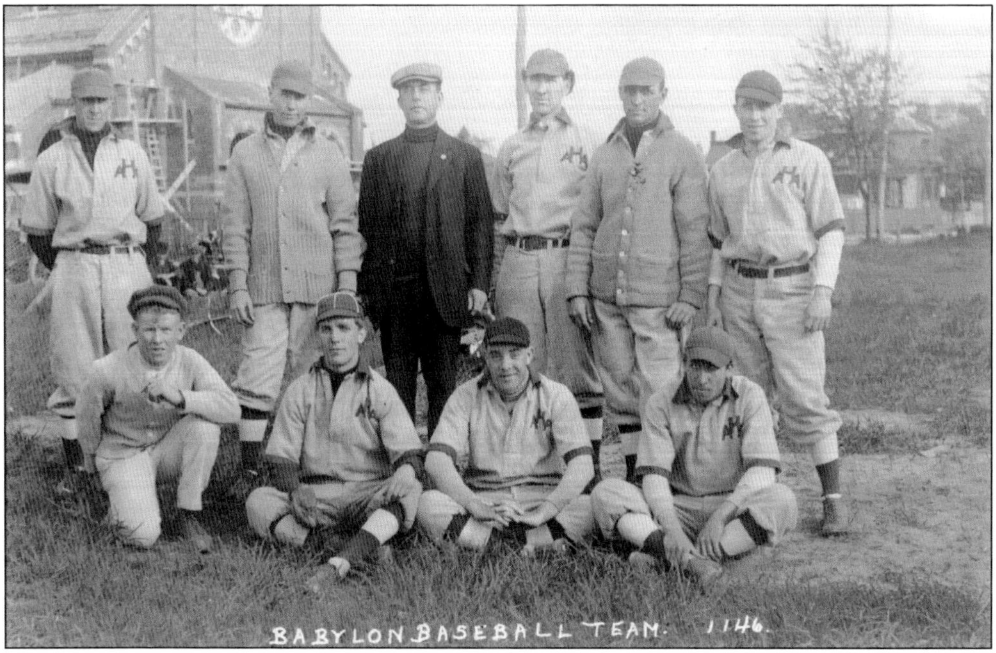

A rousing 1910 account from the *Signal* read: "The baseball team of the Halcyon Athletic Association gave the Bay Shore nine a severe drubbing on the local diamond last Saturday, as the score, 24 to 8, would indicate. The heaving and timely hitting of the local players was responsible for the victory of the home team, and if the locals keep up their batting streak the Babylon fans will be filled with joy throughout the season."

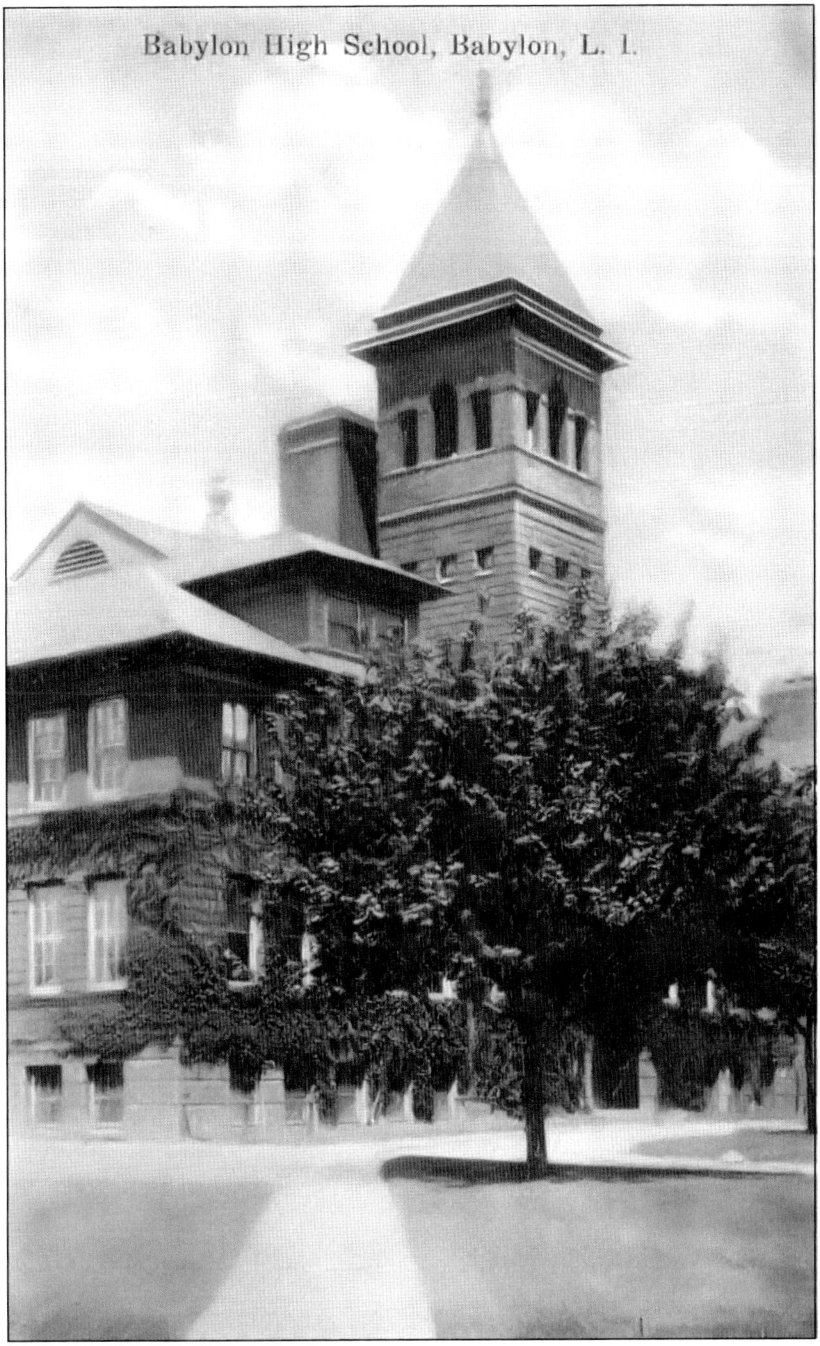

Babylon's first school was erected in 1805. The small frame Main Street school was privately owned by a stock company made up of local residents. The stockholders sold the school to Huntington Town School District No. 21 in 1818 for public use. A handful of private schools were also established around the village, including some that boarded pupils. In 1859, the public school was relocated to George Street, where a new school was soon erected to accommodate the ever-growing school population. In 1893, taxpayers authorized the purchase of a plot fronting Railroad and Carll Avenues and Grove Place, as shown.

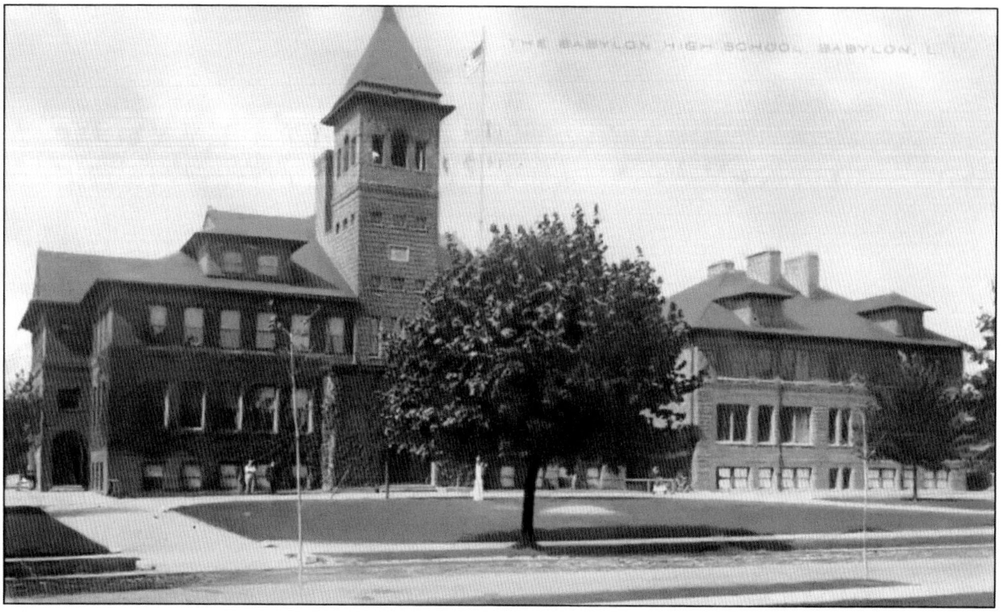

The mammoth redbrick school, designed by Palliser, Palliser & Company and built by Frank Mapes, was formally dedicated on April 14, 1894, "a 'great day' in the education annals of Babylon," "a model school building," and "an ornament to the village and a credit to the district," declared the *Signal*. An east wing was added to the school in 1912, designed by Amityville architect Lewis Inglee. (TOB.)

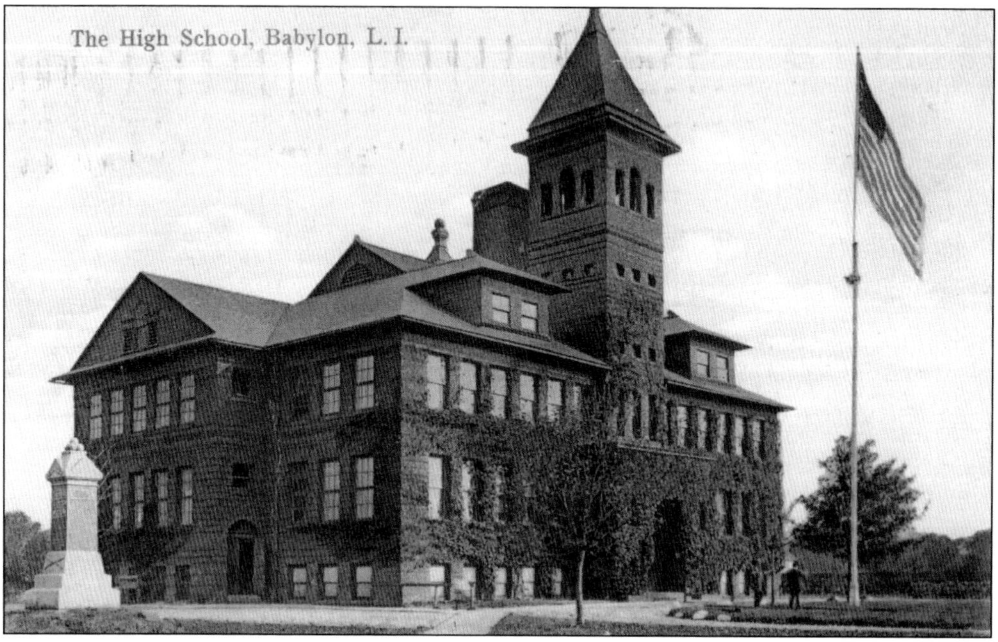

On November 24, 1907, the Joel Cook Monument Association, led by Judge James B. Cooper, dedicated an impressive granite monument in tribute to Revolutionary War soldier Captain Cook "to perpetuate in this community the memory of a lover of his country, a brave defender of his native land." Originally placed on the grounds of the Babylon High School on Grove Place, expansion of the school building later necessitated the relocation of the monument to Argyle Park. (TOB.)

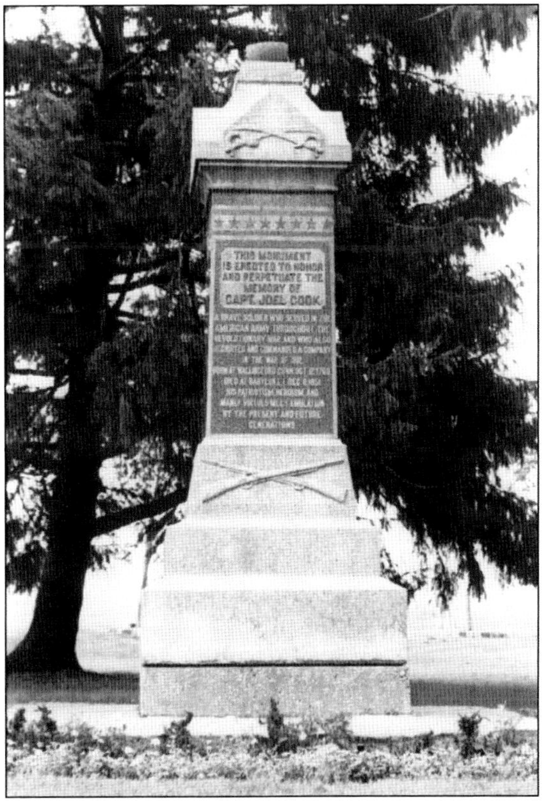

Joel Cook died, aged 91, in 1851 after living in the Babylon area for less than two years. Just 16 when the Revolutionary War began, he was initially rejected for service. Instead, he spent a year as a Continental officer's body servant before joining the ranks for the remainder of the war. In the War of 1812, he formed a company in his native Connecticut, was commissioned captain, and fought in several engagements, including the Battle of Tippecanoe. (TOB.)

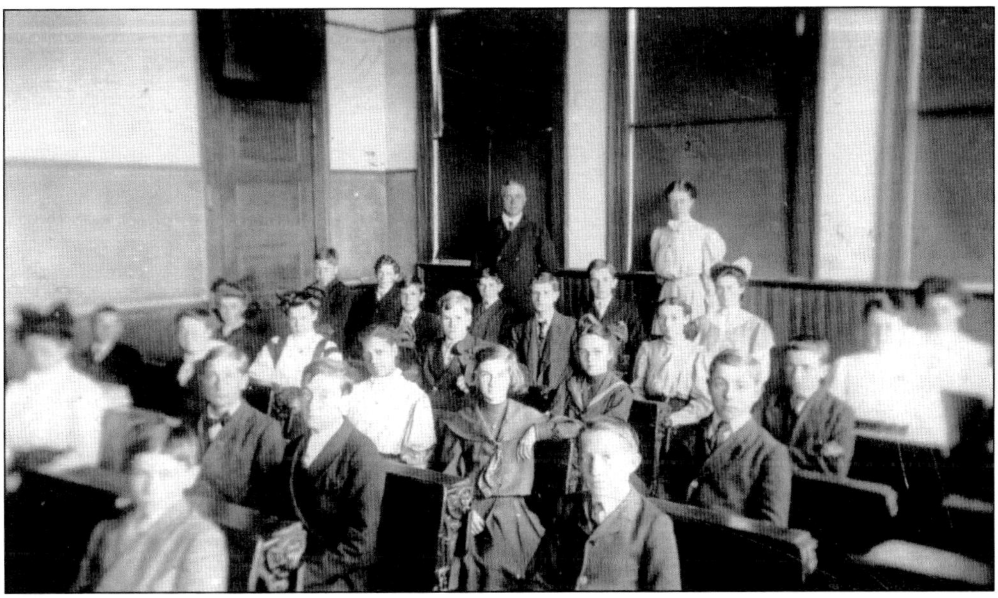

This class is pictured in the 1894 Babylon High School. Tall windows afforded natural light for the students and teachers. The school enrolled students of all grades until the separate elementary schools were built—Babylon Memorial Grade School in 1954 and Babylon Elementary School in 1965. Through the 1950s, high school enrollment included students from Deer Park, North Babylon, West Babylon, and West Islip until neighboring districts built their own high schools.

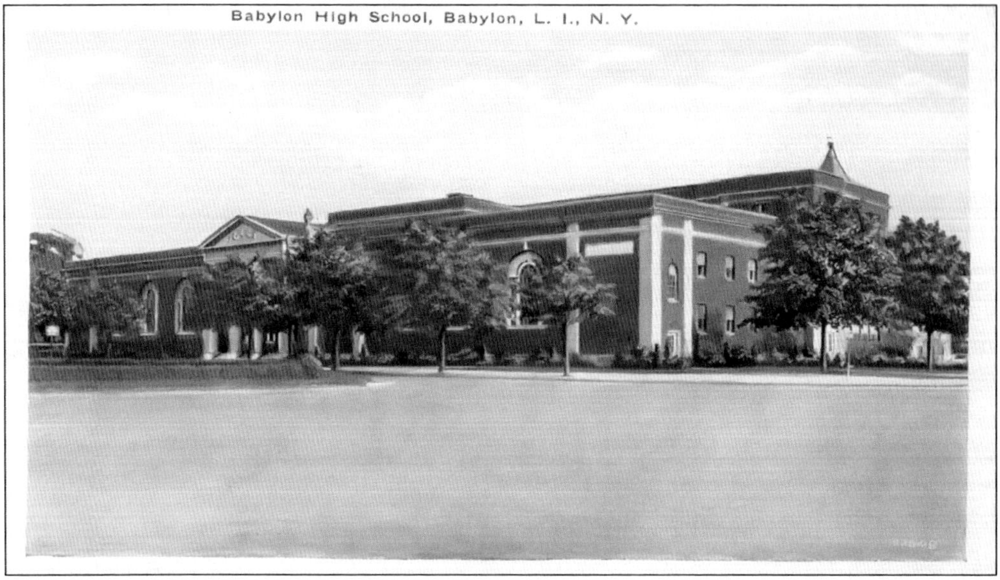

The north-end expansion of the Grove Place school, facing Railroad Avenue, was designed by Tooker and Marsh. The old school tower is seen peeking above the structure. Demolition of the 1894 school began in 1957, followed by renovation and enlargement of the entire junior-senior high school under the designs of Eggers and Higgins. In the years that followed, building cornerstones from 1893, 1925, and 1957 were incorporated into interior walls of the school.

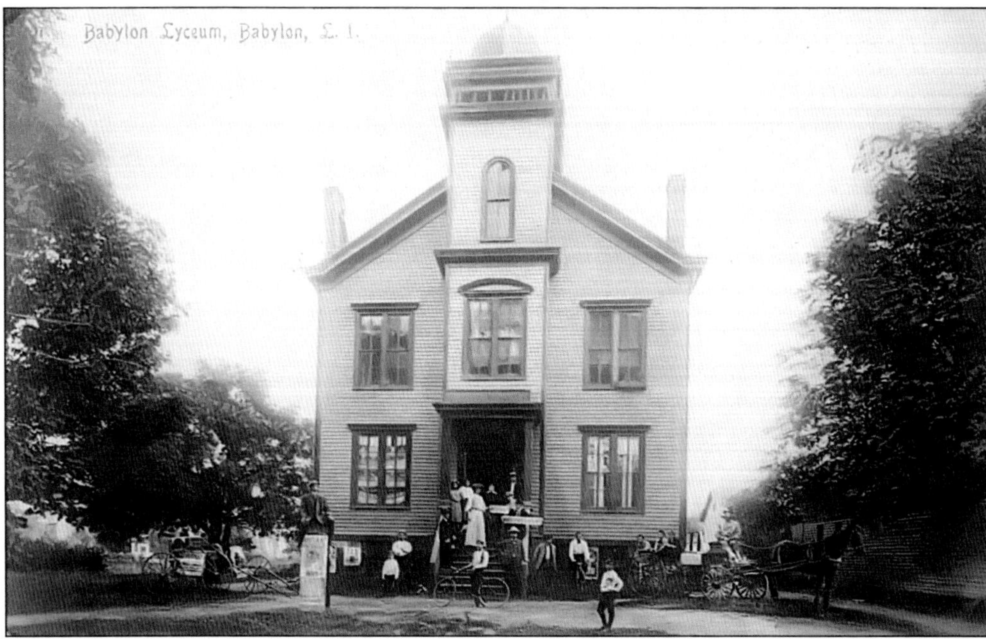

The late 1800s lyceum movement promoted community education through public lectures and performances. In 1869, many Babylon residents encouraged the establishment of a lyceum, which included a reading room where, the *South Side Signal* declared, "our young men and women can spend their spare time pleasantly and profitably, without any of the contaminating influences of many other places of public entertainment." The wholesome organization held meetings at the Methodist church before taking occupancy of the old school on George Street. (Steve Loudon.)

Eight

Spiritual Guidance
Houses of Worship

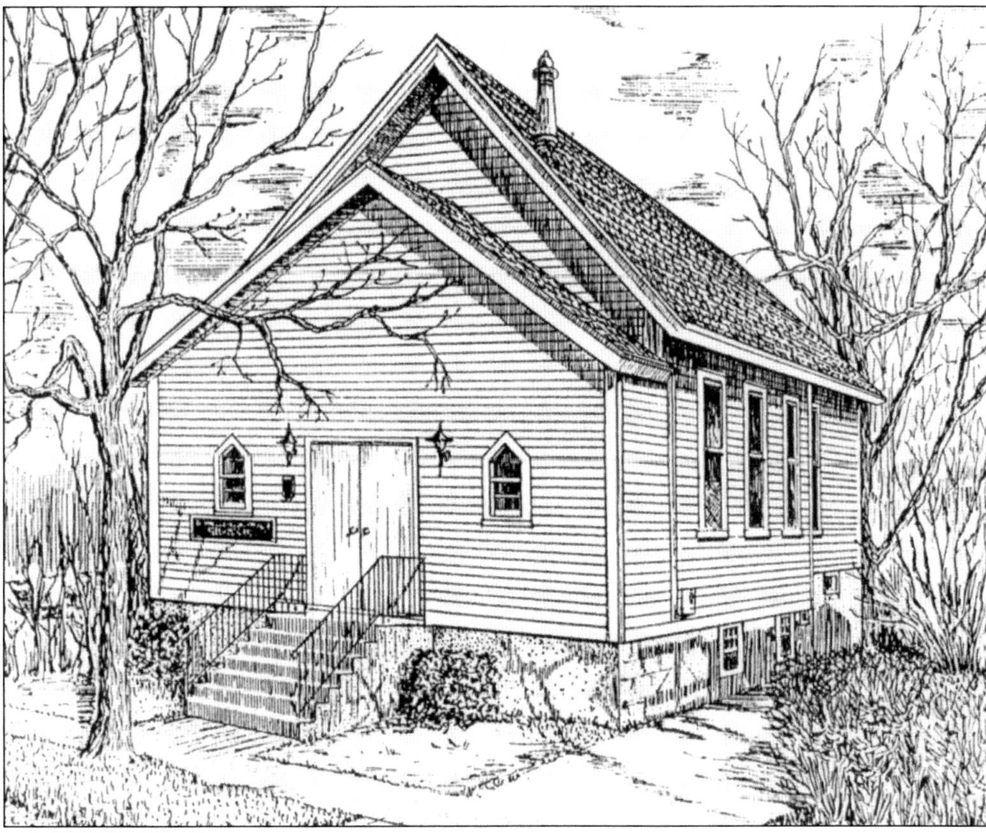

In 1906, six members of the Bethel African Methodist Episcopal Church, led by Rev. John Cuff, purchased a $700 plot on Cooper Street, and built their church the following year. The original church was destroyed by an early-morning fire on October 31, 1911. Under the leadership of Rev. G.R. Murcheson and Reverend Irons, Bethel was rebuilt in 1913. The church celebrated its centennial in 2007 and continues at its original location. (Bethel AME.)

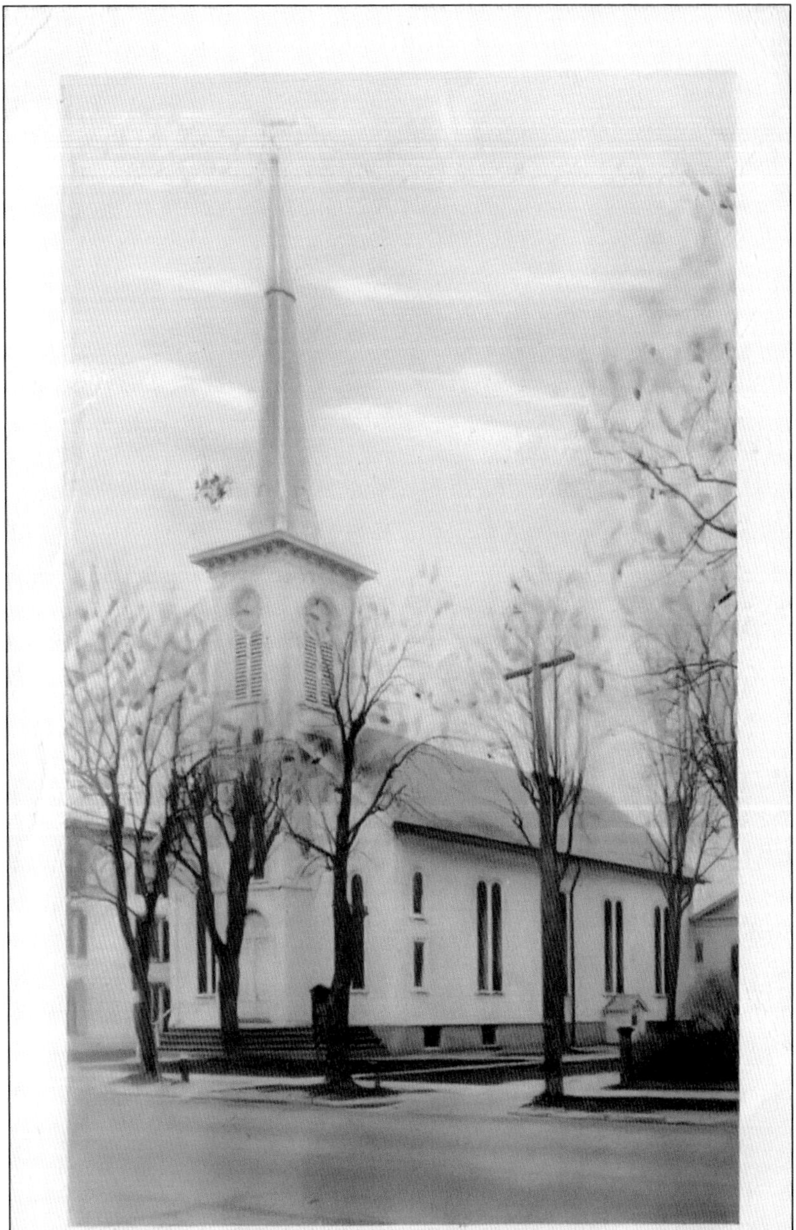

The First Presbyterian Church of Islip and Huntington South was built around 1730 on the north side of Montauk Highway in West Islip, just east of Babylon. The structure was occupied by British troops during the Revolutionary War and demolished. The congregation built a new church around 1784 on Main Street in Babylon. Around 1838, that building was moved east of the property and became the Sammis family home; it was reacquired by the church in 1951 for offices. The third and current church building, known as Fellowship Hall, was erected in 1838 at a cost of $3,410. Now known as the First Presbyterian Church of Babylon, the congregation has been a part of the greater Babylon community for over 275 years. The church's 250-foot steeple, with four-faced clock and 1898 bell, towers over East Main Street as a constant and familiar landmark.

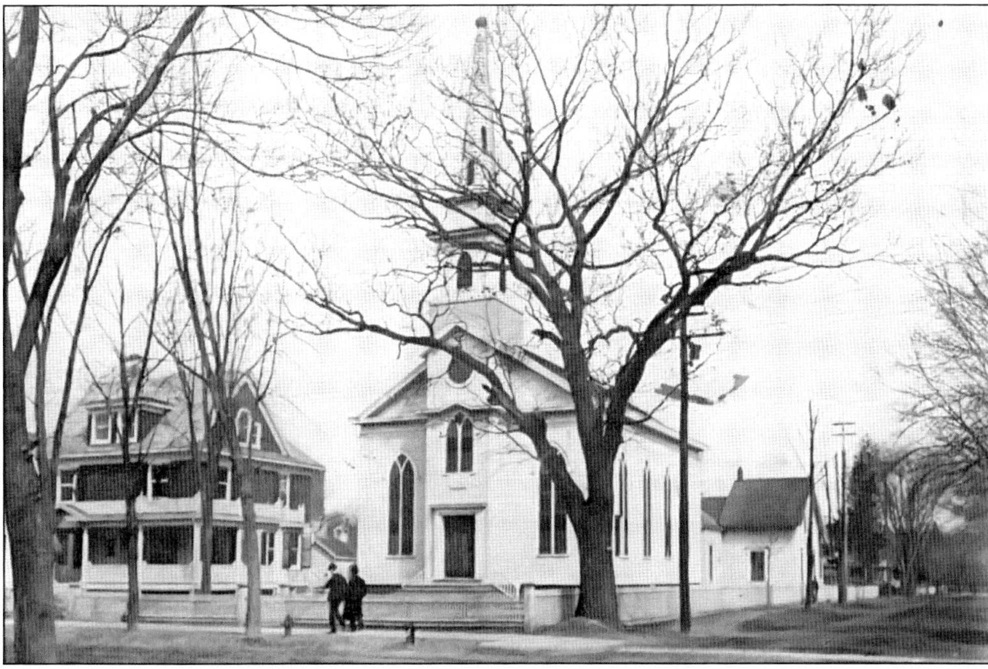

The Methodist congregation dates to 1831, when devout members Elizabeth and Stephen J. Wilson settled in Babylon. The Wilsons attended church in Amityville until interest grew in Babylon and a society was formed in 1837. By 1840, the first Babylon Methodist Church, measuring 30 feet by 40 feet, was built on Deer Park Avenue at a cost of $1,025 for land and construction. By 1859, the burgeoning congregation erected its present church at the corner of James Street.

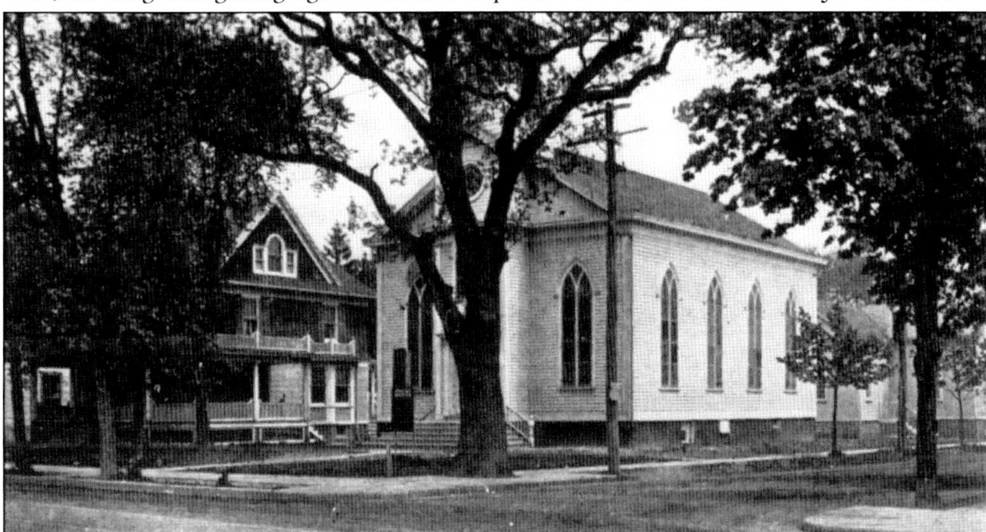

METHODIST CHURCH, Babylon, L. I.

William R. Foster, president of the New York City Bowery Bank, and his wife, Harriet, were summer residents of Babylon and fervent Methodists. The Fosters contributed generously to help fund the Gothic-inspired church. Moved to James Street, the original church was used for several years as a Sunday school. The church name has changed over the years and is currently the United Methodist Church of Babylon.

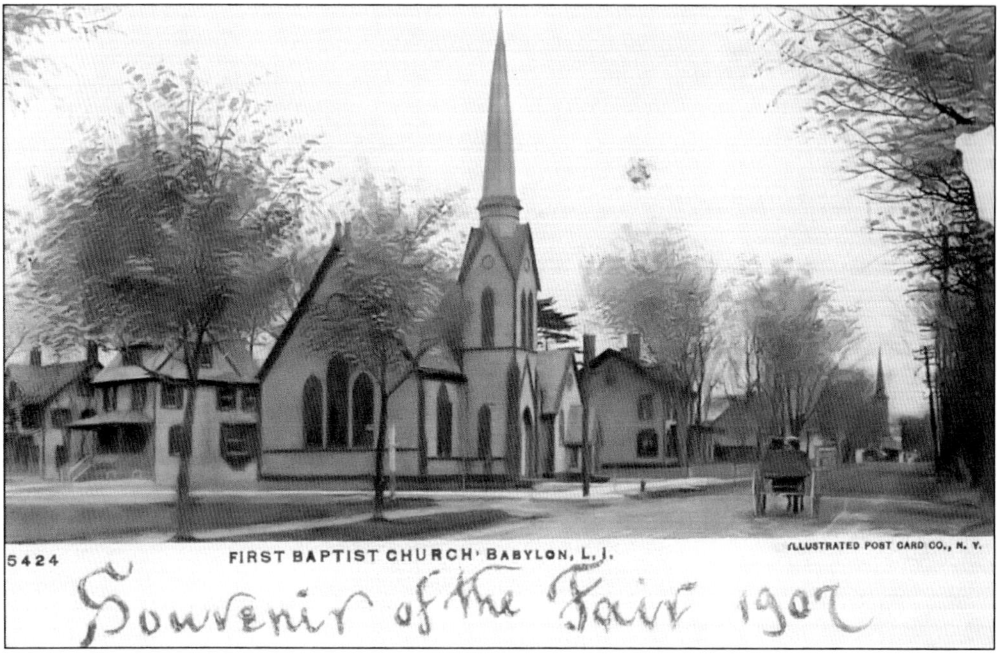

In 1872, four years after its formation, the Babylon Baptist Church Society built this church at the northeast corner of Main Street and South Carll Avenue, later changing its name to the First Baptist Church. The steeple was removed during a 1912 remodel, and a Sunday school added in 1923. E.B. Litchfield, an early owner of Argyle Lake and a church supporter, reportedly gave permission for the first members to be baptized in his lake.

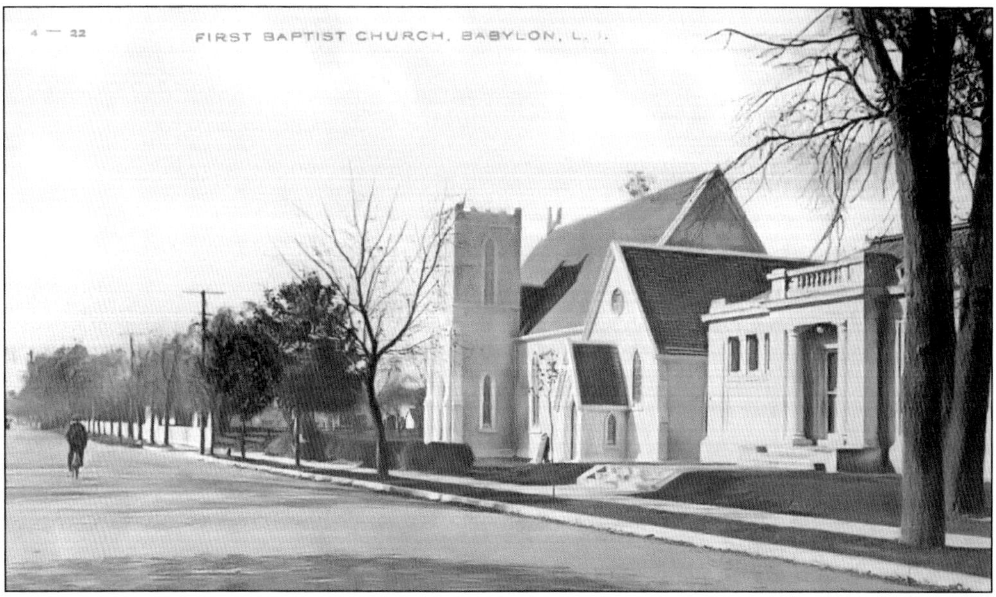

The old Baptist church is viewed from the east after the steeple removal. In 1958, the congregation relocated west on Main Street, where they remain. Rev. Wilford Fowler held the first service on Easter Sunday. The congregation moved the old parsonage to the new property and incorporated some stained-glass windows from the original church into the new structure. Eventually, the old church property was sold to the village, and is currently used for parking.

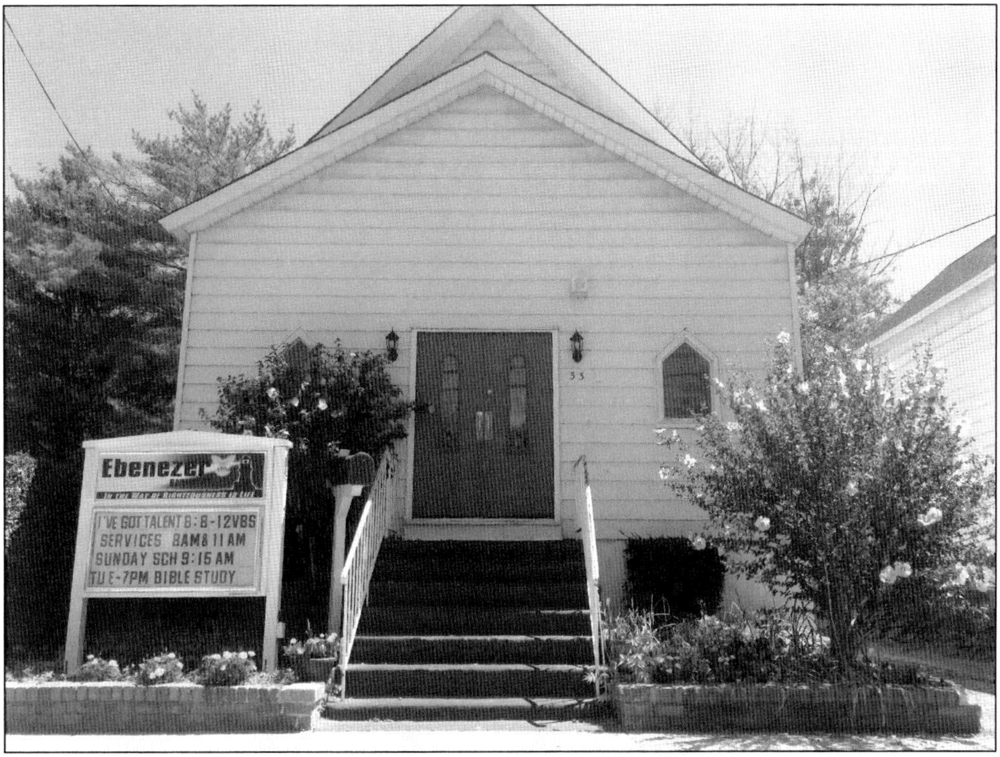

On September 19, 1874, the *South Side Signal* described a large gathering at the Baptist church where "several converts [were] immersed, and a Colored Baptist Church organized." Raising money through fairs and donations, the newspaper announced the July 16, 1883, opening of the renamed "Ebenezer Baptist Chapel, recently erected by the colored people of Babylon." Afternoon dedication services were held at the new Ebenezer chapel and an evening service at the First Baptist, where the new chapel was recognized. (TOB.)

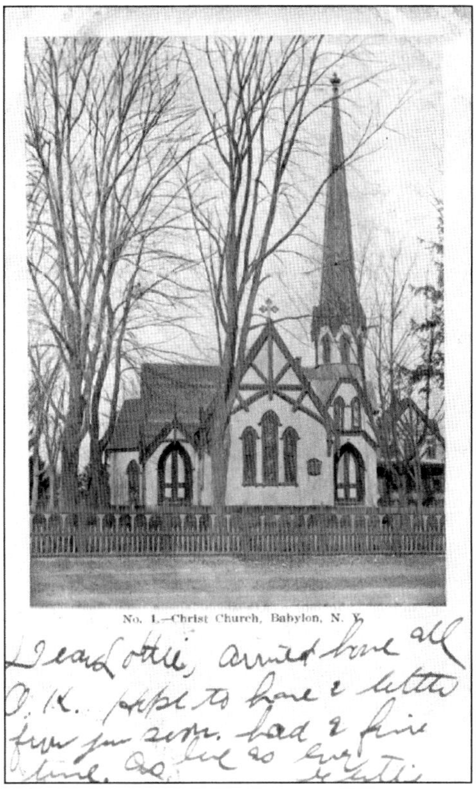

Two years after its 1869 formation, construction began for Christ Church Parish on Montauk Highway in West Islip, which was completed for Easter service in 1871. For the convenience of local residents, some felt that the church should have been built in Babylon village. Additional services were held around Babylon until 1930, when the congregation purchased the southeast corner property at Prospect Street and Carll Avenue, where it is now known as Christ Episcopal Church.

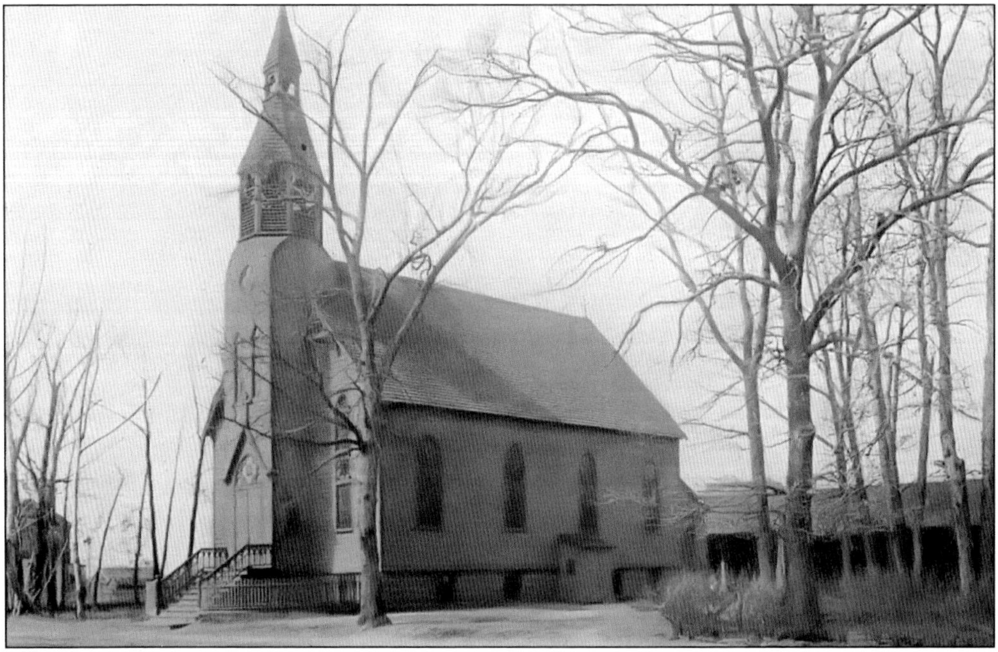

In 1877, the Catholic Society of Babylon secured lots on the north side of Grove Place, just west of Deer Park Avenue, and built a wooden church the following year. Prior to this, the congregation met in local hotels. To accommodate the expanding congregation, plans were made for a larger church on the southeast corner of Carll Avenue and Grove Place, a short distance from its original location.

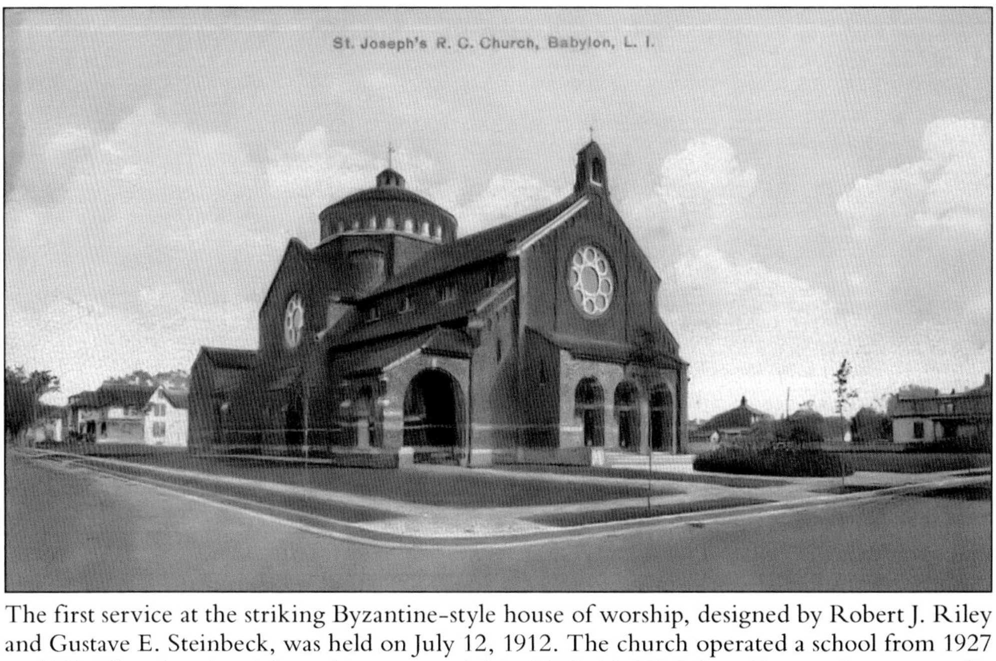

The first service at the striking Byzantine-style house of worship, designed by Robert J. Riley and Gustave E. Steinbeck, was held on July 12, 1912. The church operated a school from 1927 to 1991. The church celebrated its centennial in 2012, highlighting tile mosaics, reportedly designed by Rafael Guastavino, and stained-glass windows. The unique dome is adorned with a fresco buono by Maxwell Franz Friederang depicting St. Joseph, known as the Cyclus.

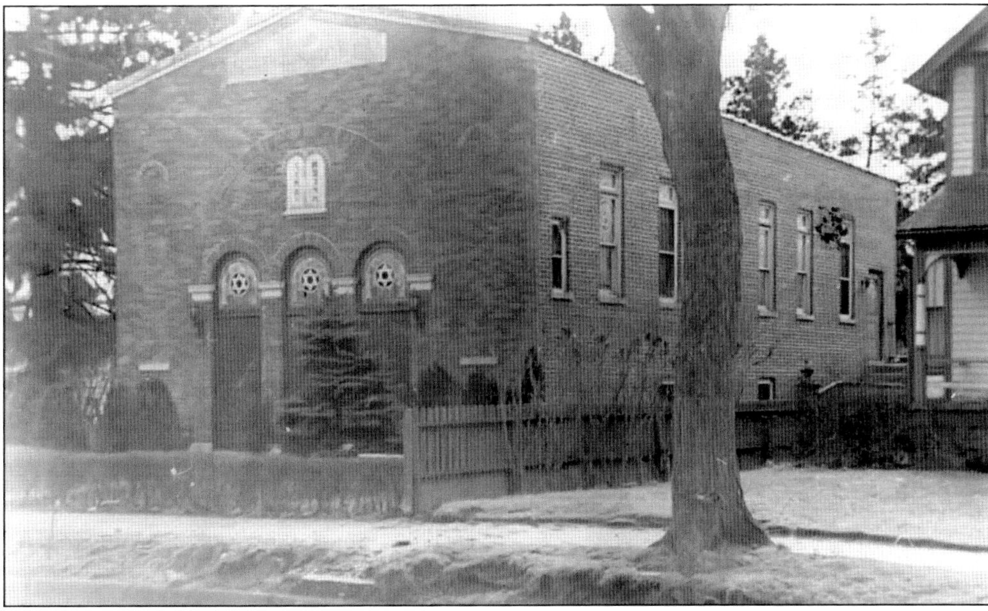

Dedication of Temple Beth Sholom on George Street took place on December 14, 1930. Attended by over 400 people, the *Babylon Leader* reported that the ceremony began with the presentation of the key for the outer door to Martin Weinstein, followed by the dedication address by Rabbi Morris M. Goldberg and a song by Ruth Weinstein. "The honor of Turning on the Lights was bought by Cadman H. Frederick and B. Press, both prominent South Shore business men."

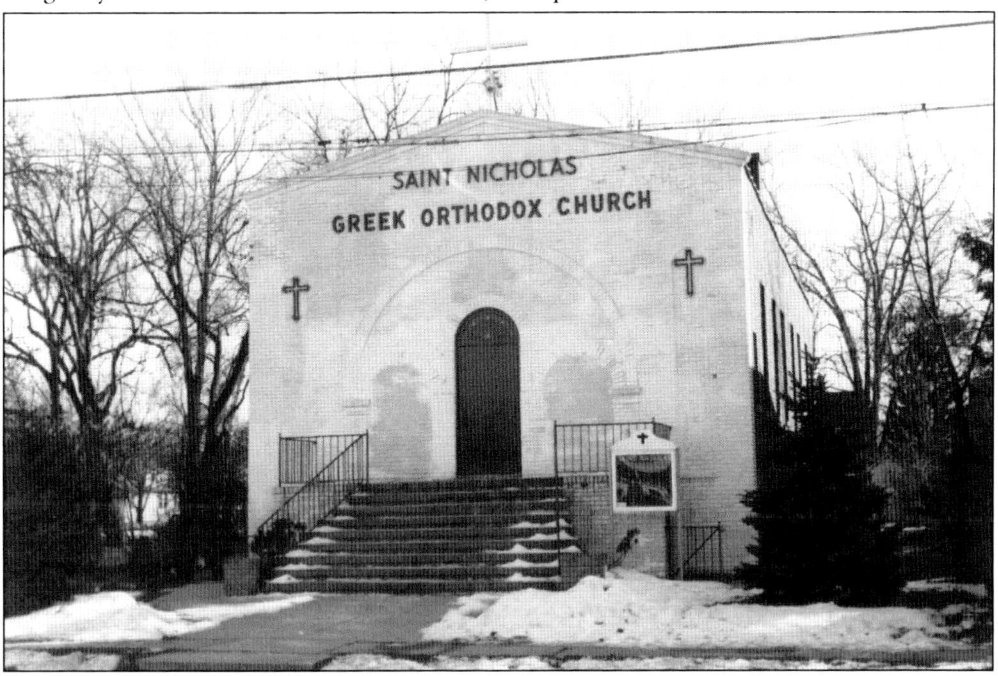

After Congregation Beth Sholom relocated to Deer Park Avenue, the Babylon Hellenic Community took occupancy of the George Street edifice in 1961. Later named the St. Nicholas Greek Orthodox Church, the congregation relocated in 1989 to a magnificent new church on Great East Neck Road in West Babylon, where it continues.

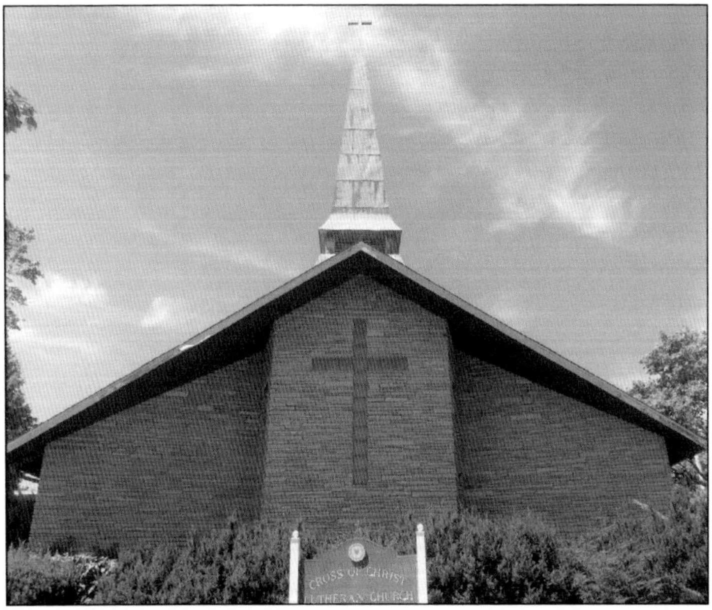

Cross of Christ Evangelical Lutheran Church formed in Babylon in 1923 as the First Lutheran Church of Babylon. The congregation worshipped in private homes before erecting its first church on Locust Avenue in 1927. Led by Pastor Albert Zetzer, the congregation relocated to Deer Park Avenue in 1957 with the opening of its educational building, which was used while raising funds for a new church edifice. (TOB.)

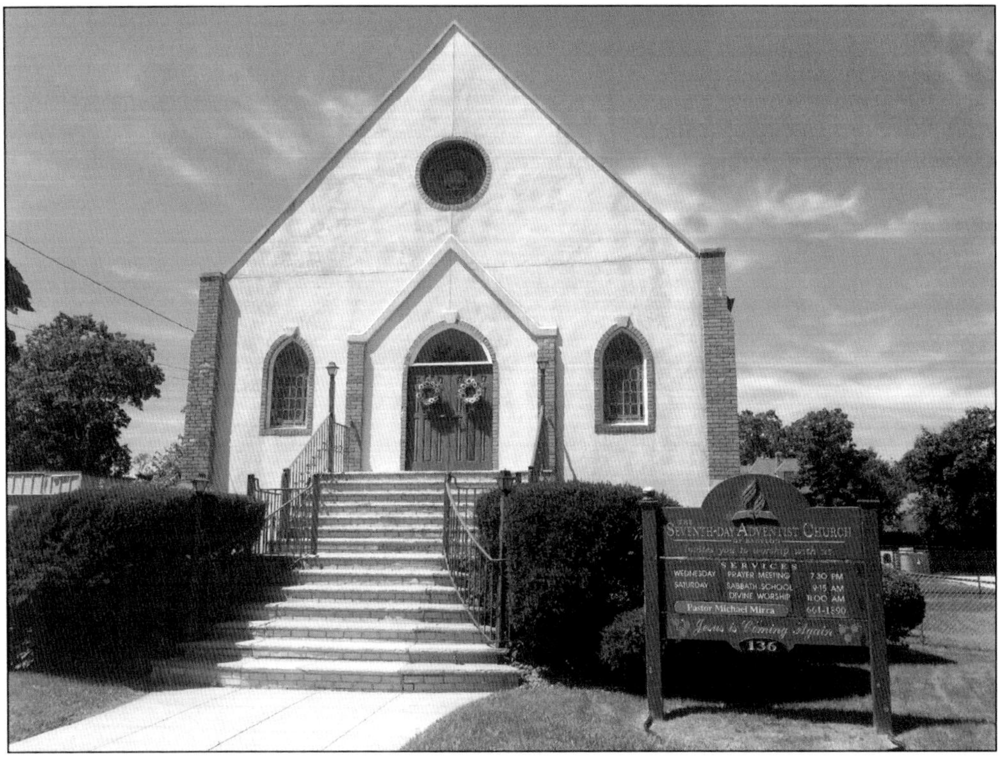

The Seventh-Day Adventist Church debuted its Fire Island Avenue auditorium on November 13–14, 1957. The *Babylon Leader* reported that the church was "largely constructed by the members . . . over a five-year period. The ground floor, first completed, served during this period of time as the worship room and school room. The newly completed auditorium was started a year ago, when funds become available through the personal sacrifice of the members and a solicitation program." (TOB.)

Nine

CELEBRATE!
PARADES AND FESTIVALS

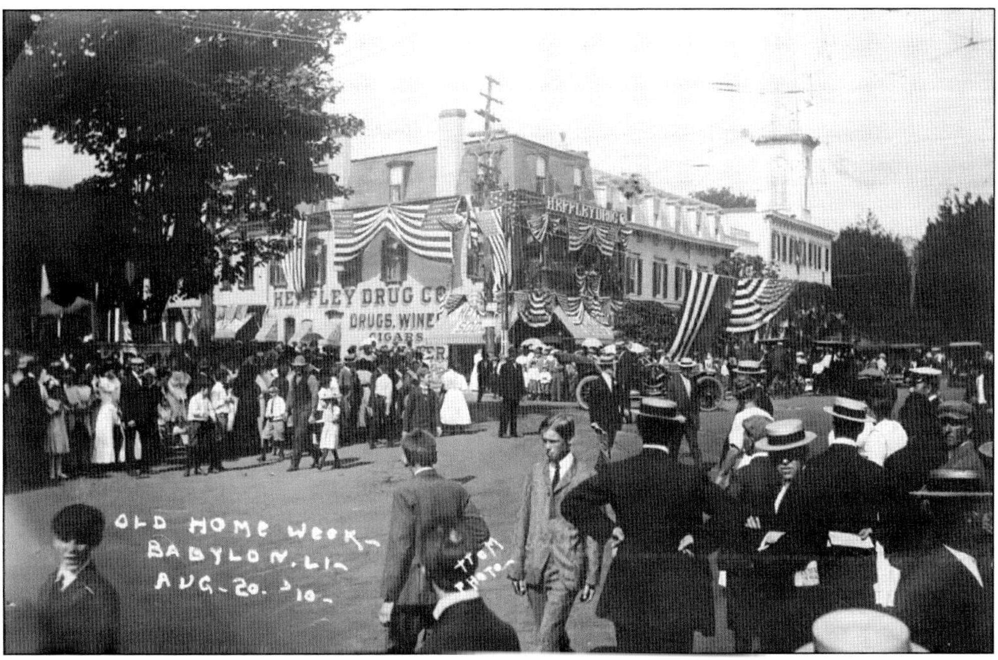

The August 19–21, 1910, Old Home Week was a three-day carnival devised by the village board of trade. An automobile parade was led by village president Chester O. Ketcham, with Babylon's two oldest residents, Samuel and William Muncie, as passengers. Prizes were awarded for the best and most uniquely decorated vehicles. The Committee on Balloons engaged the services of Professor James K. Allen, who made four successful balloon ascensions, drawing *oohs* and *ahhs* from the breathless watchers.

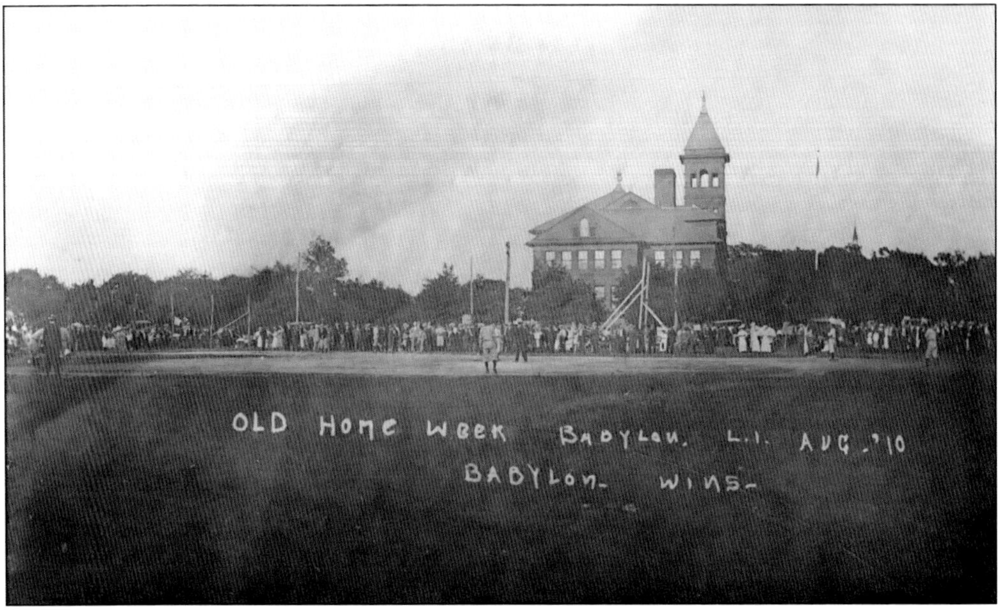

Several sporting events were held around the village, including motor boat races and a baseball game between the Married Men and Single Men. Water sports included swimming, racing, and tilting: "with their long poles . . . the contestants balanced themselves on a short stand in the bow of their respective rowboats, and it was interesting to watch one try to push the other off his stand, into the boat, or usually into the water," reported the *South Side Signal*.

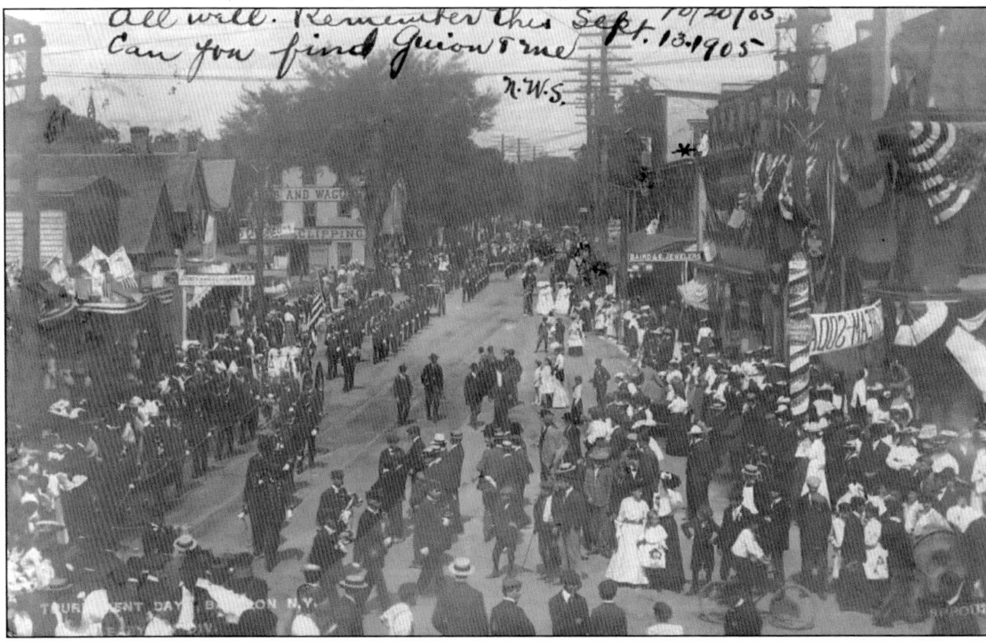

On September 21, 1883, Babylon was honored to host the first Suffolk County Firemen's Tournament. Babylon played host to the annual tournament many times, including in 1914, when the parade included over 1,600 firemen and musicians. The *Signal* deemed "the decorations along the line of the march were very good, but the most distinctive was the renovated Sherman House, where the newspaper men were entertained."

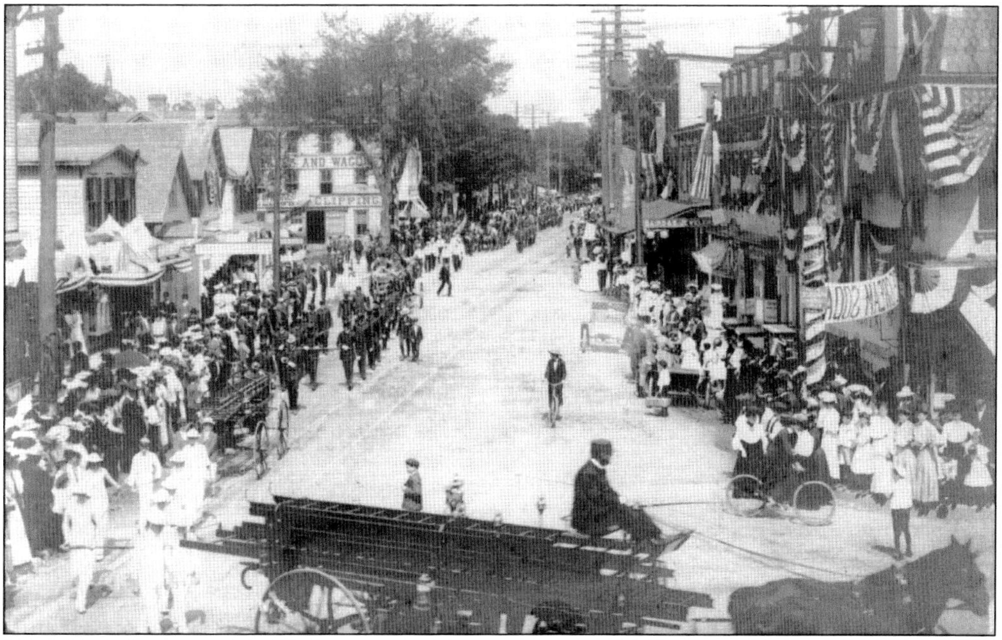

With horse-drawn wagons still common, much attention was given to an exhibition of "automobile apparatus" by the Huntington Manor fire department at the conclusion of the hose and ladder contests. The 1914 *Signal* reported that "a building was set on fire . . . north of the grand stand. At a signal the auto truck came dashing down the track, and with a length of chemical hose the fire laddies has the big blaze extinguished before the line of hose could be used."

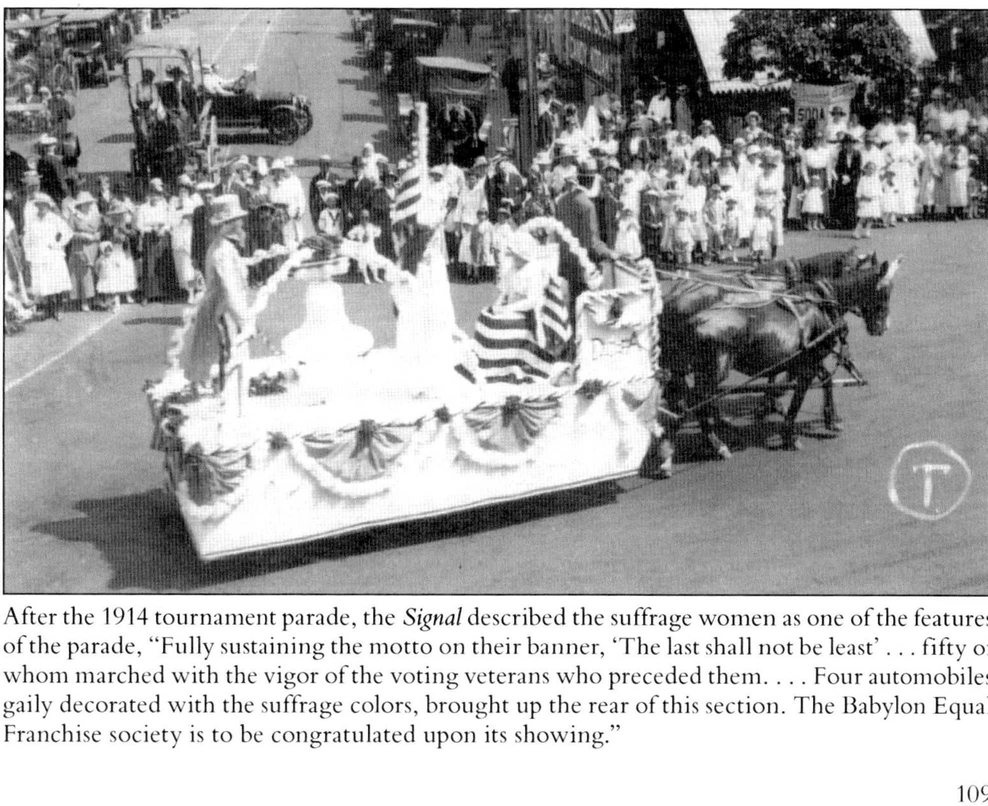

After the 1914 tournament parade, the *Signal* described the suffrage women as one of the features of the parade, "Fully sustaining the motto on their banner, 'The last shall not be least' . . . fifty of whom marched with the vigor of the voting veterans who preceded them. . . . Four automobiles gaily decorated with the suffrage colors, brought up the rear of this section. The Babylon Equal Franchise society is to be congratulated upon its showing."

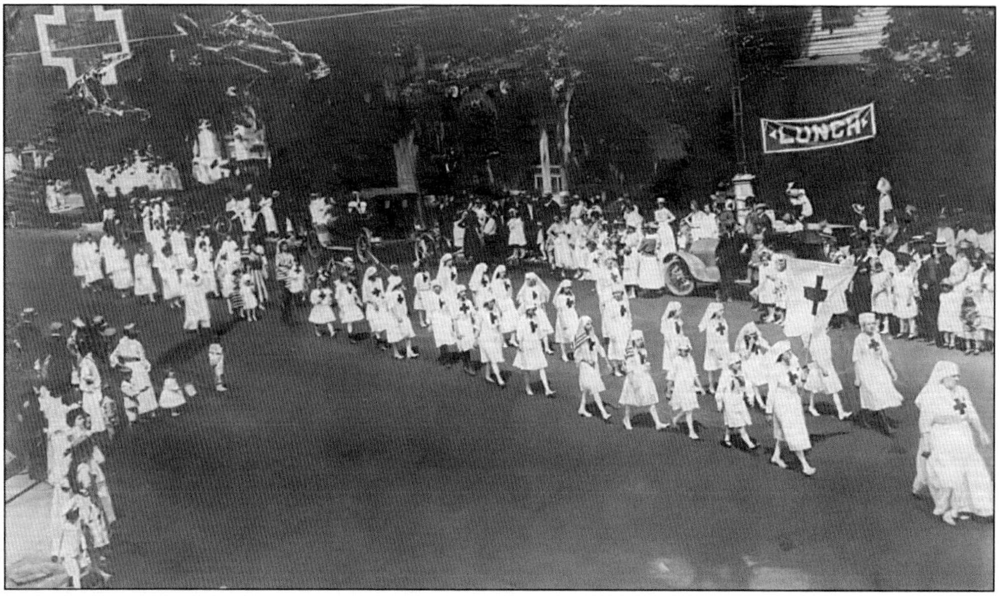

On August 23, 1919, a "welcome home" parade and reception was held in Babylon for "its world war service men and women, with fair weather it promises to be one of the biggest days in the history of the town," the *Signal* proclaimed. Representative delegations from the fire departments, Boy and Girl Scouts, and Red Cross branches came from Amityville, Lindenhurst, Babylon, and surrounding communities. Residents were asked to decorate houses and business along the parade route.

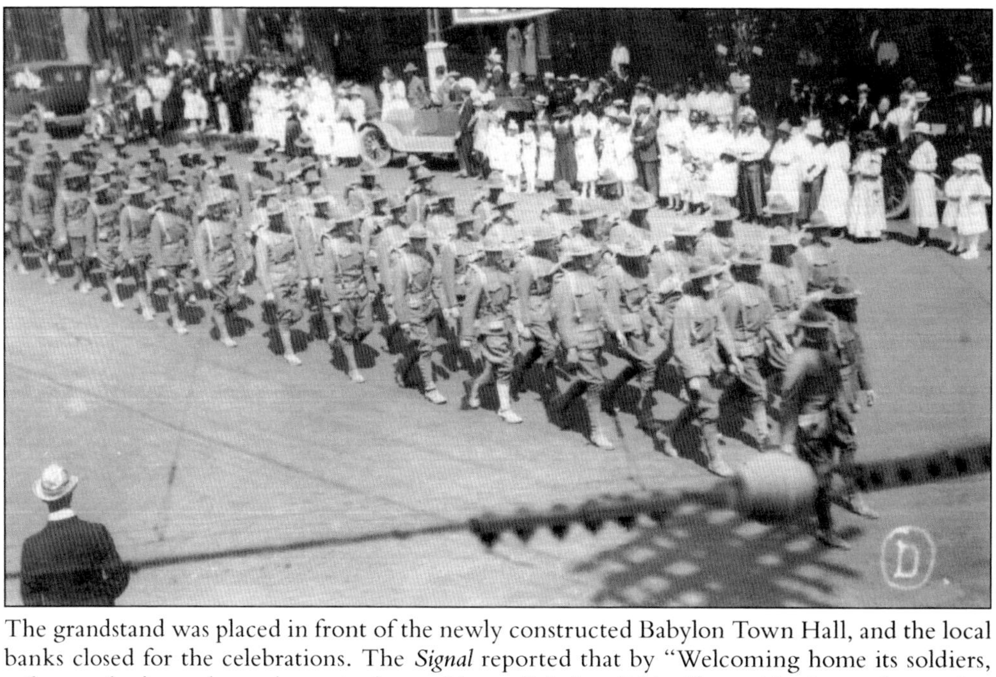

The grandstand was placed in front of the newly constructed Babylon Town Hall, and the local banks closed for the celebrations. The *Signal* reported that by "Welcoming home its soldiers, sailors, and others who took part in the world war, Babylon did itself proud in the royal reception to its special guests. Nothing was left undone to show the people's appreciation of their fighters and even the weather was kind in its treatment of the occasion."

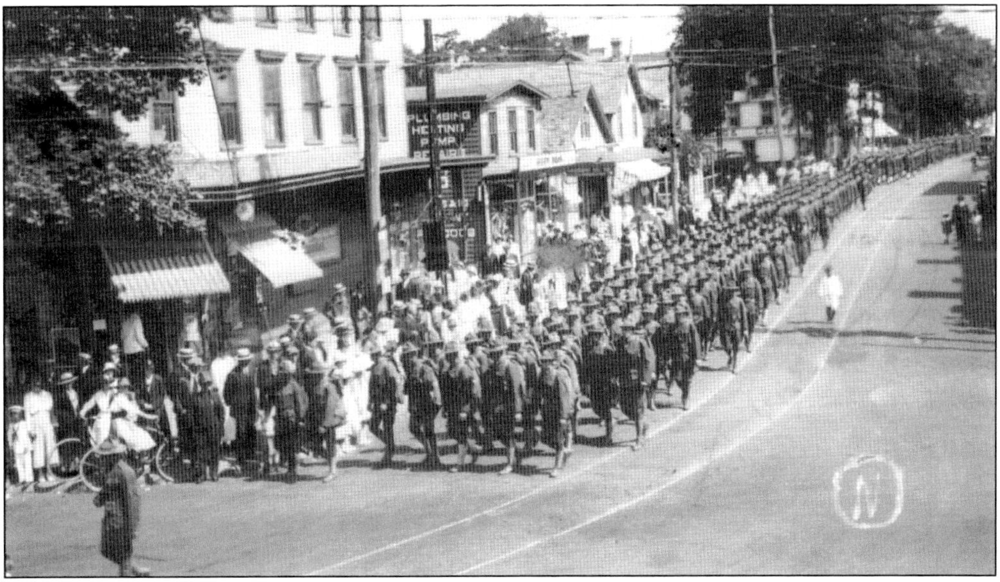

Declared "one of the best ever" by the *Signal*, the 1919 parade was led by Grand Marshal Harry VanWeelden and local officials, who were followed by the 15th Colored Infantry Band, and "a striking impersonation of Uncle Sam and Miss Columbia by Mr. and Mrs. E.J. Udall." The Daughters of America, dressed in white costumes, carried a large American flag, and school children and Girl and Boy Scouts "vied as to who could march in the most military fashion."

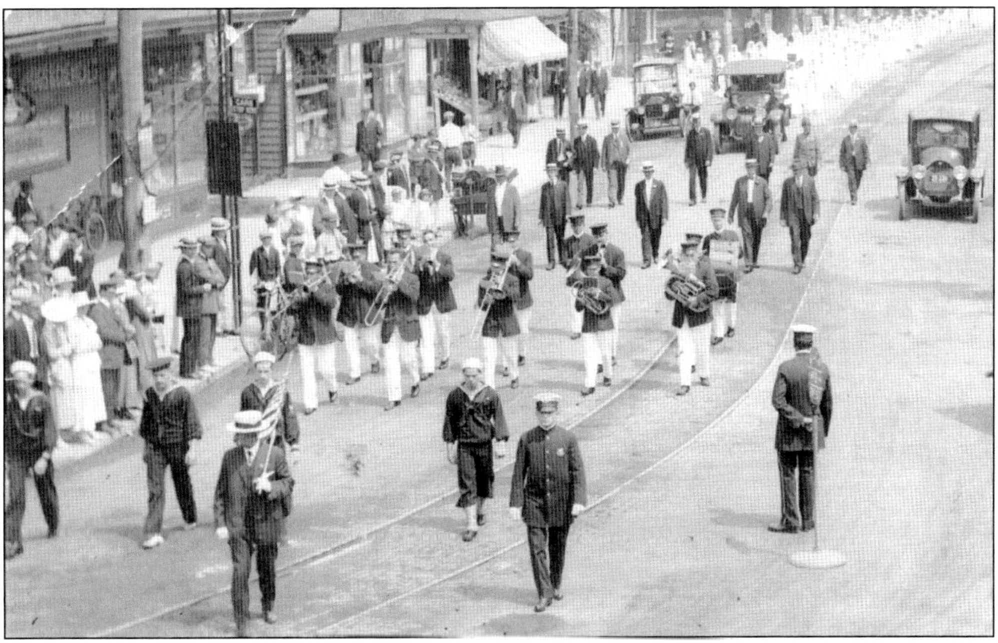

The paraders were marched twice past the grandstand before Babylon village president Chester O. Ketcham opened the ceremony and "extended a most cordial welcome home to its sons and daughters who had gone overseas or had been engaged in service on this side of the Atlantic," as summarized by the *Signal*. Maj. M. Robert Guggenheim of the 32nd Division, who owned a North Babylon country estate, was introduced as Gov. Al Smith's personal representative and shared the governor's telegram for the occasion.

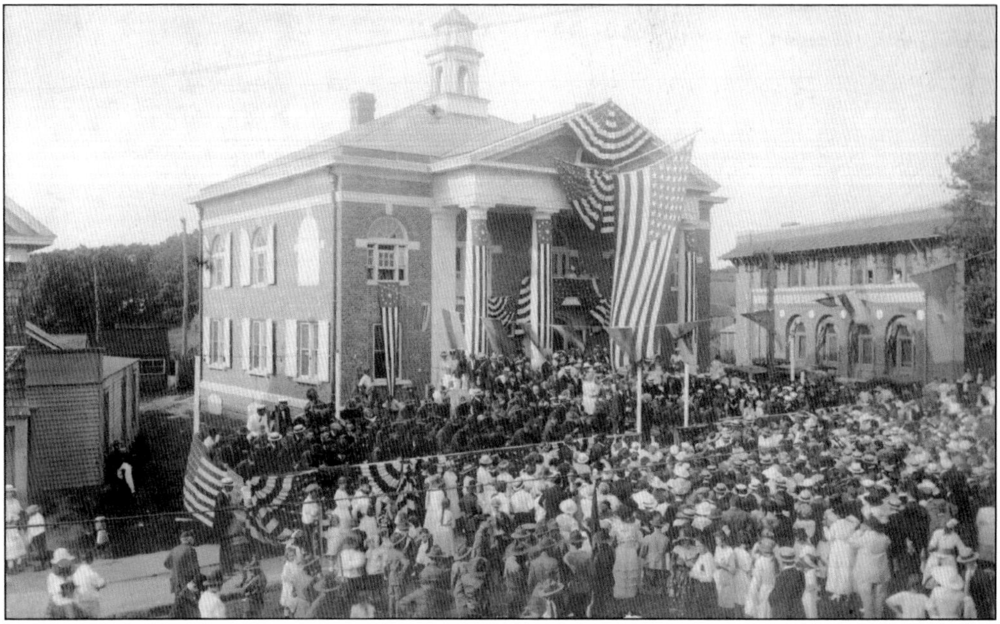

Retired baseball star John M. Ward introduced the chief speaker, Job E. Hedges, who "spoke with his characteristic straightforwardness and his own hearted Americanism struck deep in the minds of his hearers," according to the *Signal*. Representing all of the servicemen and -women, Cpl. Frederic J. Wood (later Babylon town supervisor) "extended our heartfelt thanks and appreciation for what the people of Babylon and the U.S.A. have done in every line of war service."

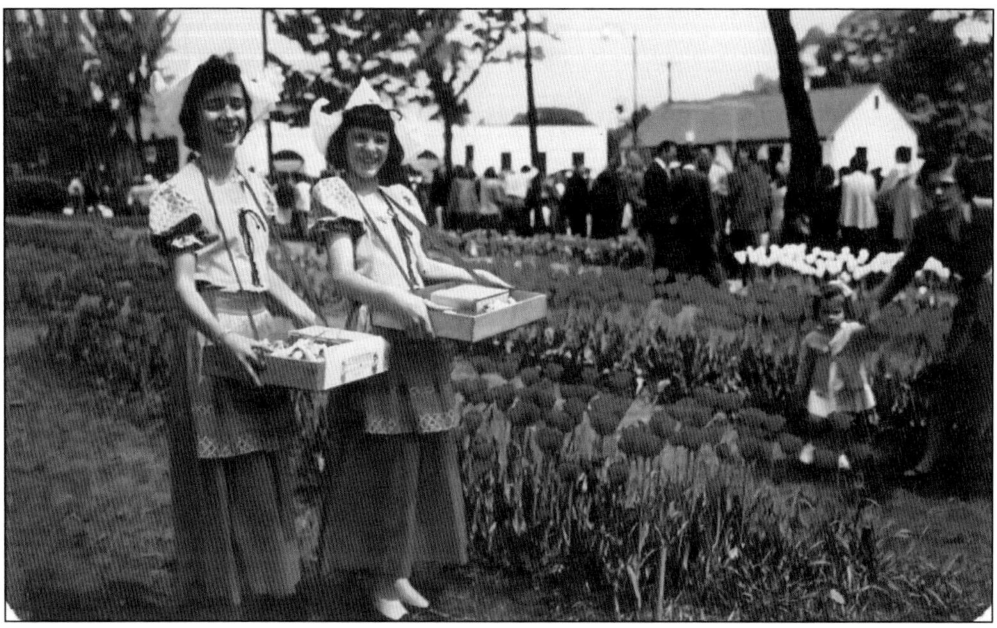

Originally organized by the Babylon Rotary Club and later by the Babylon Tulip Festival Committee, tulip festivals were held in Babylon each spring starting in 1947. The committee facilitated the planting of tens of thousands bulbs around the village and public buildings, and many homes followed suit. Announcing "Maytime is Tuliptime in Babylon," the committee touted Babylon as the largest tulip-growing area in the eastern United States.

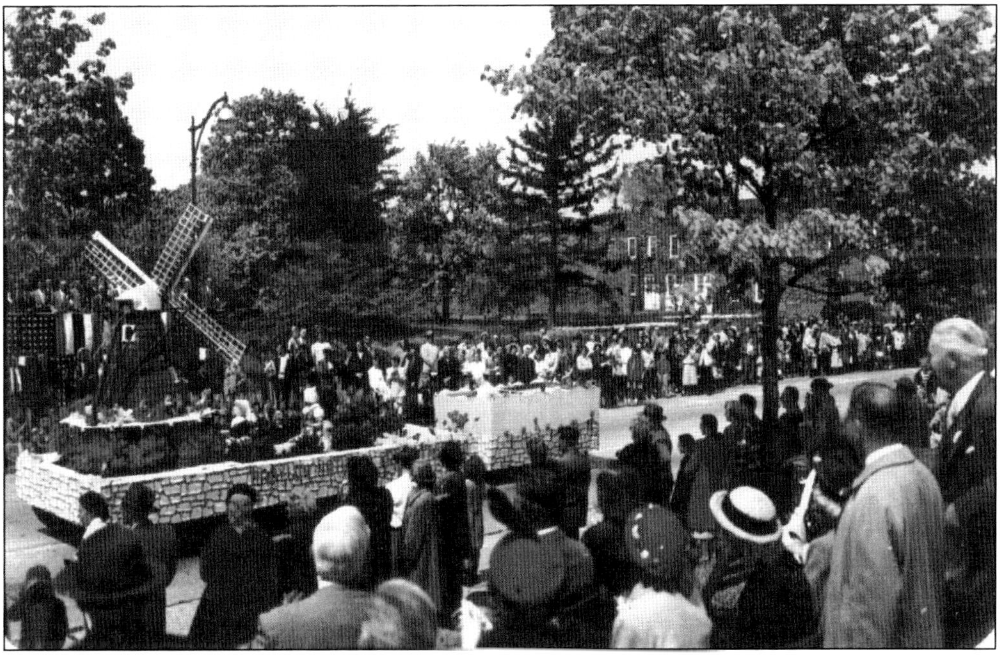

In 1952, the committee recalled, "Babylon is ablaze with thousands of tulips, daffodils and other flowers. People come from all over just to drive through our village and visit our parks to see these displays. Each year everyone cooperates in putting on a tremendous parade for your enjoyment. There were beautiful floats decorated with tulips and pretty girls, many costumed in brilliant colored uniforms, and horses with riders in western apparel."

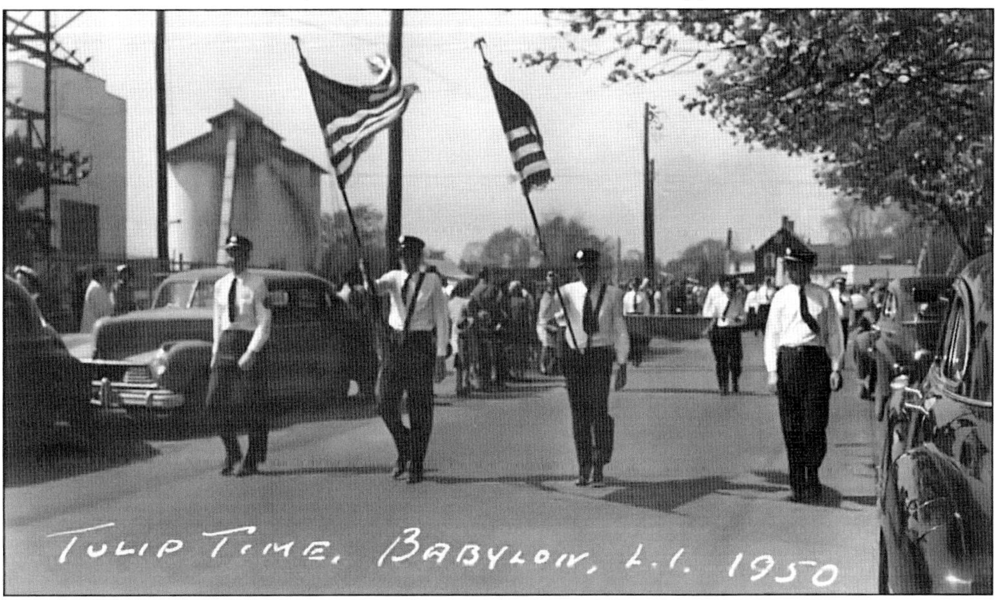

Parade floats and organizations typically lined up near Little East Neck Road, proceeding east down Main Street to Willow Street, south to Robbins Avenue, then west to Fire Island Avenue. Continuing north, the procession crossed Main Street to Deer Park Avenue and west on Railroad Avenue, concluding at the high school athletic field. The route traversed most of downtown, affording residents and celebrants a view of the nearly two-hour festivities.

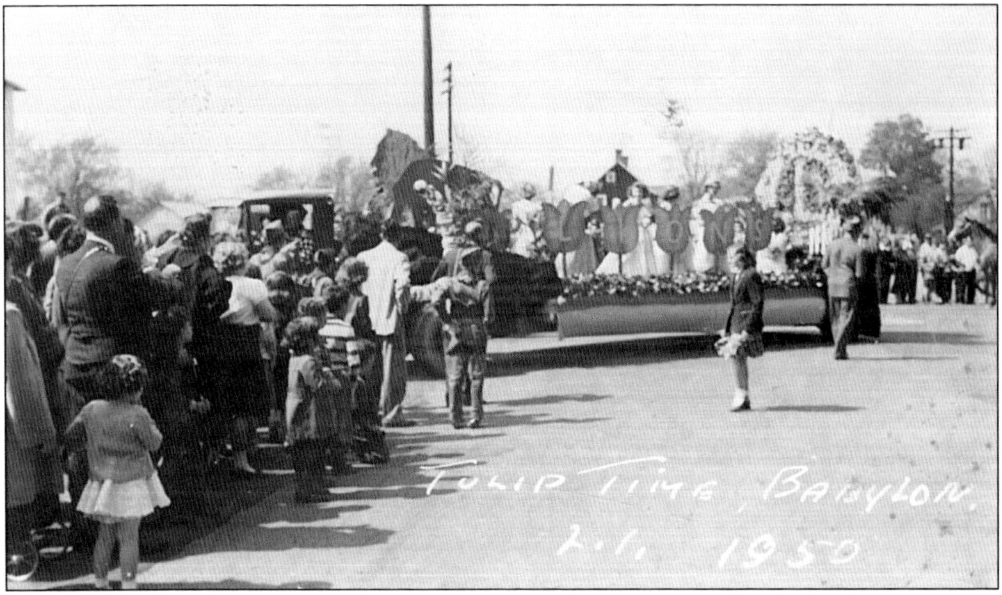

Celebrations were adapted each year, including a performance of "Tulip Follies." An original song, "Tulip Time in Babylon," was written by Dr. W.G. Hansen for the Babylon Chamber of Commerce: "In old Babylon town by the Great South Bay / There's a lot go-in' on when spring's on the way. / Then the tulips will bloom at ev'ry way-side and the neighborhoods bright and gay. . . . 'Cause the tulips are bloomin' and ev'rything's boomin', / its tulip time once again."

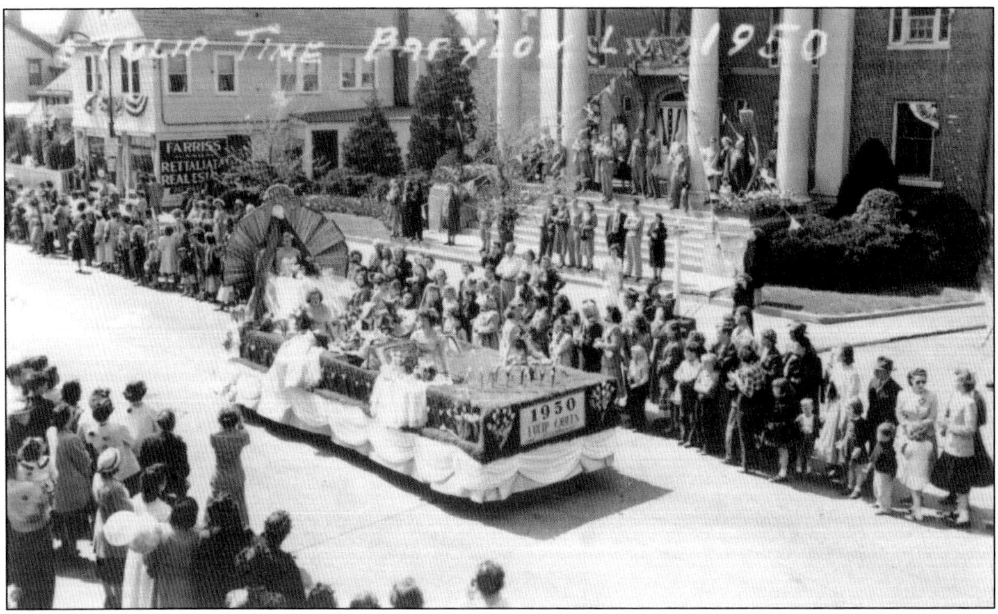

Starting in 1948, a highlight of the Tulip Festival was the crowning of the Tulip Queen and court. The five Tulip Queens were Arlene Snedeker (1948), Joan Billings (1949), Janet Kelly (1950), Joan Healy (1951), and Pat Gardner (1952). By 1953, Tulip fervor quieted, and there was no festival. There had been some grumbling over the 1952 selection of a Tulip Queen who was not a local resident.

Ten

Getting Around Town
Local Transportation

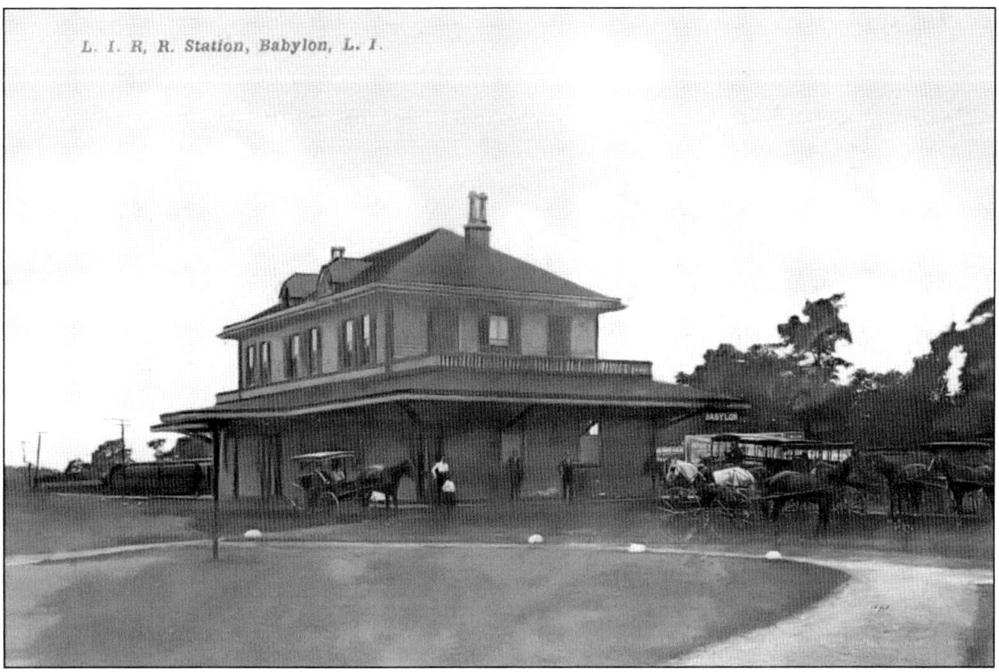

The formal opening of the South Side Railroad of Long Island from Jamaica to Babylon took place on November 14, 1867. Reporting on the inaugural trip, the *Brooklyn Daily Eagle* described Babylon as "one of those quaint old towns which has a life of its own and looks through sleepy eyes upon the rest of creation," and predicted that the new rail line would make Babylon "a popular sea-side resort for families in summer."

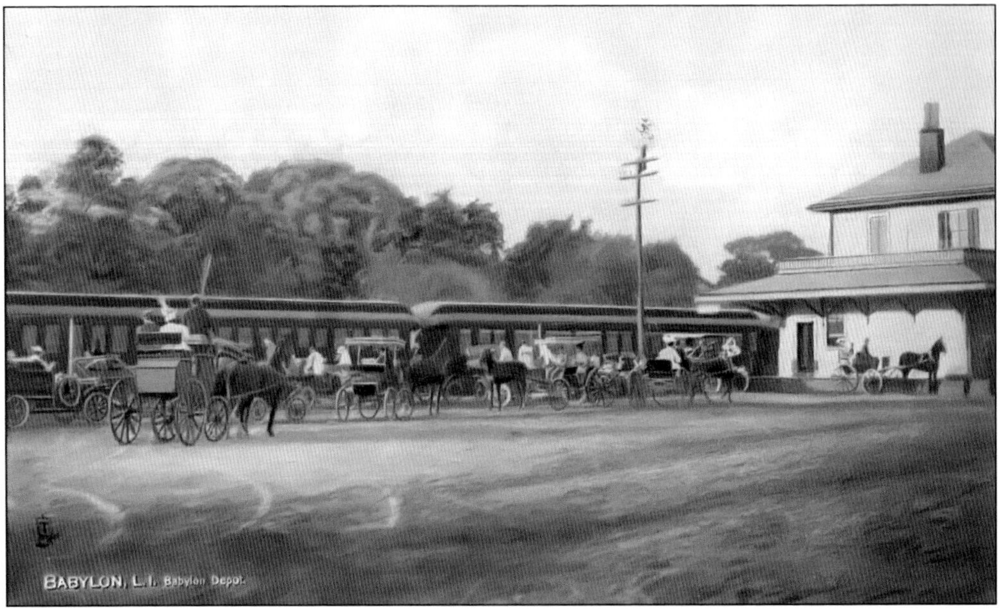

However, the *Eagle* also reported that "an old resident" declared that the name "Babylon" had fallen out of favor, claiming "that from the Biblical reputation of Babylon, city people concluded that its Long Island namesake must be very wicked," attracting those who "carouse and play at cards with the few who are among those always ready to take a friendly game or a social glass." He hoped that a name change would "change the tastes of the inhabitants."

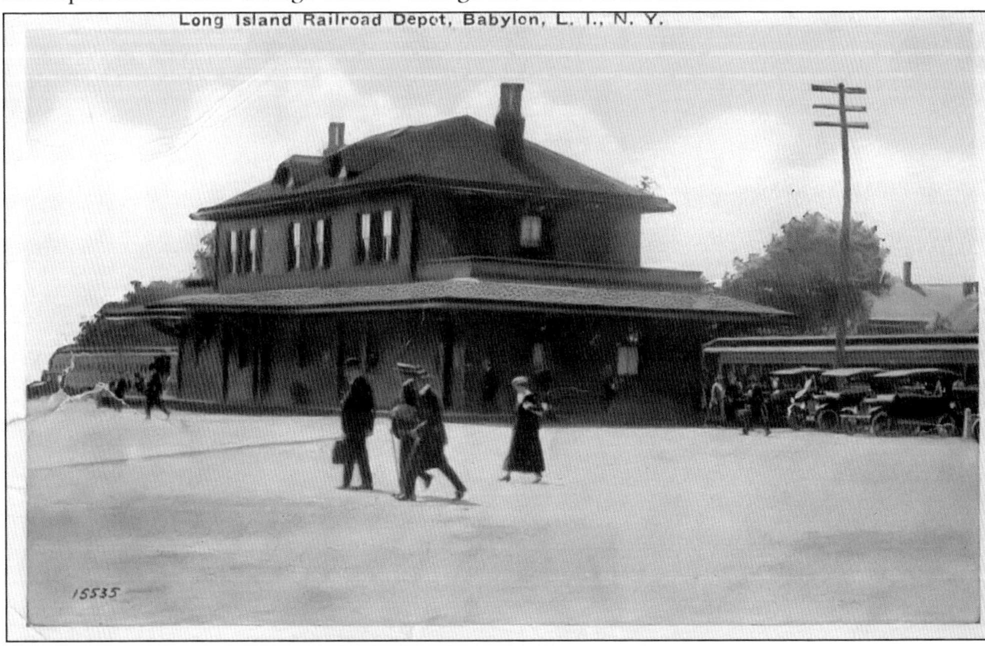

Efforts to change the name of Babylon to Seaside were quickly defeated. In 1932, Henry J. Kellum, a young boy during the controversy, recalled that Babylon "received an unfavorable reputation because of certain overt acts of the New York sporting fraternity who . . . made Babylon a point of rendezvous. Wives of the gentry, it is said, put their two feet down hard whenever their husbands remarked that they were going to Babylon!"

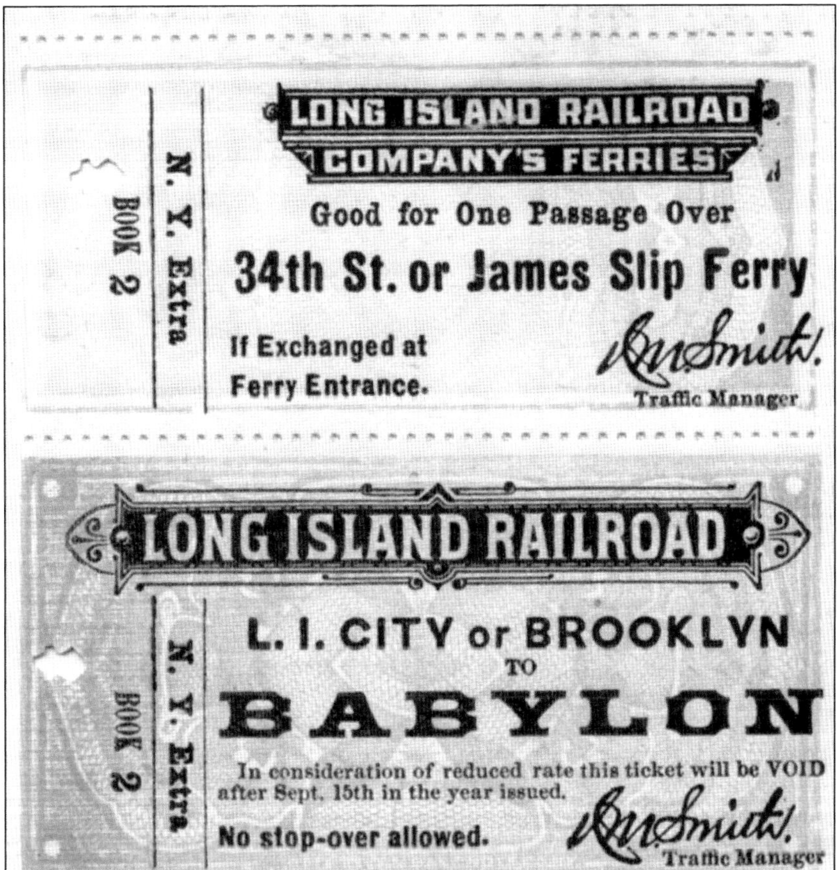

This four-part ticket illustrates a vacationer's journey from New York City, through Babylon, to the beach resorts around 1880. Starting from Manhattan, ferries shuttled passengers to Long Island City or Brooklyn for transport on the Long Island Rail Road. Arriving at the Babylon railroad station, passengers transferred to a horsecar that delivered them to the Babylon docks. Waiting ferries then carried visitors to Fire Island. (TOB.)

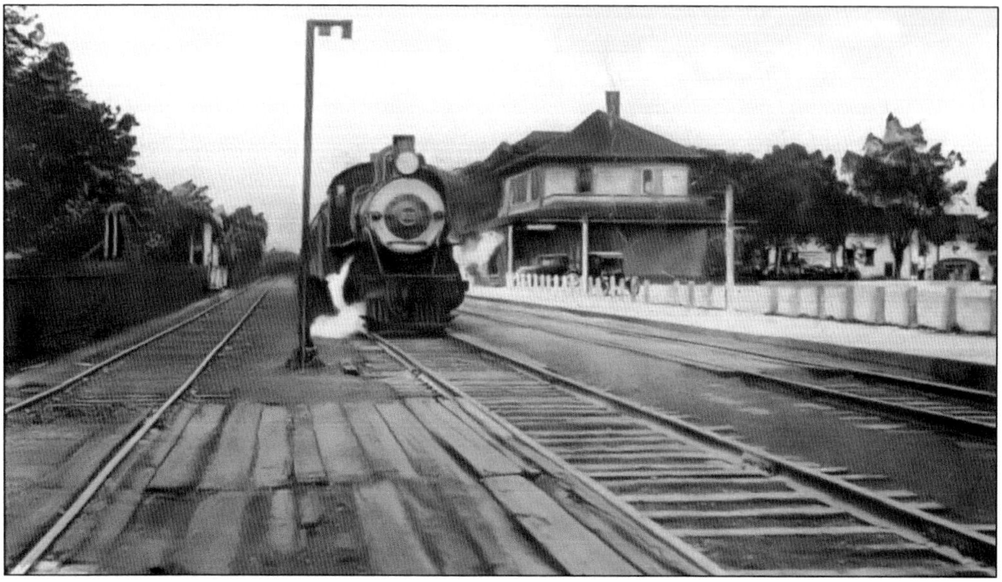

Long Island–The Sunrise Homeland, published by the Long Island Chamber of Commerce in 1929, promoted Babylon's amenities, including 72 weekday trains, running 60–87 minutes to and from Manhattan. A 60-trip monthly ticket was $13.81. According to the book, "the accessibility of the village in this connection has made it popular with commuters, not only during the summer, but also during the winter months. As a result, it has a large permanent population made up of New York businessmen."

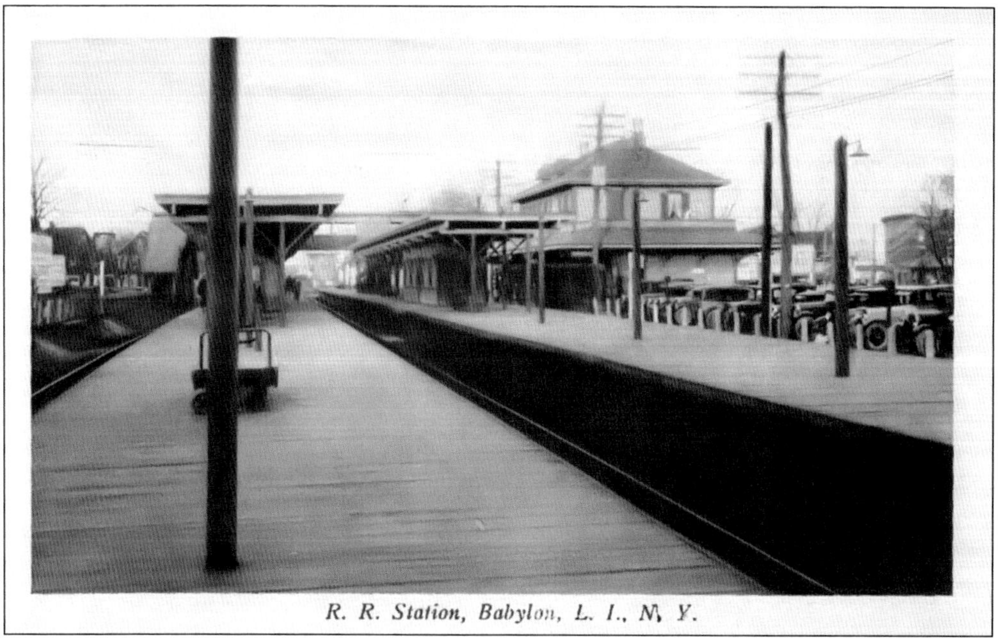

A similar community survey in 1954 described Babylon as having 1,549 monthly commuter passengers, "fire and police protection, electric, gas and water systems . . . conveniently located berths on public water frontage." "Transportation facilities are excellent. Babylon is an express stop for steam and electric trains . . . a short distance to the Belmont Lake State Park. . . . Village roads are well paved and cared for, as are the highways to all points on the Island."

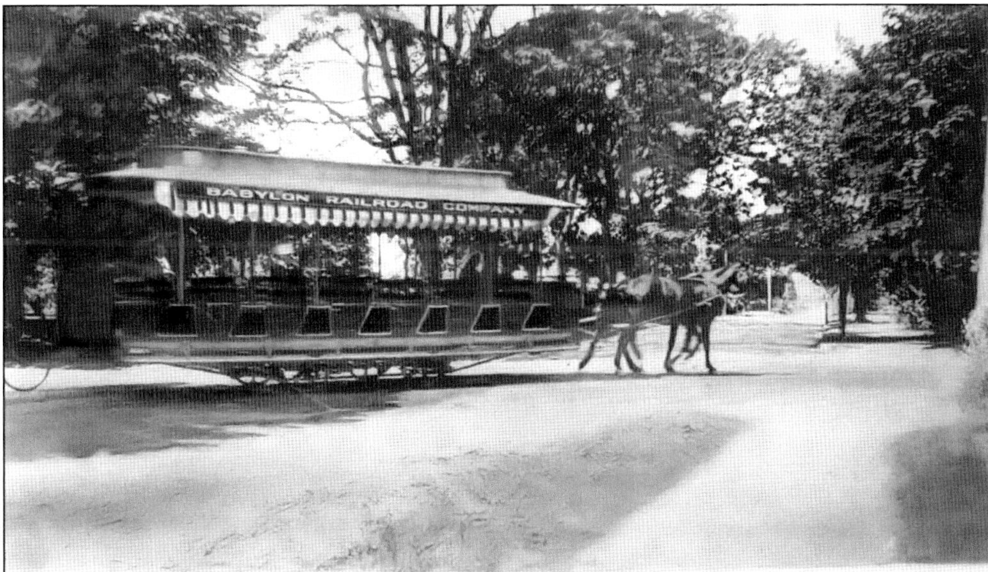

Rapid Transit to Oak Island, Babylon, L. I.

In 1871, David Sturges Sprague Sammis established a horsecar line in order to ease the transport of visitors to his Surf Hotel on Fire Island. Known as the Babylon Railroad, the line consisted of two horses and two carriages pulled on street rails. Passengers paid 6¢ for the 1.5-mile ride from the railroad station down Deer Park Avenue to Fire Island Avenue and the Babylon Dock for ferries to the ocean beaches.

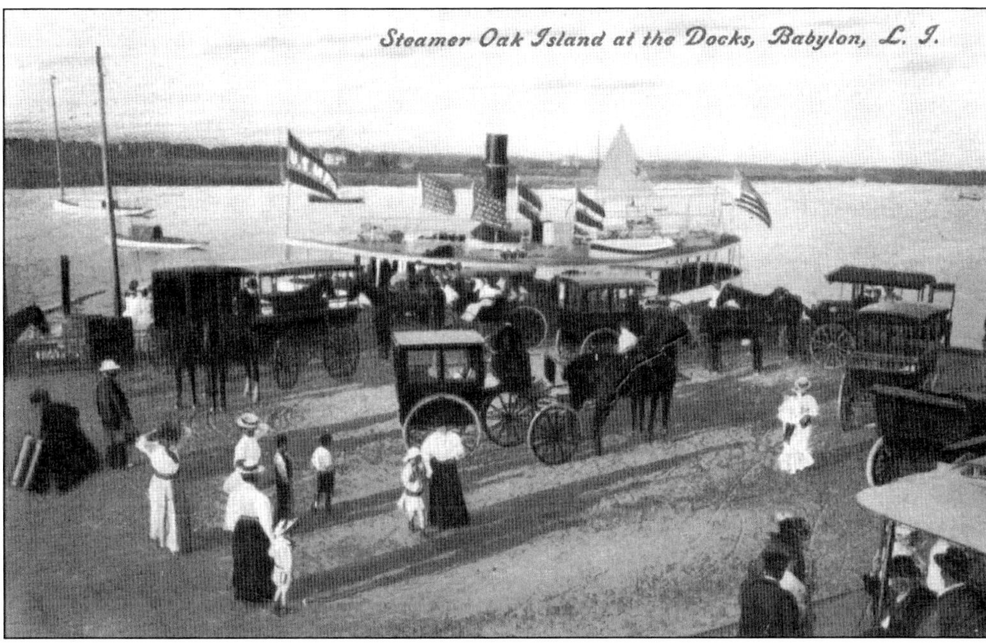

In 1876, the South Side Railroad was leased to the Long Island Rail Road, and it merged with LIRR in 1889. During the 1910 summer season, the steamer *Oak Island* advertised five daily trips from the Babylon Dock to the Association Dock on Oak Island—50 minutes—and the Government Dock at Oak Beach—one hour from Babylon. A one-way trip was 15¢, and a round trip was 25¢.

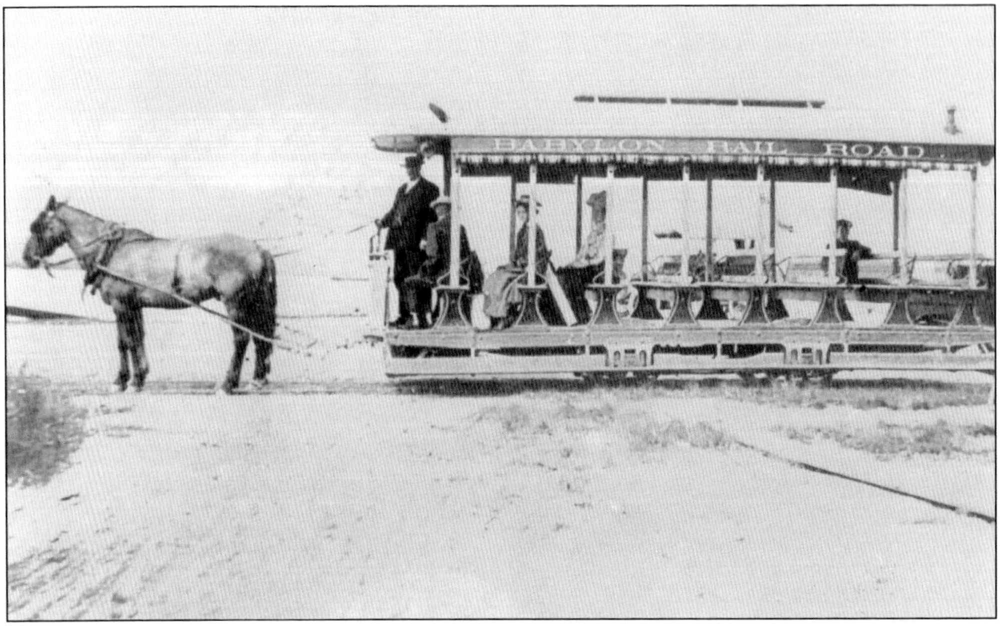

Although the Surf Hotel closed in 1892, the horsecars continued. In 1898, a Manhattan firm purchased the line and installed steam power motors. Steam power was effective, but it was unpredictable. After just two years of steam operation, William DeGarmo leased the company and reinstated the horse-drawn service. While horses may have seemed a backwards choice, DeGarmo's initial year of operation realized the first profit for the Babylon Railroad—a total of $1.

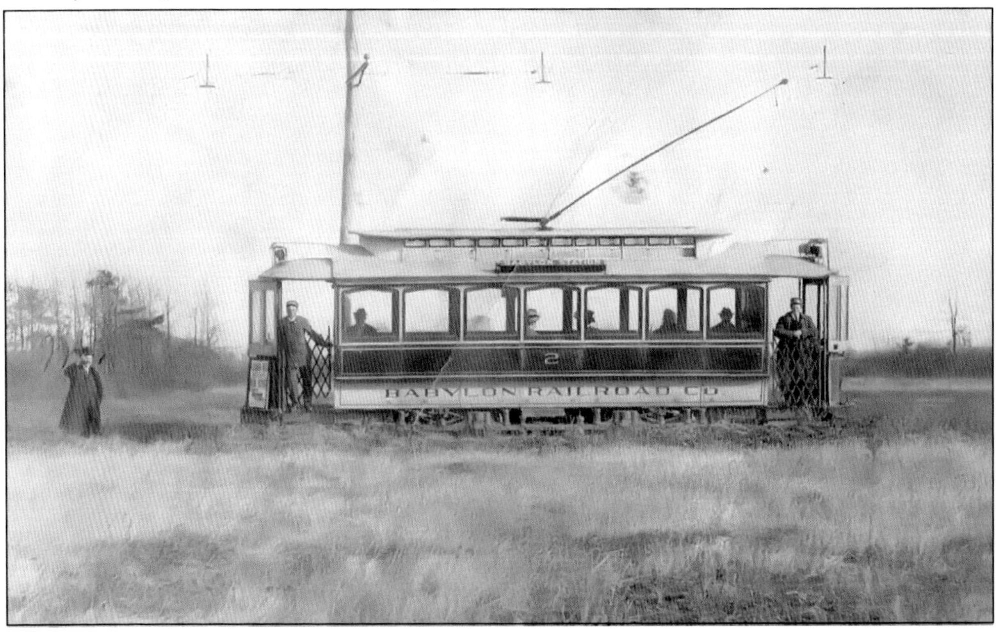

The next owner of the Babylon Railroad was the Long Island Consolidated Electrical Company, which planned to electrify the line, but the financial panic of 1907 hindered those plans. In 1909, the line was purchased by the South Shore Traction Company. Additional rail was laid west to Amityville, where passengers could transfer to the Cross-Island trolley route, which extended 18.5 miles north to Huntington along the approximate route of the present-day Route 110.

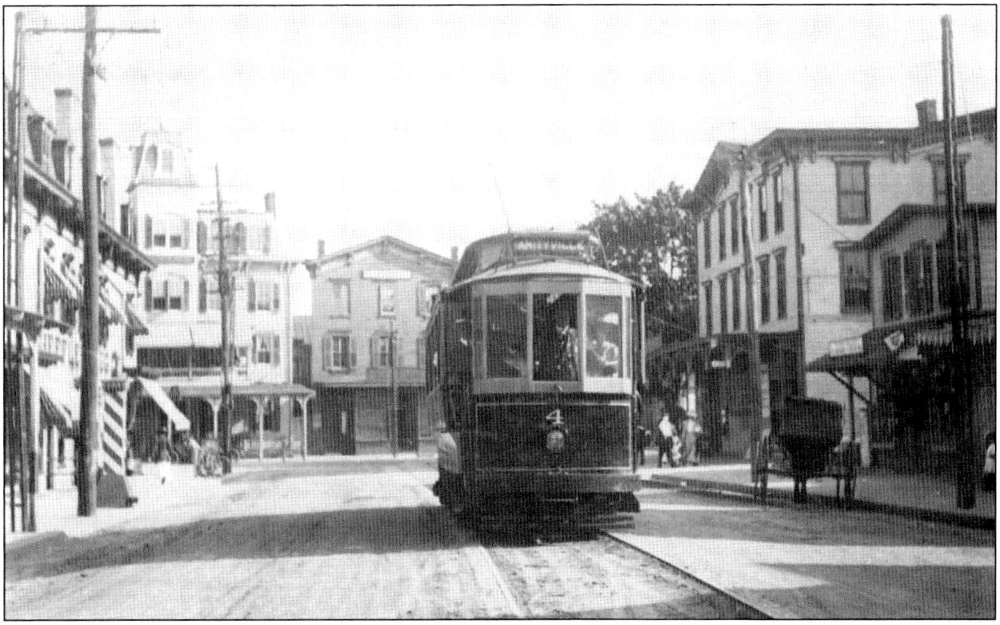

Still operating under the name Babylon Railroad, the new electrified trolley line officially opened on June 11, 1910, with five small trolley cars, each with a capacity of 28 passengers. The fare for stops at West Babylon, Lindenhurst, and Copiague was 5¢, while the full trip from Amityville to Babylon cost 10¢. The full trip took approximately 35 minutes, and trolley cars operated at an average of one per hour.

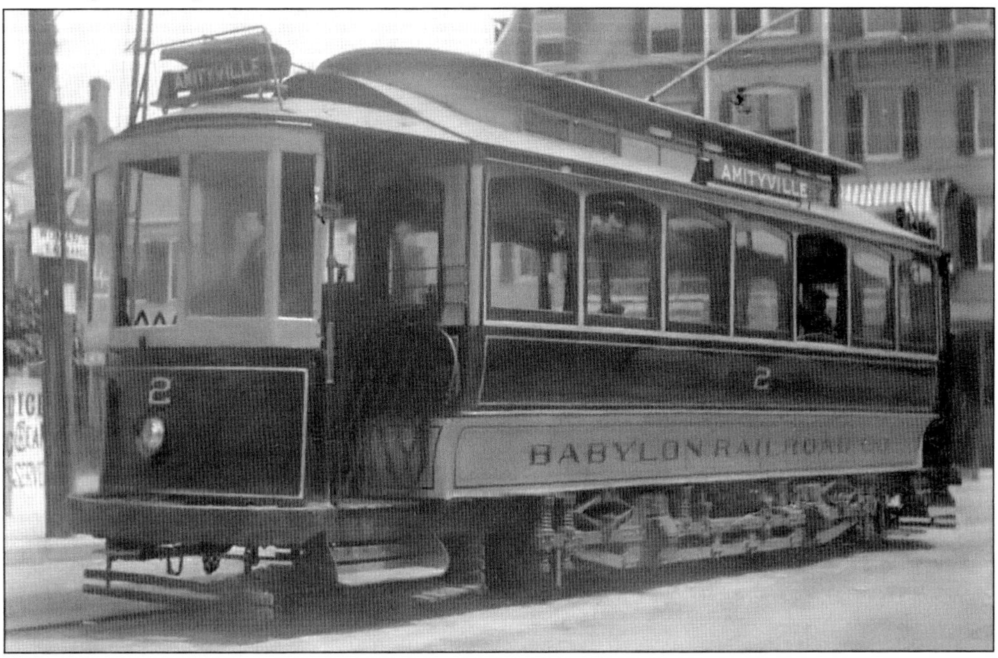

Stories of trolley mishaps abound. Henry Ellis Willmont, a former motorman, recalled that the trolley "used to jump off quite a bit and we'd have to run it back on." Sometimes, passengers helped to lift the car back on the tracks. A former commuter, Shepard Farrington of Babylon, recalled "When there was too much a load in the back, the front would tip up. The passengers had to be evenly distributed."

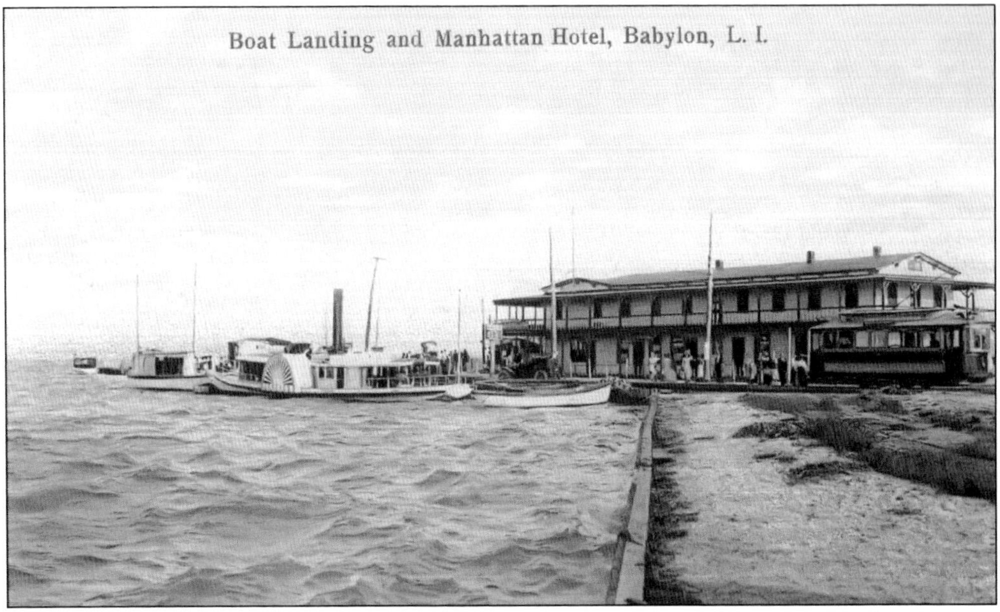

Horsecars and, later, electrified trolleys transported passengers from the Babylon railroad station to the ferry docks. Here, a Babylon Railroad trolley car passes the Manhattan House while the *Oak Island* steamer is moored at the pier. The 1910 guide ***Suburban Trolley Lines within Fifty Miles of New York City*** directed passengers that the docks were a 10¢, five-minute trip from the railroad station to the docks, with connections to steamboats for Oak Island.

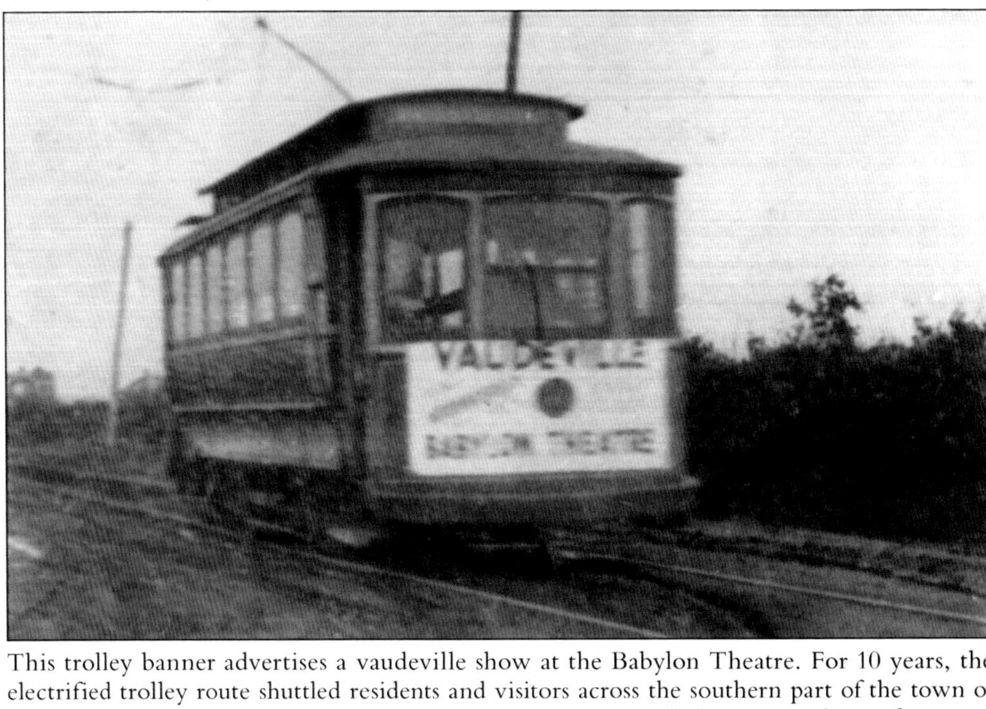

This trolley banner advertises a vaudeville show at the Babylon Theatre. For 10 years, the electrified trolley route shuttled residents and visitors across the southern part of the town of Babylon. However, the trolley business could not compete with the increased use of personal automobiles. Despite its decade-long service, the route was never a profit-making enterprise. On May 25, 1920, the operations of the Babylon Railroad ended.

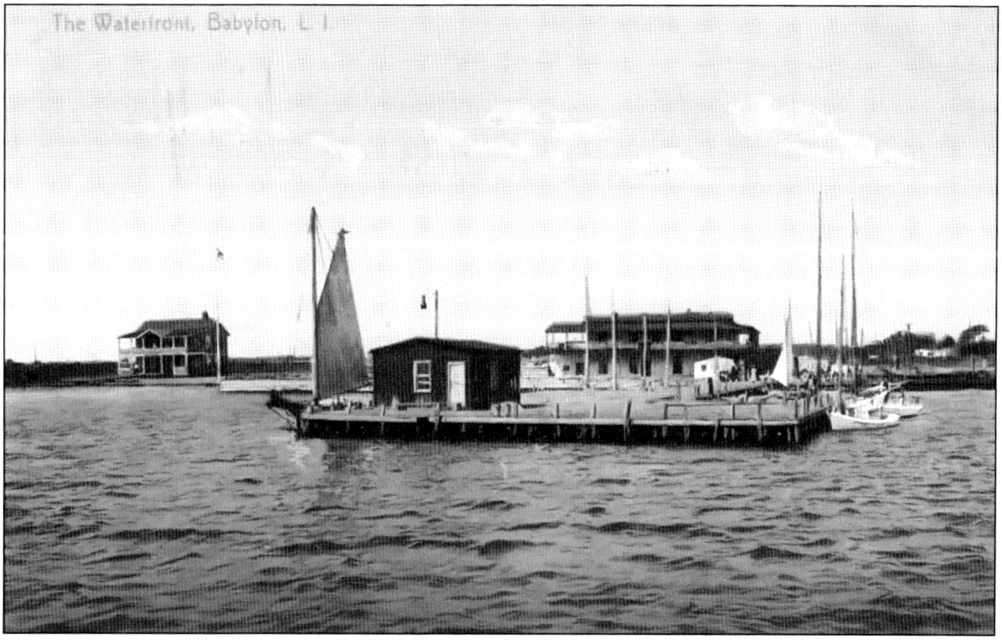

The Babylon Dock was the focal point of vacation travel. Carriages, horsecars, and sailboats later gave way to automobiles, electric trolleys, and steam ferries. The docks were bustling with travel-weary passengers anxiously awaiting the start of their oceanfront vacations mixing with visitors heading home after their own sojourns. (TOB.)

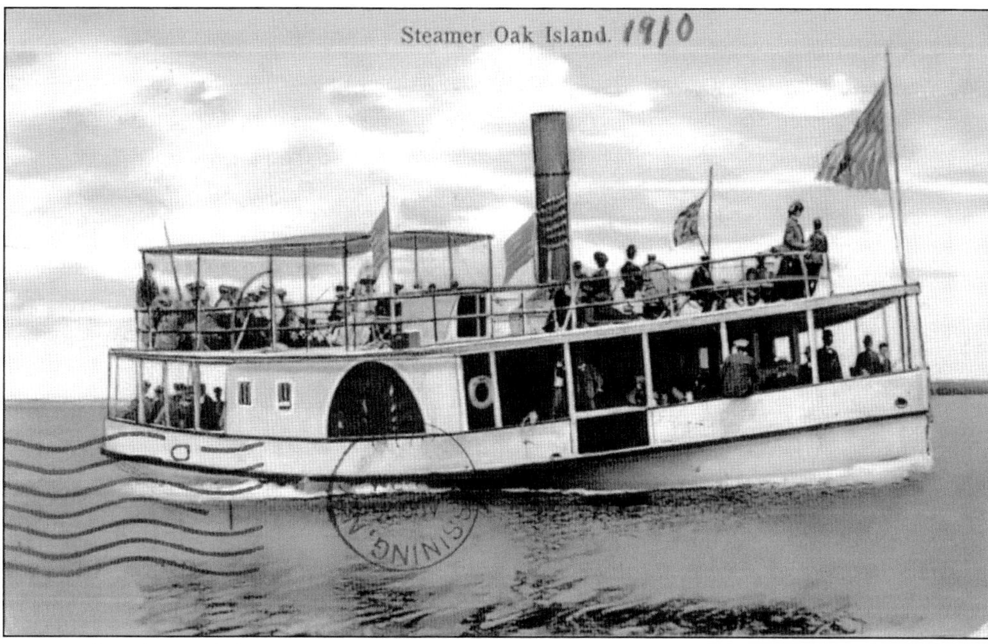

Edgar Albin debuted the steamer *Oak Island* in 1894, later adding a gasoline motor. Over time, the ferry was enlarged from 52 feet to 78 feet. The ferry was problem-prone, suffering mechanical breakdowns and often running late. The *Oak Island* was also prone to running aground in the Great South Bay, necessitating the crew of the US Life-Saving Station at Oak Island Beach to dash to the aid of the ferry and its passengers.

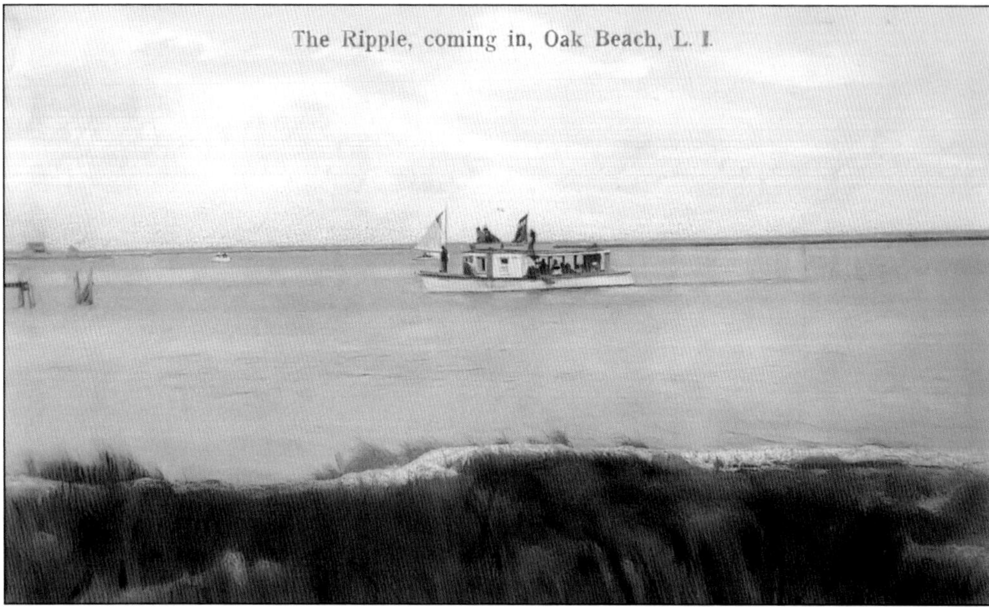

Noticing the increasing popularity of Oak Island and Oak Beach cottages and beach vacationers, Albert S. Haff and Norman H. Smith seized the opportunity to expand ferry services between Babylon and the barrier beach communities. By that time, the aging steamer *Oak Island* was less than reliable. Designed by Haff and built with his business partner Smith, the *Ripple* was a 45-foot ferry powered by a 24-horsepower engine, which also made several trips to Florida.

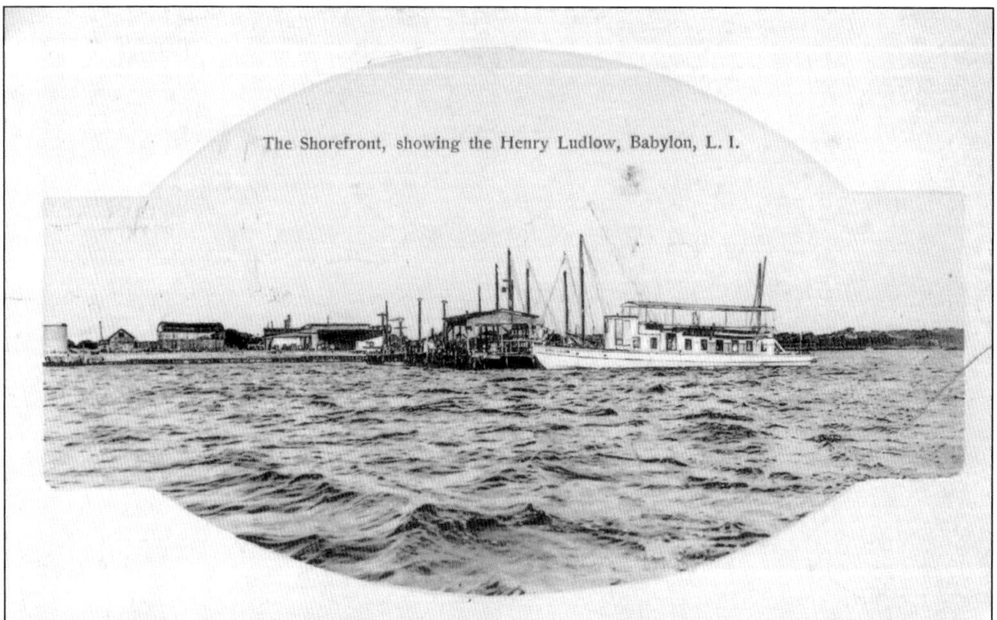

The following year, the success of the *Ripple* inspired Smith and Haff to construct a larger, 70-foot, double-decker ferry, the *Henry Ludlow*, named after Smith's father, Henry Ludlow Smith. Smith and Haff had deep Babylon and beach connections. Albert S. Haff later operated the Oak Island House hotel. Norman H. Smith was the great-grandson of David Smith, a local tailor who had served in the American Revolution.

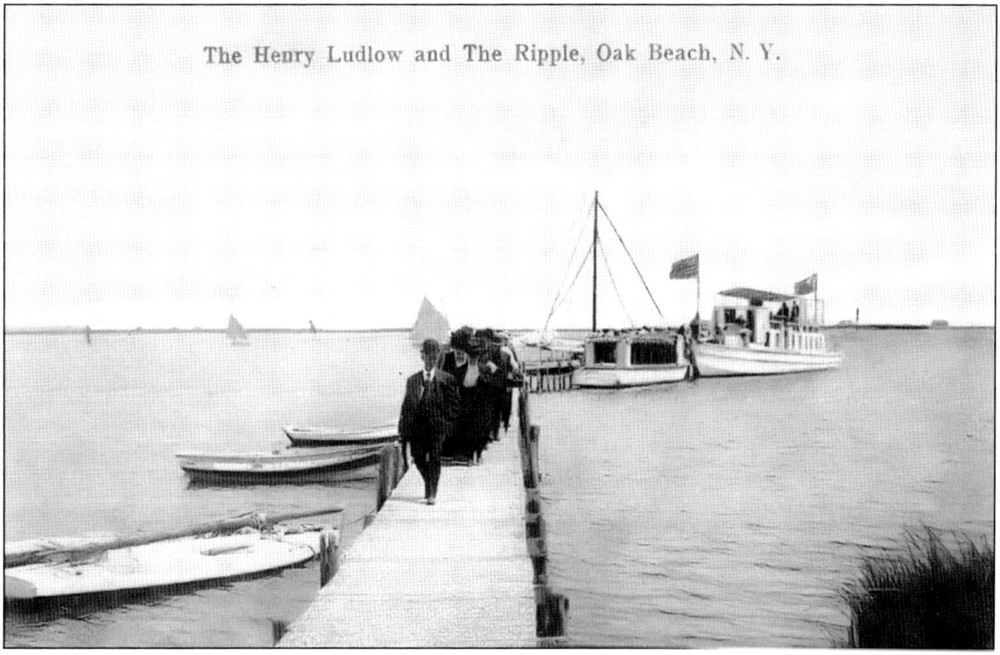

After decades of transporting residents and visitors across the bay, the ease of driving automobiles on the new Ocean Parkway led to the demise of the ferry services. The once-popular ferries made their last cross-bay trips by 1935 and were sold to a Bay Shore boater. The *Ludlow* met an unceremonious end "under a wrecker's axe" in 1938, as announced by the *Babylon Leader.*

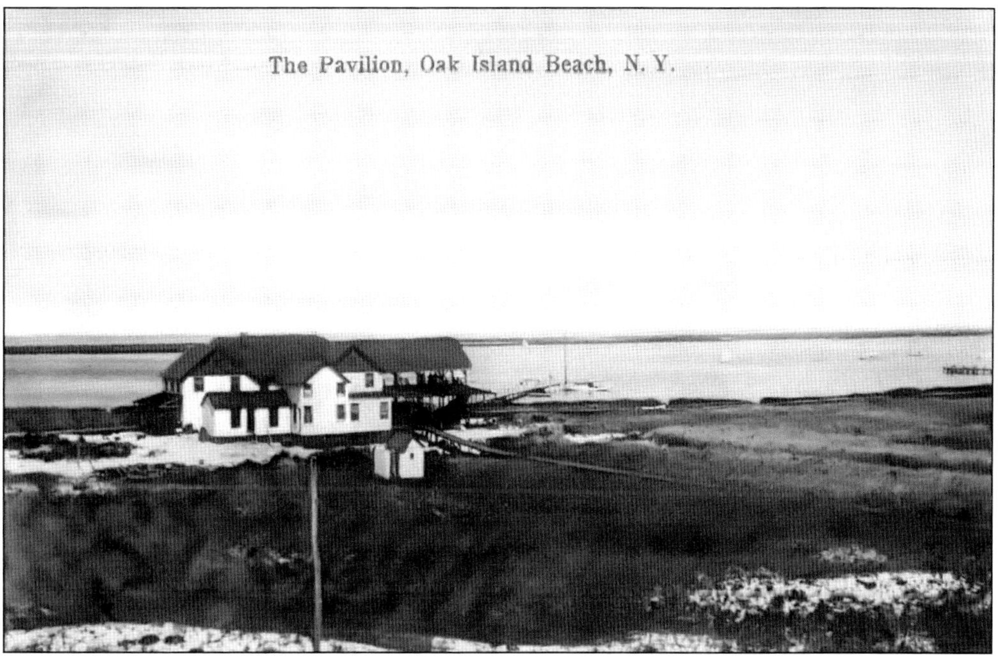

A popular destination on the barrier islands was Van Nostrand's Pavilion. In 1889, Amityville brothers Sidney and Wesley Van Nostrand opened a small Oak Beach restaurant. After the brothers separated their business ventures, Sidney built a larger clubhouse with 30 bathhouses in 1900. Declining business, hampered by Prohibition, led to the destruction of the pavilion in 1937.

Bibliography

Babylon Leader. 1910–1958.

Brooklyn Daily Eagle. November 15, 1867; August 30, 1905; April 10, 1916; February 26, 1922; December 10, 1922; January 30, 1927.

Bayles, Richard M. *History of Suffolk County, New York, with Illustrations, Portraits, and Sketches of Prominent Families and Individuals.* New York, NY: W.W. Munsell and Company, 1882.

Eaton, James Waterbury. *History of the First Presbyterian Church of Babylon, Long Island, from 1730–1912.* Babylon, NY: Babylon Publishing Company, 1912.

Field, Benjamin P. *Babylon Reminiscences.* Babylon, NY: Babylon Publishing Company, 1911.

The New York Times. September 27, 1869; September 4, 1910; December 6, 1921; November 15, 1924; January 11, 1929.

Newsday. August 24, 1967.

Pulling, Anne Frances. *Babylon by the Sea.* Charleston, SC: Arcadia Publishing, 1999.

Sammis, Romanah. *Huntington-Babylon Town History.* Huntington, NY: Huntington Historical Society, 1937.

South Side Signal. 1869–1920.

Village of Babylon Centennial Book. Babylon, NY: Village of Babylon, 1993.

About the Authors

The Village of Babylon Historical and Preservation Society formed in 1974 and has operated a local history museum ever since, offering visitors a glimpse into the village's past, from baymen and boats to its role as a vacation resort community and suburban boomtown. The historical society museum is located in the old Babylon Library at 117 West Main Street, which was listed in the National Register of Historic Places in 2015.

Mary Cascone is the historian for the town of Babylon and manages the Town of Babylon History Museum, which opened in June 2010 with exhibits pertaining to the entire town of Babylon, including the communities of Amityville, Babylon village, Copiague, Deer Park, East Farmingdale, Lindenhurst, North Amityville, North Babylon, North Lindenhurst, West Babylon, Wheatley Heights, Wyandanch, and the barrier beach communities of Captree Island, Gilgo Beach, West Gilgo, Oak Beach, and Oak Island. The Town of Babylon History Museum is located in the Old Town Hall at 47 West Main Street, which was nominated to the National Register of Historic Places in 2005.

Discover Thousands of Local History Books Featuring Millions of Vintage Images

Arcadia Publishing, the leading local history publisher in the United States, is committed to making history accessible and meaningful through publishing books that celebrate and preserve the heritage of America's people and places.

Find more books like this at
www.arcadiapublishing.com

Search for your hometown history, your old stomping grounds, and even your favorite sports team.

Consistent with our mission to preserve history on a local level, this book was printed in South Carolina on American-made paper and manufactured entirely in the United States. Products carrying the accredited Forest Stewardship Council (FSC) label are printed on 100 percent FSC-certified paper.

MADE IN THE USA